THE BEST OF SAIL CRUISING

THE BEST
OF SAIL CRUISING

Edited by Anne Madden

*With acknowledgment to the entire staff
of Sail Magazine, whose expert collective
hand contributed greatly to this effort.*

SAIL Books

BOSTON

Third Printing 1982

SAIL Books are published by Sail Publications, Inc.

ISBN 0-914814-11-7

Printed in the USA

Library of Congress Cataloging in Publication Data

The Best of SAIL Cruising

   Anthology of articles from Sail Magazine
   1. Sailing — Addresses, essays, lectures.
I. Madden, Anne. II. Sail
GV811.B44   1978   797.1'24   78-7936

Contents

3.   NAVIGATION

7.   IMPROVEMENTS

1

Choosing a Boat

Cruiser or Racer?

Is there a satisfactory compromise?   George Nichols

More and more "big boat" sailors are drawing a clear line between racing and cruising boats. But is this division necessary? Offshore racing was started by sailors in cruising boats who wanted to add the spice of friendly competition to the joys of voyaging to some distant point. Must such seaworthy designs be replaced by a new breed of boat in which comfort, maneuverability and strength are totally sacrificed to speed and rating requirements if one wants to win a race? Must the yachtsman choose *either* a cruising boat or a racing boat; or is some compromise still possible?

I contend first, that many changes in the design of ocean racing yachts were not caused by the IOR (many preceded it) or any other rule, but rather by the increasingly competitive attitude of the participants in the sport; and second, that it is just as possible to design and build a boat suitable for cruising *and* racing under the IOR as it ever was under the old rules as long as that is what you want to do.

I believe that the ocean racing sailor should be well steeped in cruising knowledge and experience for several reasons. Cruising means sailing under all conditions of weather and sea, expected or unexpected. So the cruising sailor learns to face emergencies, to keep his head and to maneuver out of danger. Because his breakdowns often occur far from home, he learns to rely upon his own ability to make repairs; he learns what to carry for spare parts, tools, etc.

And he learns what is unnecessary, too. He learns piloting and (if he wants to sail offshore to distant parts) celestial navigation as well. In

addition he learns, at his own pace, how to live comfortably — cook, sleep, dress, get along with others — in the very different environment of a small boat.

Because cruising crews tend to be small and selected, the cruising skipper learns quickly the *simple* ways to sail his boat, ways which both can be easily explained *and* executed by inexperienced crew members, not all of whom are racing gorillas. In other words, cruising teaches self reliance, and good judgment. But most of all cruising gives the sailor the leisure to study his boat, the sea, the wind and how they interact, and so to develop a "feel" for her — something which every racing skipper knows means the difference between winning and losing.

What do I mean by "feel"? The event that to me best illustrates that illusive term occurred a few years ago when, having been over the line too early, I started well behind my class in a local ocean race. My position seemed especially bad since the onshore breeze blowing over the outgoing tide had created a nasty chop in the narrow sound leading to the open sea. What little wind could penetrate between the high islands on each side of the sound was hopelessly broken up by the mass of racers fruitlessly trying to make their way dead to windward. The confused head sea repeatedly killed what little way they had.

Knowing from years of cruising in the strong tidal streams of the New England coast that such conditions were especially prone to stop my boat (a view amply confirmed by the sight of a couple of sister-ships totally stalled in mid channel), we slacked sheets and headed off the

15 or so degrees needed to put the sea more abeam and so to preserve boat speed. Twenty minutes later (despite reaching off) we were out in clear wind and smooth water ahead not only of our own class but of all but a very few of the two larger classes which had started ahead of us — a lead we never lost.

Just as cruising is good for the racing sailor, racing teaches important lessons to the cruising person. I believe that racing teaches him better seamanship. For the skipper to get maximum performance from the boat and to maneuver safely in the close quarters of the starting line and race course, precision and speed in boat and sail handling are required.

Precision and speed in navigation are equally important. Racing also teaches the auxiliary owner how to get himself out of a tight spot using *sails alone* — a skill which may save the cruiser's boat for him one day when his engine fails to start as he is being swept onto a lee shore by a sudden squall or wind shift. The bones of the lovely brigantine *Yankee* lie on the reef at Raratonga today for lack of such knowledge.

And important contributions to cruising pleasure and safety have come from racing's influence on hull and rig design. The need for speed under all conditions, implicit in racing, has led to notable developments in hull form which have contributed both to boat speed and sea-keeping ability. While the desirability of the latter for the cruising yachtsman is obvious, the importance of the former to his pleasure is often forgotten. A faster boat means his range is extended, more ports are available to him and he has more time to enjoy them when he gets there — quite aside from the zest which sailing a lively boat instead of a logy one contributes to the actual passage itself. Finally, Dacron sails, two-speed winches, aluminum spars, and compact reliable electronic navigational equipment of many sorts, all developed originally for racing, have contributed enormously to the pleasure and safety of the cruising yachtsman.

Anyone who remembers the backbreaking labor of swaying up a wet cotton mainsail on one of John Alden's winch-less pre-WW II schooners . . . or who remembers wondering how to explain to a "landlubber" boss that when the buoy failed to appear out of the fog when the distance was run out on the taffrail log there was nothing to do about getting home in time but, wait, hove-to, for dawn and clearing weather . . . can tell you what a difference such equipment has made.

Racing and cruising have contributed so much to each other why can't a single boat be suitable for both, I asked myself early in the summer of 1971. I enjoy both cruising and ocean racing. My 1946-designed boat had been fine for both when I built her in 1956, but design had progressed and she was no longer competitive. Besides, I had some longer voyages in mind and felt that a slightly larger, roomier and (especially) more buoyant hull would be better for these. With proper planning, I thought, a vessel suitable for my cruising needs should be possible which *also* would be fast and rate well under the IOR rule. The Rule's provisions tend to dictate many features I want for comfort: high sides, great beam, medium to light displacement, small mainsails, etc. So I needed to think out a program, discuss it with various designers, and then see what I could afford.

The procedure I followed was simple. I listed the characteristics which were *essential,* in my view, for each purpose — racing and cruising — and which were *nonessential.* To my surprise the two lists turned out to be remarkably similar.

The points I found essential for racing were, of course, a "good" hull design. This meant in my mind a boat of about 40′ overall length

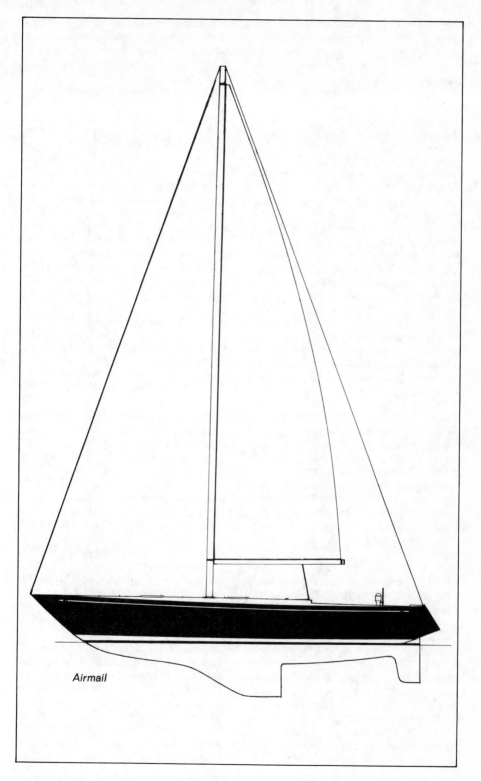

Airmail

with relatively short ends (better looking to my eye as well as more sea kindly), great beam and high freeboard for rating, stability and dryness. Under water, the divided keel and rudder configuration was obvious (to keep wetted surface down), but in addition, I sought a fine entrance and relatively deep sections which I felt would improve windward performance and comfort in a head sea. The very long flat run so popular with several designers I was less enthusiastic about despite its apparent advantage running because I felt it might impair windward ability. The rudder I felt strongly should have a skeg in front of it which reached all the way to its bottom to forestall the cavitation which spoils the effectiveness of the free-standing rudder and tends to make boats equipped with them unmanageable downwind in any kind of breeze and sea. I favored a flush deck if possible for the working space it affords, and a cockpit roomy enough for effective crew work on winches.

The masthead sloop rig was my choice from the start, both for its simplicity and its strength. A high aspect ratio seemed desirable, too, for effective use of sail area, as did a large foretriangle. Moreover, I knew I wanted a large enough rig for the boat to be lively in light going without my having to resort to oversized jibs and spinnaker poles with their attached rating and other penalties.

Below, I felt that good navigational space was essential, but also so were the living "amenities" needed to make the crew comfortable: a modicum of privacy, quiet, good lighting, comfortable bunks (with *big* leeboards so there is no fear of falling out at sea), and a locker for each person's personal gear, as well as an adequate galley. Without proper rest and food no crew lasts very long at peak efficiency and a few years of ocean racing have convinced me that the seconds lost by carrying an extra

100 lbs of "comfort gear" is more than made up for by the time gained when a well-fed, rested crew makes a single *good* tack compared to a bad one!

Other requirements were more obvious: excellent sails in adequate (but not confusing) numbers and *strong*, *light* construction. Both words were underlined on my list. I was raised in the era of Herreshoff boats in which these two features were combined, thanks to superlative craftsmanship. Nowadays, the same results can be achieved by *judicious* use of new materials — fiberglass, plastic foam, aluminum. Unfortunately, all of us also have seen or read about what can happen when the principles of good ship construction are violated in an effort to achieve lightness or economy.

One final qualifier completed my list. It was the word *simplicity*. I feel that too many gadgets, winches, and leads merely distract the crew and skipper from their main jobs: sail setting and trimming, and helmsmanship.

The things which I felt were *not* essential for racing were several. Extremes of design in hull, rig, and sails more often than not prove to be more detriment than help. At best they produce a boat good for only one purpose; even when they "work" the rule makers soon penalize them so their effective life is brief. I found I placed inadequate fuel and water tanks, inconvenient engine locations, miniature propellers and "stripping out" in the same category. Five minutes of bad helmsmanship is worth 0.1 of a foot of rating in a 100-mile race and 7 to 8 times that in a 20-miler.

When I began to write my list of essentials for cruising I found I had little to change or add to what I had already put down. The boat had to be well and strongly built and rigged. She needed to be a good sea boat, roomy, with comfortable accommodations, simple enough to be easily sailed by a small crew, as well as being (for my tastes) reasonably lively and fast enough to get me there before I starved or got bored to death. Even the cabin heater which I put on that list looked pretty good for some races, too! The only places where "essentials" seemed in potential conflict was in tankage and perhaps in certain details of rig.

Big tanks, water and fuel, are a big help cruising locally and a necessity for long passages, but their extra weight is a detriment racing and (depending on their location) may be bad from a rating measurement point of view. However, compromises are possible by using divided tanks and suitable valving so that only *some* are used for racing. *Airmail*, for example, carries 170 gallons of water when all tanks are full at the start of an offshore cruise, but only 100 gallons when starting a race. Her fuel arrangements are not so flexible and so she is penalized by having to leave the full 60 gallons of fuel in her under-cockpit tank when measured.

Grooved forestays *are* quicker (though not much) for headsail changes and therefore good for racing. Cruising, they are a nuisance because more crew is needed to handle headsails and they *do* jam occasionally. Otherwise, the sloop rig that races well nowadays can also cruise well thanks to roller-reefing and good winches.

For my cruising I find a lot of things often found on cruising boats less than necessary: pressure hot- and cold-water systems, showers, hot-water heaters, over-sized engines, fixed three-blade propellers, fancy trail boards and other "scroll work," mechanical self-steering vanes heavy electronics such as radar, rigid dinghys and outboard motors.

Generally, I have found that the more gear there is on the boat the more time I spend being a mechanic and the less I spend sailing.

The outcome of my program is my present boat *Airmail*.

Airmail is a Dick Carter-designed sloop, 42′ LOA, 32′ measured but nearer 34′ actual LWL, 12½′ beam and 7′ draft, flush deck with small house aft. Her interior is unusual only in that there is a small aft cabin with double bunk for the skipper to starboard of the companionway. This is just aft of a big chart table with comfortable seat and plenty of room for electronic and standard navigating gear as well as charts.

Opposite is a big U-shaped galley with an alcohol-burning gimballed stove with oven (anyone who has cooked at sea with an oven knows what a useful and labor-saving device it really is). All this is under the small deck house.

Moving forward one steps down eight inches into the main salon under the flush deck. A pilot berth and a setee on each side are separated by a central table. Next forward is the head to port and hanging lockers to starboard. Still farther forward are sail bins and two pipe berths for use in port.

There are no cockpit seat lockers. The starboard space is occupied by the skipper's bunk, while the space on the port side is entered from the galley area. This makes for a stronger boat, a drier area for sails, and a large oilskin locker. There is even a pipe berth in there much favored for its quiet when racing at sea and generally assigned to the cook. Heat is supplied by a diesel-fuel-burning bus heater made by the Eberspacher Corporation in West Germany.

Airmail's history up to the time of this writing, September of 1974, may indicate the "program's" evident success. She has sailed nearly 15,000 miles since I picked her up from the builder's yard on the east coast of Sweden in late July 1972. That summer we sailed her around the south end of Sweden to Copenhagen, north to Marstrand on Sweden's west coast. Thence across the Skagerak around the south tip of Norway and northward to Bergen's yachting haven at Godöysund 20 miles south of the city, then back through the fjords and islands to Oslo, leaving her for the winter in Vikene at the entrance to the Oslofjord. During those 1500 miles of cruising the crew ranged in number from 1 to 8. All sorts of weather was encountered and learned a lot about how to sail her. I was impressed by her ability as a sea boat and by the comfort of her spacious accommodations.

I, too, was reassured by the experience that this was indeed a suitable boat in which to assay my long-term dream of crossing the north Atlantic along the route the Vikings used. As a result, six of us set forth from Stavanger, Norway, on June 7, 1973, bound for Manchester, Massachusetts, via the northern islands. In the next five weeks we visited successively Unst (the northern-most Shetland island), Torshavn, capitol of the Faroe Islands, Reykjavik, capitol of Iceland, and St. John's, Newfoundland, to arrive home July 13th after 30½ days at sea. We experienced four gales; three required us to heave-to, but except for troubles with the heater which meant we were cold at times we had no difficulty while viewing some of the most spectacular land and ocean scenery any of us had ever seen. The level of confidence which we developed during the voyage in *Airmail*'s ability to take us anywhere under any conditions in safety and comfort is perhaps best illustrated as follows.

When three members of the crew found it necessary for business reasons to leave the ship in St. John's, Newfoundland, the remaining three (two girls and the author) set off for Manchester without waiting for additional help to arrive from Boston, even though hurricane Alice was proceeding toward the Nova Scotia coast at the time. Having been hove-to twice by then in gales of 45 to 55 knots with seas upward of 25' without ever taking green water aboard (or missing a hot meal), we felt the ship equal to nearly anything.

When three days later we were hove-to in the trough which extended south from the hurricane's center, we celebrated the occasion (as we had the two previous occasions) with a party complete with a freshly-baked cake and a rousing "skoal to the Mayor of the North Atlantic!" which finished off the last inch of aquavit in our bottle!

Since then *Airmail*'s cruising has taken her down the Intracoastal Waterway, through the Bahamas to Haiti and home via Bermuda much of it with only two crew aboard. Clearly, the cruising part of the program was successful.

How about racing? To my delight *Airmail* has proved as fast as she is comfortable. Our first glimpse of this came in September, 1972, when we raced informally in the Kattegat outside of Hanko against some of Norway's best ocean racing boats. There were other hints the next summer, too, but the real proof came in the SORC early in 1974 where her record was 10, 3, 2, 14, 7, and 3 in class, to yield an overall result of 3rd in class and 17th overall.

In the 1974 Onion Patch series of races her less spectacular 5, 8, 12 and 8th in class (68th in fleet) in the Bermuda race can be largely attributed to "skipper failure."

Especially pleasing to me has been her ability to foot with and point higher going upwind in moderate to fresh breezes than any of her current competition, while at the same time holding her own off wind.

What conclusions do I draw from all this? First, it is still possible under the IOR to have an able cruising boat that at the same time is competitive in top racing circles. Moreover, you don't *have* to "go all out" to race. *Airmail* has wire rigging and old-fashioned hanks for the jib. We lived aboard during the Circuit — the whole crew. We had a library of reading books, too, and some fishing gear.

This does not mean you can cut corners. We worked hard to get our

20

rating down when we were measured and when we race we race hard — *really* hard. But when we cruise we gunk-hole or go to sea as the spirit moves with friends for crew if they can make it or alone with equal ease, pleasure and safety.

Our only concession to offshore sailing — maybe "luxury" would be a better word — is an electric self-steering device that works on a wind vane and handles our tiller through tiller lines day after day (if we wish) even though it only weighs 10 lbs.

Finally, remember that the design of your boat will depend upon what you want and what you emphasize to your designer or salesman. If what you want is a racing "machine" not suitable for anything else you can get it. But it is not necessary to have a "machine" to enjoy or to win races.

Try Before You Buy

Putting a prospective purchase to the test

Jeff Spranger

Not long ago a buyer with only small-boat daysailing experience thought he had found what he wanted for his next boat, a small cruising sloop for his family of five. The boat had loads of room, modest sail area and lead ballast (important because his wife did not care for the daysailer that to her seemed to heel excessively), five berths, and an inboard engine — all at a price the family could afford with the help of a bank loan.

He bought the boat after a couple of visits to the local dealer's showroom, one by himself and another with his enthusiastic family, interspersed with close scrutiny of a lovely four-color brochure.

The transaction complete, the family climbed happily aboard for their first sail on their new boat. The wind was blowing about 14 knots — briskly but typical of the conditions that were common in the area — and the harbor was choppy, not bad, though. The buyer was pleased with how little spray came over the high topsides. His wife was likewise pleased with how little the boat heeled and how sturdy the boat felt in contrast to their "old" boat just sold.

Then, with a word to his family, the skipper put the helm over. The bow eased up into the wind and the boat slowed and stopped. Finally it fell off on the previous tack. Again, he put the helm over and again the bow would not go through the wind.

A shallow keel, the expanse of topsides, a small rudder, and too little sail combined to prevent the boat from tacking. Only by wearing his boat around in a gybe or by starting the engine could the owner bring his new boat about.

His boat had everything he wanted in a boat except the most important quality: performance under sail.

This is obviously an extreme example of poor performance, but had he taken a sistership sailing before making his decision, he might have avoided an expensive and disappointing experience.

The best judge of whether a boat performs satisfactorily is the sailor who will be handling it. Advice of sailing friends is valuable but not nearly so valuable as firsthand sailing. A boat that to one sailor has performance may to another be a clunker; to one a boat may be logy, to another seakindly.

The last and most crucial test of a boat before purchase should be a trial sail. Preferably such a sail should be in the prevailing conditions where most of the sailing will take place. Thus, if the winds are predominantly light, the boat should be tried in those conditions to see if it has reasonable speed and can drive through slop.

If the wind typically blows 15 knots and kicks up a nasty chop, then there is little sense sailing the boat in five knots of wind and a smooth sea.

A sea trial begins as soon as the docklines are cast off. While you are powering out to clear water, walk forward to the bow. The deck should be unobstructed and the footing should feel secure. At the bow the weight of one man should not drastically cause bowdown trim, an especially important consideration if auxiliary power is an outboard whose lower unit could be lifted out of the water while a crew member is forward to pick up a mooring, lower the jib, or fend off a dock.

Check the speed under engine

while heading into the wind. If the rpm is in the normal cruising range and the boat speed is below what is acceptable, that may be enough reason either to reject the boat despite other possible virtues or to consider an optional engine with higher horsepower.

Before hoisting sails the prospective buyer should take the helm to feel the response of the boat under power. Try putting the engine in reverse and steering with the boat making sternway; most sailboats are difficult to handle going astern but the handling should not be impossible.

The sails set for a trial should be similar to those the buyer is considering for his new boat. If he is looking for performance in moderate airs for which a large genoa jib is appropriate, a trial with a small working jib in those same moderate winds would not prove much. Likewise, for more distant cruising with a short-handed crew and working sails, a trial with a large jib might be misleading.

Once under sail the most important factors to look at — or perhaps better, to feel — are the motion of the boat and the response of the helm. If the boat heels too far to give a feeling of security, that tenderness, while not necessarily dangerous or unseaworthy, may make even day-sailing uncomfortable for guests and family members already a bit nervous about being afloat. Many boats, however, are designed to heel a few degrees initially but then become stiff and heel very little more even with substantially more wind strength. If in doubt about such stiffness, sheet the sails in tight and try to increase the amount of heel. The tension caused by a boat that doesn't stop heeling until the deck is awash in moderate winds may more than outweigh the excitement and send the buyer ashore to look for a stiffer craft.

What the helm of a good boat feels like is the subject of much controversy among sailors. Some like a helm — whether a tiller or a wheel — that even in heavy winds requires no sustained muscle power. Others like a firm feeling that is a reminder that the boat needs to be steered.

Having jib and main sheets within easy reach of the helmsman can make shorthanded cruising easier for the crew

Mainsail furling on a 30-footer can be a job for one crew member but cabin top should be free of obstructions and companionway hatch be capable of being readily closed for safety sake

Above all, the steering of a boat should not demand the undivided attention for cruising or daysailing that it might for successful racing. If the helm feels as if it is always losing the battle of keeping the boat on course, either the design of the boat or the tuning of the rig is apt to be faulty. Having to fight the helm may be acceptable for a few minutes, but would it be acceptable for an afternoon?

Only experience on the helm of a variety of boats gives a helmsman the perspective to judge a specific boat. However, on a trial the feel of the helm, as subjective as that re-

sponse may be, either does or does not fall into tolerable limits. Remember, unless the boat is to be used as something other than a sailboat, more hours will be spent at the helm and more pleasure is apt to be derived from steering it than all the other time and pleasure of a boat put together.

As the boat heels to the breeze and sails to windward, the helm should continue to be comfortable to handle — no hyper-extension of the elbow and no crooked arm that quickly tires, nor should the helmsman feel that he is going to fall off the windward cockpit seat because he cannot brace his feet conveniently.

In moderate winds the touch of a few fingers can hold a well-balanced boat on course without the helmsman's having to move the helm so much that sailing to windward feels like an exercise to strengthen a bad back.

For sensitivity, a tiller is more effective than wheel steering. However, a tiller takes up much more cockpit space because of its swing, so much so that it may make tacking difficult in a crowded cockpit, painfully so if it cracks a crew member across the shins or jams him or her against the coaming.

Wheel steering is more compact, a bit difficult to adapt to after experience with a tiller, in itself a cockpit obstruction, and relatively expensive. It should, however, make steering less a physical chore, particularly on larger boats.

While the boat is still heeled on the wind is the time to make one's way forward. If the sidedeck is narrow and windward stanchions obstruct passage, the only alternative route may be over the trunk cabin top. Such a trip should be safe with proper handrails for aid and no need to jump, shinny, or crawl except in heavy winds. Other than during a race there is seldom a need to leave the cockpit. However, when a trip forward is necessary, it is usually to do tasks that may require alacrity, surefootedness, and both hands. Such a test cannot be done adequately with the boat in a marina slip but only under actual sailing conditions.

As the boat sails to windward, heeled and pitching, is also the time to slip below decks to see if the interior, the one that looked so comfortable with the boat upright at the dock, is as pleasant and, more importantly, if it is safe under sail.

There should be sturdy handrails (not merely decorative shelf trim) as a safeguard against crew members' falling. Edges of counters and bulkheads should be rounded to prevent maiming if someone is thrown against them. Locker slides, drawers, and doors should not stick or jam as the hull works. Undue flexing and ominous creaking are suspect. If wind and sea conditions are too calm to throw water on deck, a few bucketfuls sloshed down the sidedecks and over the cabin roof may indicate leaks that occur as the hull works under sail.

Before falling off the wind, tack

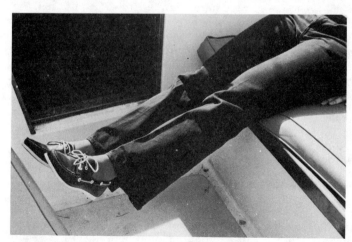

A cockpit too wide to permit bracing with one's feet can make sitting to windward precarious and tiring

To reach the bottom of this icebox requires short person to brace herself over stove burner, inconvenient if not downright dangerous — and not noticed until under way

the boat a couple of times. The angle between one tack and the other should not be appreciably more than 90 degrees unless the boat is meant to power to windward rather than sail. A careful look at the wake as the boat sails upwind will tell whether it is making much leeway. If the wake leaves the transom at a perceptible angle to windward, it indicates leeway that may make windward sailing frustrating and slow.

Tacking affords an excellent opportunity to judge the capabilities of the sheet winches. Too small a winch makes jib sheeting a job for behemoths, not for a couple of children or a wife and her husband. If in doubt the solution may be to note the winch size and plan to pay the difference for the next larger size. The same applies to the mainsheet winch.

Another feature to note while tacking is the location of the mainsheet. Roller travelers can be dangerous to a crew member as the carriage rolls from one side to the other during a tack or gybe.

Any boat should feel at her fastest and smoothest with the wind about abeam. Merely sea testing a boat by reaching back and forth is virtually a waste of time; to be a successful boat under sail it is more important that she handle well sailing upwind and downwind. On a broad reach or run in moderate winds the boat should not feel as if it wants to fly out of control into the wind even in swells or in the wake of a passing powerboat.

As the sails are doused take the opportunity to note again the security of the foredeck and the convenience of gathering the jib aboard and of furling the mainsail. These are jobs that frequently must be done in a squall, in a crowded fleet, or when the crew is tired.

While the dealer is handy, discuss with him exactly what gear will be on a new boat compared with the one you just sailed. A boat used as a demonstrator probably is equipped with optional equipment. For instance, on many new boats the genoa sheeting fittings and track are options at additional cost and yet the sailing performance of the demonstrator may have been impressive because of the power afforded by a large overlapping jib.

Finally, before stepping off the boat, stop and evaluate your reactions to how the boat performed. Some awkwardness may have been caused by unfamiliarity with the boat and perhaps with any boat that size. If doubt about the sailing performance lingers, ask for another trial sail. After all, a boat is a large investment and its purchase should be as free as possible from reservations.

At the same time it is not fair to monopolize a dealer's time and his demonstration boat in numerous trial sails, taking advantage of his desire to make a sale. His is often a seasonal business and other potential customers may be waiting for good wind conditions in which to make their own trials.

A sailor in the market for a new boat is entitled to a reasonable opportunity to try a boat he is considering purchasing. Without such a trial he has largely himself to blame if later sailing performance does not measure up to his expectations. No amount of subtle interior decor, go-fast fittings, persuasive chatter of a salesman, superficial eyeballing of hull shape, or endorsements from other owners will make a sweet sailing boat out of a clunker.

If a dealer does not have a boat available to sail before purchasing, ask him to find out where one might be sailed from the marketing director of the builder. A good dealer wants you to be satisfied with the boats he handles; he wants your business when you move up to a larger boat in the future. As a general rule beware of the dealer who shows little enthusiasm for your request for a trial sail. His concern for you may be no greater when you need warranty work done after taking delivery.

More Than a Glance Below

A checklist for cabin features or follies

Edward Brewer

A **close look at the** interior of a boat can tell a sailor a great deal about the amount of thought and care that a builder puts into his product. Here is where the crew will spend considerable time if the boat is to be used for anything but daysailing. Moreover, the space below decks should foster comfort and livability both under way and at anchor.

On first going below on a boat get an impression about how spacious the interior seems, given the limitations imposed by the size of the boat. Even a small boat can create the effect of spaciousness while a large boat may suffer from a sense of clutter and cramping.

Then look at the galley. It should have plenty of dry, accessible stowage for dishes and food and a place for all the utensils, silverware and condiments that make cooking and eating a pleasure. The teak finish in the galley should be varnished or oiled. If not, ugly grease stains will quickly spoil that as-new appearance. Counter tops covered with a plastic laminate are durable and easily cleaned.

The stove should be gimbaled to swing through a 40° to 45° arc.

Pull-out cutting board is a thoughtful idea for the galley but the varnished countertop is difficult to maintain compared to a more durable plastic laminate surface

Swing it to test. If it only gimbals through 20° to 30°, there is a chance that someone will have a mess to clean up or even be scalded in case of a knockdown. The stove space must be asbestos-lined for safety and sheathed with monel, stainless steel or, at the very least, formica so that spilled fuel and food does not seep into the woodwork. Metal sheathing is much to be preferred in case of fire, of course.

If the stove is fitted with a remote propane, alcohol or kerosene fuel tank, there must be a shutoff valve at both the stove and tank. Moreover, the fuel line must have a flexible section near the stove to avoid cracking of the lines from the action of the gimbals. Some means of fitting a safety belt is necessary if the vessel is to go offshore to prevent the cook's being thrown against the stove. A U-shaped galley is the most suitable for use offshore although a well planned L-shaped setup can also be fitted with safety straps without much difficulty.

The icebox is another check point. The food particles in ice water develop odors if it drains into the bilge. The drain should run off into a pan or it should drain into a plastic bottle or jug that is easy to empty. Within the icebox the shelves should be of fiberglass, stainless steel or scrubbable ash or teak. A top opening icebox spills less cold air than a closet type so the ice lasts longer.

Another point in preserving ice is adequate insulation; 3″ thickness PVC foam is desirable and 4″ is better. Many boats get by with 2″ of insulation but it is minimal for serious cruising.

The sink also deserves an inspection. Many are too small and shallow.

For average use an inside measurement of 12" x 15" x 7" deep is satisfactory. Round basins or small shallow bowls are not ideal and the cook will be the first to complain.

If the galley has a pressure water system, it is desirable to have a manual backup pump, either hand or foot operated, so that fresh water still can be drawn in case of electrical or pump failure. Another useful fitting is a through-hull water pump so that overboard water can be used for dish washing to conserve the fresh water in the tank.

Two items builders often overlook in the galley are a garbage bin and a dust trap, usually because of lack of space in smaller craft. Both will make the cook more content with life aboard and are very worthwhile if space permits. The garbage bin should prevent its contents tipping over onto the cabin sole. The best location for a dust bin is at the foot of the companion way where it also can serve as a drain as crew members take off oilskins on coming below.

In the main saloon check out the berths and settees for size. A berth should have a length of more than 6' and a minimum of 20" for comfort with 24" as preferable. Mattresses should be 4" foam. Mattress covers of cloth often are best as vinyl may be sticky and uncomfortable in hot weather, although this is a matter of choice to a large extent.

In the interest of providing as many berths as possible, builders often make use of the area under the cockpit seat for a quarter berth. Such berths can be virtually impossible to get in and out of if they are recessed too far or if they are too narrow. Climb into a quarter berth to test it and then check to see if stowage at the end is accessible since this is where bedding will probably be stowed. A quarter berth should also have ventilation at the foot to permit air to circulate its entire length.

Lee boards on canvases are essential if the berths are to be usable at any angle of heel. These can be cloth or wood but the heavy Dacron type are more comfortable. Few production boats fit these as standard equipment so they are usually owner-installed as an afterthought. However, if the builder has not provided strong handrails over the berths the lee boards will have to be tied up to padeyes fastened with bolts through the cabin roof, a possible source of leaks, particularly where the roof has an inner liner.

The handrails along the underside of the cabin roof are essential for another purpose, of course, as they enable one to move fore and aft in relative safety when the boat is rolling. They should be through-bolted, usually to the deck handrails, as screws are simply not strong enough and may pull out.

The saloon table should be of adequate size to seat the number of people for which there are berths in the boat and it should be heavily built to resist the impact of a person slamming into it in a seaway. Deep fiddles or rails around are a necessity if it is to be used at sea. If the table converts to a berth, the conversion process should be easy for a single person to do and the cushions should make a comfortable mattress.

Toilets facing fore and aft are better than those facing athwartships although the latter are more common in smaller craft since they use less valuable fore-and-aft space. The problem with the athwartships head, of course, is that when the boat is well heeled in a good breeze it can be rather uncomfortable to sit with your knees higher than your chin. It is not easy to arise from such a head either and a handrail can ease the chore of using the head in heavy weather.

Washbasins in many craft are undersized and too shallow so it is a good idea to try them for size. Check that toilet and basin through-hull seacocks are fitted and easily accessible in an emergency. Most craft now have holding tanks or self-contained toilets so seacocks are going out of style, but these toilets have been known to develop odors. Adequate ventilation with some type of spray and rain-proof vent is a must in the head area.

On smaller craft the navigation is usually done on the icebox top or the cabin table. If so, the ice hatch or table top should be a flush, smooth fit. On larger yachts a separate chart table is provided and this should have ample stowage for charts in a flat bin or drawer under the table top plus room for electronic equipment and navigation tools. The quarter berth often is used as a navigator's seat and should be checked out for comfortable height and knee room.

While near the companionway, look around for an oilskin locker or hanging space as it is one of the first things to be left out in the builder's or designer's quest for that extra unnecessary berth.

Now that you've checked out the big items in the layout, look at the small but equally important ones. Is ventilation adequate throughout the interior including screened opening ports and perhaps a screened skylight over the saloon or galley? Is there a satisfactory place to store the necessary tools for engine and boat maintenance? Look for high, solid fiddles. Turned rails are cute if your taste runs to that, but they don't keep small objects where they belong and they are often weak when a person grabs them to prevent himself from falling.

Oiled or varnished wood below gives a feeling of warmth and quality but it should be ruggedly built and easily maintained

Do the drawers have positive locks, either elbow catches or a notch that requires that the drawers lift ¼″ or so to open? Drawers of the latter type can be difficult to open if the drawer is short or filled with heavy objects. Are the drawer slides lubricated and is a center rail fitted to keep the drawers running smoothly?

Lockers should have positive elbow catches. Spring catches have the habit of strewing the contents of the locker all over the cabin sole in heavy seas and magnetic catches are worse than useless.

Give one last glance around to see if the corners of the bureaus and other joinerwork are well rounded, if durable reading lights are fitted over the berths, if there is a mirror light in the head, if sole hatches lift freely. When everything checks out, then perhaps it's time to start talking seriously to the dealer.

How Many Will She Sleep?

There's more to cruising than berths   Murray Lesser

My **black-hulled** 36′ yawl *Apsara* displaces six tons. She is a pretty boat, and attracts a lot of attention from the casual dockside strollers, as well as from the owners of other boats. In striking up a conversation, the first question most ask is, "How many will she sleep?"

I don't know what they expect, but they always seem disappointed when I tell them that she "sleeps four." I don't explain that her four berths are the maximum that should be fitted in a boat of *Apsara*'s displacement, according to my rule of thumb for extended coastwise cruising in comfort.

"Comfort" is a strange word to most small-boat cruising sailors, who spend their cruising time in a boat cluttered up with too many berths. One of the joys of cruising under sail is to be quasi-independent of the land, spending several nights anchored out without the effort of resupply, and without being subject to the exigencies of "camping out." The limiting factor is displacement per person aboard. For comfort, the space taken up by the extra, unused berths would be better utilized if given over to almost anything else.

Of course, displacement is not the only factor in determining how many berths it pays to carry. The boat must also have sufficient *tonnage* — the measure of the internal volume available to carry passengers, crew and cargo. If the displacement is concentrated on too short a waterline, there won't be room enough below to live in, for all the volume indicated by the weight-carrying ability. The minimum requirement is to be able to get the full ship's company below when they are *not* in the berths. A more restrictive, but necessary, rule is to have at least

enough room below for the entire complement to survive two days marooned at anchor during a storm — and come out sane.

Displacement is the gross weight of the whole works — structure, ballast, engine, sails, safety gear, necessary equipment, and *useful load*. Presumably, the useful load is why you want the boat in the first place. Useful load, by definition, is the people, their personal gear, food, drink and wash water, and fuel for the engine.

Unfortunately, in most stock sailboat designs, the weight of all those "optional extras" that are convenience items, not essential to the safe operation of the boat, also comes out of the weight the designer may have left for useful load. In fact, observation of the floating level of the boot tops of many "empty" small stock cruising boats will show you that some designers leave out the weight of both the heavy optional equipment and any useful load. The design displacement is a little less than the weight empty.

How much weight can you cram into a cruising sailboat without overloading it to the point of discomfort or lack of seaworthiness? Fortunately, the discomfort point usually comes first.

Henry & Miller, in their 1965 book, *Sailing Yacht Design*, made a statistical analysis indicating that the design useful load was only about 6% to 8% of the design displacement for the average "sailing yacht" capable of going to sea. However, I am sure that an overload of 5% to 10% of the design displacement can be tolerated for cruising. All that will suffer will be the performance and handling characteristics — the fun and comfort of cruising under sail. A well-designed cruising sailboat should still be reasonably seaworthy under such overloaded conditions.

Notwithstanding the statistics, stock sailboat builders are sure that your first question will be, "How many will she sleep?" Since they don't want you to be disappointed, they ask their designers to pack six berths into a boat displacing less than 10,000 lbs.

Of course, the designers do give you fair warning by limiting the water supply to about 20 gallons (approximately two days' supply for six moderately-careful inhabitants, particularly for coastwise cruising where the pollution makes the sea water unfit for anything except floating boats on). Further warnings are the icebox capacity of 50 lbs (if you don't put anything into it but ice), and the lack of sail stowage space other than in a berth.

Thus, if you are interested in a boat in which you and yours can cruise comfortably and want to compare sailboats to see how well they fit your needs and resources, you have to learn to discount the bed check. You can choose your boat and then learn to live within her limitations. Or, you can establish your load requirements first, before going out to look for your dreamboat with enough displacement to fit. In most cases, you probably can't make use of more than one berth per ton (2240 lbs) of displacement. If you are interested in more than weekend cruising, you may not want even that many.

Remember, one average adult plus the water he/she will probably use in a week of coastwise cruising will weigh about 250 lbs. Add in another 50 lbs per person for food and clothing. Allow 100 lbs of ice for the week (in a pre-cooled well-insulated top-loading icebox), plus a tank of fuel (gasoline weighs six lbs per gallon).

Then, consider how much overload you will be willing to put up with. My arithmetic produced my rule of thumb: One berth for each 1½ tons of displacement, for comfortable cruising.

This rule assumes that the "optional extra" items don't weigh more than about 3% of the displacement; this may establish the minimum size of the boat. For example, if you want many of the good (heavy) things in cruising life such as a diesel engine, wheel steering, pressure hot and cold water (which runs up the water consumption), a shower (which runs it up even more), a reasonable shelf of books, a second heavy-duty battery (in order to have enough light to read by, and still be certain of being able to start the diesel), and maybe even a small charcoal-burning fireplace, it is hard to carry all of them in a sailboat displacing less than 13,000 lbs (barely 6 tons).

At that displacement, you should also get sail lockers, at least 70 gallons of water capacity (in two tanks), an icebox that will take 200 lbs and still leave a little room for food, and 48 hours of fuel capacity (at cruising-in-a-calm speed).

Four congenial adults can spend a very civilized week away from physical replenishment in such a vessel. Two can be even more civilized, for over twice the time.

If your tastes aren't so lavish, and if you are willing to narrow your comfortable cruising circle, you can do with considerably less displacement. At near-minimum, weekending for two can be done very nicely in a boat displacing around 5000 lbs. At sub-minimum, you can always "cruise" sans civilization or comfort — which is better than not cruising at all.

The next time you go looking at cruising sailboats, don't ask, "How many *will* she sleep?" Look at the boat and her specifications, ask her displacement, and then decide for yourself how many she *should* sleep.

Building Your Own

Pitfalls of home construction   Edward Brewer

The first step in turning the dream of building your own boat into a reality is the selection of the right design. The amateur builder is looking for a boat that is within his financial reach, of course, and also within his ability to construct to reasonable standards. Moreover, he wants a design that satisfies his requirements as to size, type, rig and accommodations.

Unfortunately, the average amateur builder is often not sufficiently knowledgeable to select a plan that meets these needs and is, at the same time, a technically correct design. Too many would-be builders are attracted by a spacious and comfortable accommodation arrangement without giving sufficient thought to the hull shape that is going to carry that interior or the rig that is going to propel it. They trust that the designer has done his job properly.

Some available plans are not only designs of unattractive, poor-performing craft but also of possibly dangerously unseaworthy boats as well.

A prospective amateur builder showed me a brochure on a cruising boat in the mid-40-foot range and requested that I comment on the merits of the vessel. The builder of this boat could have been in serious trouble without some sound advice.

The boat featured in the brochure may have been an outstanding example of innocence and ignorance on the part of a so-called "yacht designer," but I fear that it was just one of a number of such plans that are being pushed at amateur builders. Briefly a few of the faults of the design were as follows:

—boat was of excessively heavy displacement (displacement-length ratio of 455), very small sail area (sail area-displacement ratio of 10.5), and of unusually low ballast-displacement ratio (18.5%). Its performance at best would be disappointing and at worst, hazardous, hardly satisfactory for what the brochure described as a "seagoing auxiliary."

—the mainmast was stepped directly on the keel with no mast step to spread the load, a dangerously weak construction inviting serious future problems.

—the propeller shaft was over 12' long with no sign of an intermediate bearing. This would probably lead to major problems of shaft whipping.

—the lateral plane was a rather curious shape, the keel being deepest at its forward end and shoalest at the rudder post. This configuration is typical of Arabian dhows, but Fenger was the only modern designer to use such a shape as he felt it worked well with his "Fenger" rig. The design in question was not Fenger rigged. My feeling is that the unusual lateral plane would pose sail balance problems and possibly poor steering under quartering wind and sea conditions.

—the mooring cleats intended to hold a 25-ton boat were only of 8" size, not really adequate for a yacht of half that displacement.

—the winches for a rig of almost 1100 sq. ft. consisted of only two Merriman #3's for the jib sheets, about what one would see today on a 25 footer. There were no indications of a mainsheet winch, a staysail sheet winch, or any cleats for these sails.

—the bow pulpit was formed of "half inch diameter stainless steel or brass tubing," not even remotely adequate for a 20' trailer cruiser,

33

much less a boat over twice that length.

—the deck layout showed no genoa tracks, jib sheet pad-eyes, cleats, staysail sheet fairleads or other useful hardware normally fitted to a sailboat.

—ventilation consisted of only two small dorade vents for three cabins plus heads. There was no sign of engine room ventilators.

The above faults were evident on a cursory examination of the brochure. A thorough review of the complete set of plans would undoubtedly reveal a great many more.

In short, this boat appeared to have been designed by someone without the slightest experience of sailing or sailing yacht design, yet it was offered as a sea-going vessel suitable for amateur construction. Surprisingly, it was not offered by some unknown young designer but by a supposedly reputable firm. It is interesting to note, though, that the brochure did not give the name of the "expert" who drew up this dream ship.

The ethics of a firm that would try to sell a design of such poor quality to amateur builders is open to serious question. I am angry to discover that my profession contains such men.

Of more immediate interest, however, is a method by which amateur builders can identify and avoid the purchase of similar plans.

The first step is to familiarize yourself with the proportions and details of sound, well designed boats so that you can spot the few that are obviously incompetently designed. A study of the design sections of the boating magazines and directories can supply a wealth of information on average displacements, LOA/LWL ratios, beam/waterline ratios, draft, ballast ratios, sail area, rig proportions, power plants, and other details.

Clip out the designs of particular interest and start a "crib" file so that you have a basis for serious comparison when you consider plans for your own boat.

Next, obtain some good books on yacht design and read them thoroughly with emphasis on the sections dealing with proportion, construction, and details of deck layouts, rigs, machinery, etc. In particular, I recommend *Sailing Yachts* by Juan Baader, *Elements of Yacht Design* by Francis Kinney, *Sailing Yacht Design* by Douglas Phillips-Birt, *Offshore* by John Illingworth or any of Eric Hiscock's fine books.

For information on wood construction study *Boatbuilding* by Howard Chapelle or Robert Steward's *Manual of Boatbuilding;* for ferrocement, Jay Benford's *Practical Ferrocement Boatbuilding.* Unfortunately, there are few good books on fiberglass other than those of a very technical nature, but Bruce Roberts' *Amateur Fiberglass Boatbuilding* contains worthwhile information for the amateur builder.

There are many other books available covering various aspects of design and construction and the ones mentioned above are just a sampling. I realize that working your way through such a pile of reading matter is a tedious step for someone anxious to start building his own boat, but a month of study could well save several years of wasted labor along with thousands of dollars worth of material.

Finally, visit all the boat yards in your area and again study closely the type of yacht which you intend to build. Look carefully at hardware, deck layouts, rigging and, if it is off season, underwater shapes and proportions. While giving these craft a thorough going over, it is a good idea to have a notebook and camera in hand to record particularly interesting details and ideas which you can incorporate in your own boat while under construction. Few designs are so good that they cannot be improved upon.

While you acquire knowledge of yacht design, you probably will already have begun collecting brochures on plans of the type of craft that interest you. First, discard any that do not bear the designer's name.

It is evident from the brochure I saw that at least one firm is using inexperienced draftsmen to draw up plans and then is selling these plans as "company" designs without checking on the quality of the work. A legitimate naval architect would not allow a firm to sell his designs without insisting that he be acknowledged as the designer. If you cannot ascertain the architect's name, you have no way of looking into his technical ability, his reputation or his experience.

The second step is to study the details of the designs to the degree that the small scale drawings in the brochures permit. Check the adequacy of deck hardware, such as cleats, winches, sheet fittings, ventilation, etc. If you find a number of minor details that are obviously poor, the chances are good that some of the major points in the plans will also be wrong although they may not be so obvious to an amateur builder. Here your crib files will be useful.

You can be reasonably certain that the work of leading designers such as Olin Stephens, George Cuthbertson, Dick Carter, Alan Gurney, Gary Mull, John Atkin, and McCurdy & Rhodes is technically correct. If the plans you are considering do not match their work in accuracy of detail, proportions, styling (according to type) and other particulars, take a second, closer look at them and discard those that do not match up to reasonable standards.

On the other hand, do not shy from an otherwise suitable set of plans simply because the designer is relatively unknown. There will always be a new crop of promising young architects trying to get a start and many of these have both the talent and knowledge to design an excellent yacht.

Do not hesitate to write the designer to ask about his qualifications, experience and previously successfully designed craft. A reasonably long apprenticeship with a well-known yacht designer or design firm is an excellent recommendation as is membership in the Society of Naval Architects and Marine Engineers or the Society of Small Craft Designers. However, such societies have "student" and "associate" members who may or may not be as well qualified in yacht design as a designer with the status of a full member. Even graduation from a recognized school of yacht design, whether by correspondence or at the university level, is not necessarily a sign of competence since it does not guarantee that the designer has the necessary practical background.

At Yacht Design Institute we recommend that our students work for a successful designer for several years before setting up their own office. We feel this is the best possible way to obtain the practical experience necessary to meet the needs of future clients. The capable architect will also have considerable sailing time aboard both his own designs and other vessels, but this is a qualification that can be difficult to check.

Obviously, the finest recommendation for a designer's work is a successful boat already built to the plans in which you are interested. However, many successful designers do not like to release client's names and addresses since it can be an imposition upon the owner to be asked to show his boat or to have to answer long inquiries. Of course, it does not hurt to try to see the boat or write the owner, particularly if you are doubtful about the suitability of the design for your needs.

If you are very much interested in the design, the architect may sell study plans at a fraction of the cost of the full set of drawings. As a rule, the cost of the study plans is applicable against the design fee, so you lose nothing if you go ahead at a later date.

The study plans normally include a large scale sail plan, arrangement plan, inboard profile and some construction drawings, possibly a construction section and/or profile. These plans should let you determine whether the designer knows his business. If there is still any doubt, consult with a more experienced amateur builder, a professional builder, or another designer. However, be prepared to pay a consultation fee when you seek professional advice, although it will be well worth the cost if such advice saves you from an expensive mistake.

In summary, the best way to avoid a dud design is to increase your own expertise to the point where you can recognize incompetence when you see it. Then, if in doubt, obtain professional advice. Nothing could be more to the point than the adage "look before you leap." A blind leap into building a poorly designed craft will give you more agony, expense and frustration than any man needs in one lifetime, yet it is a simple matter to avoid such problems if you plan ahead.

Recycling the Ocean Racer

Ways to convert to a cruising boat   Michel G. Emmanuel

During the past 10 years, offshore racing has undergone greater change, at a more rapid pace, than in any prior period. Breakthroughs in hull design, coupled with rapid-fire alterations in the racing rules have left tumbling in their wakes a multitude of yachts that are outmoded for racing.

What do you do with a tired racing yacht? The search for an answer has caused anguished gnashing of teeth in many households.

To the dedicated racing sailor there are only three acceptable solutions: (1) Sell the old boat and buy one that is competitive; (2) compete with other boats of similar vintage under a more comfortable rule; or (3) convert the old boat to cruising and satisfy your urge for combat on someone else's boat. We chose the third alternative.

My wife Betty and I bought *Reef Runner,* our Sparkman and Stephens-designed Tartan 34, in 1969. Her hull shape and rig were up to date; she was fast and quite competitive under our Florida west coast conditions. We campaigned her locally until 1972 when, still fast but no longer competitive under the Mark III version of the International Offshore Rule, we listed her for sale.

But then we went to several boat shows and after a lot of close looking we reached the conclusion that *Reef Runner* was the best boat around, for our purposes. This decision followed an introspective evaluation of what our purposes really were. Putting aside dreams of long, offshore passages to exotic islands, we faced up to the fact that coastwise cruising was what we enjoyed and all we were ever likely to do. After all, if a couple is completely happy anchored behind Anclote Key or among the Dry Tortugas, why languish over an unattainable, far-off shore? We took *Reef Runner* off the market.

Once we defined our objectives, the next question was how heavily we should commit ourselves. We decided to make a list of additions which would make *Reef Runner* handier and more habitable, rank them as to priority, and tackle them one at a time. Each year we would make a considered decision about whether to keep the boat another year, then establish the amount we were willing to spend for improvements during that year.

This approach has worked very satisfactorily. Because of the limitations placed on our annual financial commitment, we have managed to avoid a number of mistakes by carefully thinking through each improvement during the year or two it was working its way up our priority list.

Of course, priorities have changed from time to time. For example, we had not expected to make any changes in the rig for several years until we spent one hard, dusty night beating down the coast under #3 genoa and reefed main. The necessity for waking the spouse below each time we tacked made for a long night. It was some time between three and four in the morning that priorities shifted. The next time we went into the yard we installed a self-tending, loose-footed jib that has been a joy ever since. Using an integral turnbuckle and jib-boom fitting on the headstay permits quick removal of the working jib and its club when a genoa or reacher is called for. When the wind pipes up, it is helpful to be able to reef the club-footed jib down to a practical storm sail.

The first task we addressed ourselves to was improving our ground tackle. Our warm Florida climate makes it more comfortable to anchor out during most of the year; and good holding power equals a good night's sleep. During the summer thunderstorm season we usually put two anchors out ahead of us at good angles off the bow.

Reef Runner actually carries five anchors: A 35-pound CQR plow, a 20-pound high tensile Danforth, a 20-pound folding stainless steel Northill, a 15-pound plow and a 12-pound high-tensile Danforth. As a concession to my 55-year-old back we installed a heavy stainless steel bow fitting with integral roller, beautifully fabricated for us by a custom hardware manufacturer. The big plow anchor hangs over the bow on the roller where it is always ready to let go at the pull of a quick release pin, along with 60 feet of 5/16-inch chain bent to 300 feet of 5/8-inch nylon warp. The chain is BBB link in anticipation of the windlass which will inevitably be required. The 20-pound Danforth shackles to 20 feet of chain and its own 5/8-inch line. All line is marked at 10-foot intervals, both visually and to the touch, with marline seizings. While under way we always carry the small 12-pound Danforth on the stern pulpit fastened to six feet of light chain and a tub full of 3/8-inch nylon. In case of grounding on one of

Detail of custom-fabricated bow roller with anchor in place

Florida's ubiquitous sand bars, one can quickly swim out the light anchor on a cockpit cushion, plant it, and winch off stern first.

An analysis of our log demonstrated that, from May through September of each year, *Reef Runner* was under power 80 percent of the time. In an attempt to improve performance while using the "iron jib" we removed our Martec folding prop and replaced it with a three-bladed wheel of flatter pitch. A year later we concluded that the Martec pushed us along slightly faster and was less noisy, even though the three-blader did give more rapid response in reverse and better performance against a head sea. So we reinstalled the Martec.

Early on, we assigned a high priority to improving ventilation in the main cabin. This dictated the installation of the largest practicable hatch through the cabin top. After debating the merits of the various stock metal hatches available, we decided to have a teak-framed Lucite hatch built. This choice was facilitated when our yacht yard made available to us a first-class ship's carpenter who fabricated and installed a beautiful 24-inch-square, double-opening hatch. Its stream of air makes the main cabin a delightful place at anchor, while under way in moderate seas it may be left open, facing aft. Our carpenter also blessed us with heavy teak gratings for the cockpit and head, and a number of other woodworking goodies. Notable among the miscellany is a series of hand holds he carved into the teak cockpit coamings which transform them into effective grab rails.

With her long centerboard and full width traveler *Reef Runner* balances nicely under most conditions. On a screaming beam reach, however, her tiller becomes a little heavy for lighter muscles to handle. It was on one such occasion that Betty suggested installing a wheel. This started the traditional debate that has been going on since the wheel first went to sea. Because our generous cockpit will seat eight people comfortably at a sundown raft-up, the need for additional space was not a major inducement. Actually, by throwing the tiller straight up against the mainsheet tackle, it is less obtrusive at anchor than a wheel would be. But under way, a wheel decidedly has the edge, with the pedestal providing bonus facilities in the way of folding tables, binocular cases and gadget pouches. The final decision still is open, though we have installed a Tillermaster 12-volt automatic pilot and she has stood her watch well for many hours on end without complaining about either the chow or the weather. Electrical consumption is negligible except when we are spanked by a quartering sea. At such times Tillie toils pretty steadily.

Our greatest dilemma turned out to be the refrigeration problem. As the availability of ice has declined in our cruising area, mechanical refrigeration appears more and more to be an attractive and practical solution. However, the more I studied the problem, the more complicated it appeared and the more it seemed to violate the principle that simplicity always should be the objective—to be departed from only for good and compelling reasons. Long ago a friend, wise in cruising lore, pointed out that a simple boat will leave the slip more often than a more complex one.

In due course we considered every form of seagoing refrigeration including LP gas, which had proven quite satisfactory on one of our earlier boats. Because of the snug fit of our engine under its box, there was too little space to belt on a compressor. This left electric power as the most acceptable al-ternative and we finally selected a refrigeration unit which operates on either 12 volts DC or 110 volts AC. Its two compressors, each driven by a separate motor of different voltage, fit neatly and unobtrusively behind the port quarter berth in a little-used corner of the lazarette. There is sufficient ventilation there and neither noise nor vibration is a problem. The evaporator and ice trays occupy half of what was formerly the ice compartment of the cockpit loading box, leaving the other half for cold drinks. The food compartment stays at about 45 degrees Fahrenheit on a typical Florida summer day with an average current draw of 4.5 ampere hours on 12 volts.

Of course, the advent of electric refrigeration required us to beef up our entire electrical system. First, we wired our two 105-ampere-hour batteries in parallel to double their capacity as our #1 battery bank, which is used for all purposes *except* engine starting. A new 85-ampere-hour battery was connected to the #2 side of the master switch, solely for starting use, and a volt-meter was wired into the system to give instantaneous readings of battery condition at a flick of the switch. An expanded scale ammeter was let into the switch panel to provide a constant indication of the load on the system to within a quarter of an amp. On the input side, the original 35-amp. alternator was replaced with one having a 55-amp. capacity, which was as large as we could pack under the engine box. In a way it is fortunate we couldn't in-

Handholds carved in teak coaming transform them into effective grab rails

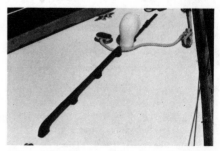

Teak grab rail on foredeck is handy for attaching things to, and for extra support and safety when deck is pitching

stall a larger one because the RPM of our small four-cylinder auxiliary drops off noticeably when the new alternator picks up a full load.

Completing the installation is a 30-amp. marine converter, fitted under the cockpit, which efficiently maintains the batteries at full charge using 110-volt shore power. At the dock the refrigerator is kept running and the batteries trickle charging so that we always put to sea with a cold box and topped-off batteries. Running the engine a minimum of two hours a day provides adequate electrical power to operate the refrigerator, radios, stereo, pressure water system, anchor light and reading lights for a week of cruising. Of course the less the drain, the less use the engine gets.

Water has never been a problem on *Reef Runner*'s short cruises. Pressure salt water is available in the galley and cockpit for cleanup and wash-down purposes and saltwater showers are the rule. As part of a continuing maintenance program we have replaced the freshwater hoses with ⅜-inch copper pipe and added both an accumulator tank and a charcoal filter to the pressure water system. The header tank minimizes electrical consumption by reducing cycling of the pressure pump and smoothes the flow of water; the taste filter smoothes the sundown libation.

Like most keel centerboarders, our boat likes to sail on her bottom. It has always been our practice to roll a reef in the main when the angle of heel consistently exceeds 20 degrees. Although our roller reefing is quite efficient, we have recently added fittings for a single slab or jiffy reef down to the first batten of our mainsail, all that is needed since any further shortening of sail would normally involve reducing the fore triangle. If it should become necessary to take in additional mainsail, however, the original slab reef forms a cushion of cloth around which a beautiful, even reef can be rolled. By applying the roller-reefing handle with determination, a most effective reef can be cranked in down to storm trysail size.

Jib boom is installed but can be quickly removed for times when genoa or reacher is to be used

Just as a proper cockpit dodger is an almost required item for crew comfort under way in any cruising boat, so is a deck awning a necessity at anchor. *Reef Runner*'s dodger spans the full width of the cockpit and fastens securely to a teak coaming on the cabin trunk just forward of the companionway. Our awning, when rolled around its light battens, duplicates the dimensions of the spinnaker pole and stows neatly where the pole was formerly carried on the cabin top.

Yacht designers have complicated the problem of dinghy stowage by constantly moving the mast farther aft to accommodate progressively larger headsails. Accordingly, it has become impossible to fit a dinghy of any practical size abaft the mast on any modern boat much under 40 feet. Many of our friends have opted for inflatables, which perform well under outboard power and are easy to slither in and out of when diving for crawfish or stone crabs.

We elected to go with an eight-foot fiberglass tender with built-in flotation. At 85 pounds it is easy to launch and recover, rows and tows well, and after four years of hard use has proven virtually indestructible. It stows bottom up, forward of the mast, and provides protection for the forward hatch which may be left open beneath it in all but the heaviest seas. At anchor, the dink can be turned into an effective windsail by lashing its two transom eyes to the grab rails on each side of the cabin house

Reef Runner *with dodger spanning full width of cockpit. Note also dinghy located forward of mast. When raised into air at bow, dink can be turned into very effective windsail for forward hatch*

and hoisting its bow into the air with the jib halyard.

This winter we are poring over our voluminous library of marine catalogs, rechecking Don Street's *The Ocean Sailing Yacht* and pulling together our priorities for *Reef Runner*'s spring overhaul. In the cards is a roller-furling reacher of vast overlap to supplant the club-footed jib in light air. Next in line is a single sideband radio to supersede our trusty double sideband when it goes to that great out-of-license place in the sky. Perhaps, some morning this spring, there will be a new stove complete with oven on our front doorstep.

In the meantime, while *Reef Runner* has been performing her new tricks as a cruising boat, I continue to enjoy the thrills of offshore racing as navigator aboard other yachts. Admittedly, there is a certain satisfaction in helping sail a good race and then seeing your skipper step up to claim his silver; but it is something less than the thrill of walking up to the trophy table in one's own behalf.

Next weekend, possibly, sailing our own little jewel into a favorite anchorage, rowing the dinghy ashore and strolling down an uninhabited beach, it may occur to me that I have the best of both worlds.

Sails & Rigging

Short-Handed Cruising

Thoughts on workable rigs   Jerry Cartwright

Many **boat owners** with an aversion to carrying large crews are becoming increasingly aware that there is practically no limit to the size of sailboat that can be handled short-handed — if the rig and deck layouts are right. There have been some mind-boggling examples of big boats in the Singlehanded Transatlantic races.

A cruising boat should first be seaworthy; but part of this seaworthiness comes from having a sailplan that is sturdy, efficient, and easily handled. A rule of thumb when fitting out for a small crew is that *maximum efficiency must be sought for minimum effort expended.*

One of the most important attributes any crew can possess is confidence in their ability to handle their vessel safely and effectively in all weathers. The engine, electronics gear, and a ship-to-shore radio always should be considered realistically for what they are — helpful *aids* that can contribute to the smooth operation of a boat, but woefully unreliable when used as a crutch. When any cruising boat puts to sea, it should be with a total commitment to self-sufficiency. Everything aboard should contribute to this independence — including the attitude of the crew.

The rig and sailplan are the *modus operandi* of a short-handed boat, so what *is* the proper rig? Opinions differ, but in the field conditions of a singlehanded race, where efficiency and ability to cope are absolute requirements, rigs do fall into a general pattern.

Entries up to 35′ LOA have been almost entirely rigged as single- or double-headed sloops. On sizes up to 50′ LOA, the sloop or cutter rig is still favored, although not so strongly. Above that figure, the sail-plan is usually a ketch or some other split-rig configuration.

Whatever the rig, a basic necessity for safe and efficient handling is a reasonably small mainsail. A small crew can nearly always handle the foresail area, especially if it is broken up into a double headsail or cutter plan. But a large, long-footed main is hard work and a constant menace at sea on a short-handed boat. On a boat equipped with a well-stayed modern rig, weather helm is usually reduced and often the boat will sail very well off the wind under headsails alone. Furthermore, the potentially dangerous consequences of an accidental gybe are greatly reduced.

The full-battened mainsail can be expected to find increasing favor on various cruising boats. It greatly reduces slatting and wear when one is becalmed with an old sea running; if cut correctly, it is very efficient in light airs; and it reefs beautifully when using slab, or jiffy, reefing.

This type of reefing is especially adaptable to the modern bermuda rig with the smaller, higher-aspect mainsail. On a stiff modern cutter, the crew rarely has to reef down more than once, depending instead upon headsail changes to reduce area. Slab reefing also is cheaper to fit than roller reefing, not an unimportant consideration for most cruising boats.

A staysail is greatly improved by battens. And both the staysail and the jib should incorporate a row of reef points with extra clew and tack cringles in order to reduce sail area. It's been my experience that it's easier and faster to reef a foresail than to change it.

A deeply reefed full-battened main and reefed staysail make very efficient and manageable storm sails, and it saves the cost of two more sails. In very heavy conditions when it may be desirable or necessary to keep the boat just forging ahead, an effective method of reducing wind pressure is to set the traveler well to leeward and let out the reefed main until it begins to shake. Then sheet the main in just enough to put the sail to sleep. Lazy jacks are also useful on a full-battened main for hoisting and lowering it in heavy conditions.

A strong, well-placed boom gallows is another welcome fitting. Although it is obviously an aid for a short-handed crew when they are lowering and securing the main, its legs also can serve as mooring bitts and snatch-block attachments. In port, the gallows becomes a handy awning frame; and at sea, it makes a nice support for the navigator when taking sights (especially on a single-masted boat).

I do not think it advisable to fit wire-reel halyard winches to the mast of a short-handed boat. They are slower, particularly when dropping sails, and can develop problems a small crew can do without. An ordinary winch is also cheaper as a rule.

Spare halyards should be carried, along with a length of wire that is longer than the longest stay, and equal in strength to the forestay. A galvanized spare is cheaper than stainless; and don't forget wire clamps for quick jury-rig operations.

Several jam cleats of the type similar in appearance to an ordinary cleat but with one end snubbed off should be carefully fitted to correct positions both on the mast and in the cockpit. These can quickly secure a sheet or halyard when speed is imperative, which is most of the time. While I have never had one slip, I do doubly secure them later.

If the boat is cutter rigged, running backstays will contribute considerable extra strength to the mast. Hopefully, the rig will be designed so the runners are positioned far enough forward to permit close-hauled tacking without releasing the leeward runner each time. A helpful wrinkle is to put two small blocks on each of the aft lower shrouds: one lashed at deck level and the other secured about three feet higher. These can carry a light line connected to the runner along the deck and back to the cockpit. When the runner is released, this line is pulled tight and cleated off. This effectively hauls the runner forward against the shroud, clearing the mainsail and saving a trip forward.

A mainsheet traveler, a boom vang, and an outhaul arrangement — all operated from an inboard position — are essential for proper mainsail trim. They must work easily and well. The boom vang can be a heavy rubber mooring snubber of the type sold in many chandleries. It is looped over the boom and under the mainsail and attached to a block assembly on the rail and cleated off. It is simple, cheap, and effective.

A cunningham hole is not needed for there is no hoist restriction on a cruising boat. However, a long downhaul track that extends almost to the deck is a great help in jerking the mainsail down in a hurry (watch your shins) when the halyard is slacked off.

Some singlehanded boats are rigged with permanently attached steps leading up the mast in case one has to go aloft at sea. The trouble is they add weight and windage where it is definitely not wanted. A good alternative is a stowable ladder made up of four-strand rope with hefty wooden dowel stock cut into short lengths and used as rungs spaced about a foot apart. Each end of the rung should be pushed through the rope and seized.

The ladder should be wide enough so that a man can place both feet on the same rung, and its length should be about three feet shorter than the mast. Eyes are spliced in at each end, with the top one taking the halyard hoist and the lower end secured firmly to the deck. The ladder must be stretched tight, and when you are climbing it, it's a good idea to secure it to the mast in a couple of spots if it is blowing hard or the boat is rolling (it probably will be). Once you reach the top, you should snap on your harness for security.

All lower halyard ends should be kept permanently attached, for they do have a habit of disappearing at embarrassing moments aboard a short-handed boat. The jam cleats have a hole drilled just for this purpose.

Twin forestays are convenient for keeping an extra sail hanked on and ready to run. This arrangement can save a lot of energy, but there can be problems. Correct tensioning is difficult, and there have been instances where the hanks on the hoisted sail have been accidentally released or fouled by the other stay. If you do use two stays, they should be positioned at least six inches apart at the base.

Some singlehanders fit a connecting plate which leads both stays to a common turnbuckle and maintains equal tension. Two forestays do give extra security and often serve nicely for hoisting twin running jibs. These downwind sails can make a tradewind crossing very pleasant indeed if they are adequate in area and are correctly set up.

Whether twins are used or not, there should be at least two jib halyards available on any cruising boat. The wire part should be long enough to be carried forward and made taut to a keeper fitting on the pulpit. You should use snap shackles that can be opened under pressure and they should be swaged or spliced to the hoist end of the halyards. They are expensive but they are worth it, for speed can be important here.

A substantial topping lift can double as an emergency mainsail halyard. I carry my topping lift fall aft ($\frac{3}{8}$" dacron) to the transom where it leads through a block to a jam cleat. It saves another trip forward.

Rolling-furling genoas seem to be getting better all the time, and they do make life aboard a short-handed boat considerably easier. If one is fitted, a second forestay should be set up about a foot forward. It is good security, and can also serve as a stay for a big drifter or emergency working sails if the furling gear should go.

Probably the most important fitting nowadays on any short-handed cruising boat on a long passage is a strong and reliable self-steering vane. It can spell the difference between a pleasurable cruise and an endurance contest.

Heel and windspeed indicators, if used with vane steering, should be mounted below, but in a position where they can also be seen from the cockpit. A telltale compass (it can be a cheap model) should also be mounted below for a constant check on heading. A flashlight can be used for night observations, but asleep or awake I keep a lowered kerosene lamp burning continuously during the night.

Ideally, a constant watch should always be kept at sea, but the realities of short-handed voyaging being what they are, with a good vane and a tired crew, it probably won't be. An ordinary wind-up egg timer is a good alarm to keep from oversleeping.

A seagoing cockpit should be deep, protected, and fairly small. Large winches are a blessing as are boxes incorporated into the coaming or elsewhere to take sheet tailings. A spaghetti-like mess in the bottom of the cockpit is maddening and can be very dangerous.

A wire dacron jackstay that leads along the deck from each side of the cockpit all the way forward is advisable. This gives a clear lead on which to snap a safety harness line. This is a good habit to cultivate when sailing shorthanded.

Strong lifelines, 28" to 30" high, should attach to a bow pulpit that can be *leaned* against when lowering or setting sail. Synthetic netting should be laced to the lines forward. This netting isn't to stop someone from being washed overboard in heavy weather, but rather to keep headsails aboard when they are being lowered. As a further help, I tie several short lengths of line to the top lifeline, keeping them permanently attached and available to lash a lowered sail quickly.

Sheets can be kept permanently attached to working and storm sails, preferably with a seized bowline instead of a shackle. A shackle in the clew of a storm jib can become a lethal weapon in a good breeze. Using snatch blocks for sheet leads, with plenty of spots along the deck for their attachment, will also save time.

Always install good navigation lights and make them watertight. A xenon flasher is a good flare-up light, and a radar reflector permanently mounted aloft (try under a spreader) is a must. If it is not permanently installed, a time will come when it *should* be put up but the crew is too tired to bother.

In conclusion, all fittings and equipment should contribute both to maximum efficiency and the conservation of energy. A small crew doesn't have a great deal of energy to waste.

The rewards of short-handed sailing are well worth the occasional hardships, and there will always be quiet times at sea to watch a sunset and contemplate. At such times, a cockpit fitting designed to hold your rum mug might make that moment even sweeter.

Reef — Don't Buy

How to get the most from less sails

Larry Pardey

Sails for a pure cruising boat should be purchased with the following thoughts in mind: they must be strong, they should be reliable and hold their shape, they should be simple to reef, and easy to maintain. Above all, they must be as inexpensive as possible. Yet many designers of cruising boats show sail plans with six headsails, storm trysails, drifters, spinnakers, possibly twin running sails. The sailmakers and fitting manufacturers chuckle all the way to the bank. So, if you are planning your sail wardrobe for a cruise or if the forepeak of your small liveaboard cruiser is jammed full of seven or eight expensive, wet sail bags, and you would like to use that space for something else such as a private stateroom with a double bunk, here are some simple, well-proven ways you can save space, make sail changes easier, and save money to go cruising.

When it was time to replace the lapper on *Seraffyn*, our 24-foot cutter, we built one with a five-foot-deep set of reef points. When it's reefed it is our working jib. For the price of a set of reef points (about $25) we gained another sail. We've used this sail for over a year and found it ideal. We also put a reef in the working staysail which gives us a storm staysail that could double as a back staysail when we are riding hove-to. Our mainsail with three sets of reef points works equally well as a storm sail.

Seraffyn is cutter rigged, and designed with a large working sail plan so these three sails give us almost all

the balanced combinations we need for winds over force 2 or 3 (Fig. 1):

	sq ft
Lapper, staysail and main (all plain sail)	550
Lapper and main	450
Reefed lapper, staysail and main	430
Reefed lapper and main	325
Reefed lapper and one reef in main	300
Staysail and main with one reef	260
Staysail with double-reefed main	210
Reefed staysail and double-reefed main	182
Reefed staysail and triple-reefed main	140

Reefing a headsail is much easier than:
1. hauling down the jib
2. taking the jib off the headstay
3. bagging the jib
4. bringing the new jib on deck
5. unbagging it
6. changing the sheets
7. hanking on the new sail
8. hauling up the new sail.

With a reefing headsail you:
1. haul the jib down on deck
2. furl and tie the jib sheets into the reefing clew.
3. fasten the tack down
4. tie the reef points
5. haul the jib up reefed and ready to go.

Reefing a main is even faster and easier for you have no sheets to retie. You simply haul down the reefing clew,

49

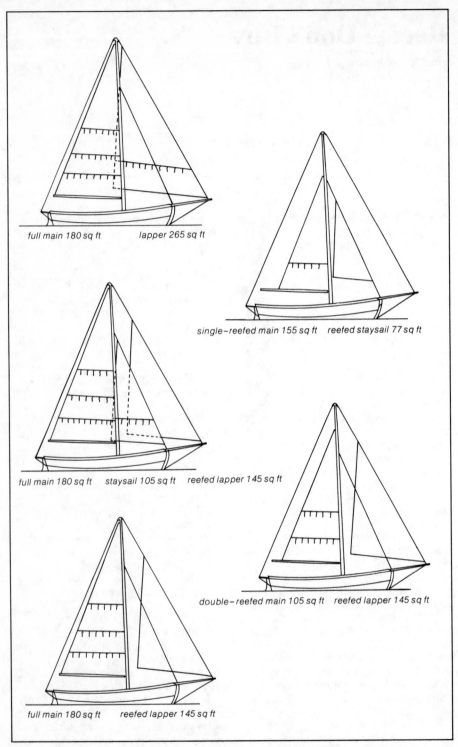

full main 180 sq ft   lapper 265 sq ft

single−reefed main 155 sq ft   reefed staysail 77 sq ft

full main 180 sq ft   staysail 105 sq ft   reefed lapper 145 sq ft

double−reefed main 105 sq ft   reefed lapper 145 sq ft

full main 180 sq ft   reefed lapper 145 sq ft

Figure 1: Seraffyn *can be shortened down in any of the following ways*

secure the reefing tack, then haul the sail up loosefooted. Your reefing pennants should be permanently rove and led to cleats near the main halyard winch. Tie your reef points in when you get around to it.

Another plus with reef points is that if any of your working sails are badly damaged in the foot area you can immediately tie in a reef and carry on. Since most sailboats rely on their main to beat off a lee shore, it's a good idea to have reef points in addition to your other reefing gear in case the foot of the sail rips or the furling gear itself breaks down.

We have never found we needed a storm trysail. During the past seven years and 20,000 miles we have only used the triple-reefed main three times, going to windward in winds of over 50 knots. For heaving-to in extreme conditions we have our reefing staysail/backstaysail (Fig. 2). I think this works well on *Seraffyn* because her stoutly built main is much smaller and farther aft than a sloop rig of similar size.

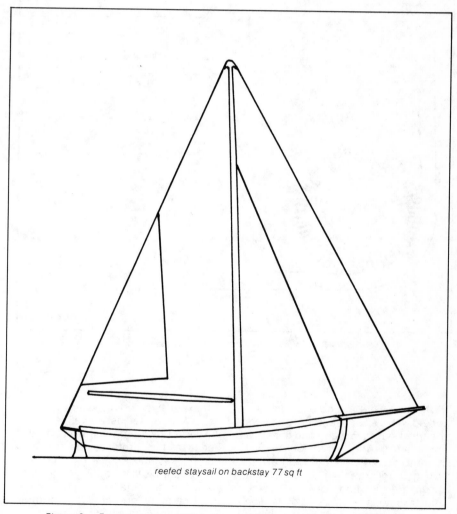

reefed staysail on backstay 77 sq ft

Figure 2:   For extreme conditions there is the reefing staysail/backstaysail

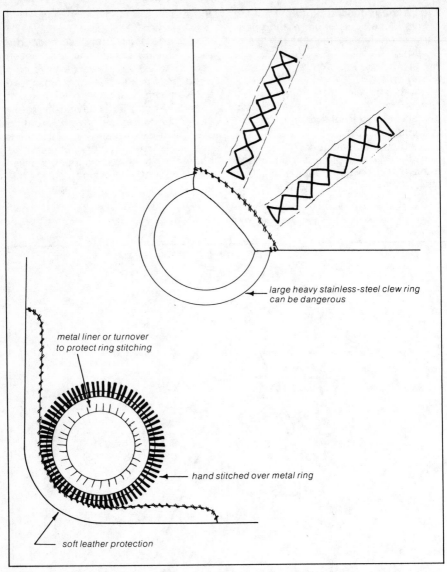

large heavy stainless-steel clew ring can be dangerous

metal liner or turnover to protect ring stitching

hand stitched over metal ring

soft leather protection

Figure 3: Two possible options for headsail clews

When we were in Poole, England, I worked with a sailmaker for two winters to learn about sailmaking and to earn a new main and lapper for *Seraffyn*. I spoke to the owner of the loft about making a roller-reefing, 110 percent lapper. He, in turn, suggested the simpler route, a set of reef points. The reasons he gave were: A reefed jib has no expensive furling gear to break down and will set just as well reefed as un-reefed. A furling sail won't do this because the draft of the sail accumulates aft as the sail is rolled. You may end up with a baggy, inefficiently shaped intermediate jib. A jib rolled on the headstay creates considerable windage forward when you are trying to heave-to, making it harder to keep your bow close to the wind. And finally, you can't hank a different jib on the headstay easily because your furling jib is in the way.

Working at the sail loft, repairing piles of damaged sails showed me various methods of sail construction that work on cruising yachts and others that don't. For offshore, long-distance cruising I want all my working sails triple-stitched. This holds the shape of the sails longer by strengthening their weakest point, the seams. And three rows of stitching are more resistant to chafe.

I like bolt ropes on all the luffs of my working sails, either hand sewn or with a rope inside a strong luff tape. This allows draft control, reefed or un-reefed, that you can't get with a wire-luffed sail. If you are using a jib down-haul, the rope-luffed sail will come down the headstay without jamming because it isn't stiff like wire. Your sails will be easier to bag and take less space to stow without wire luffs.

I prefer handsewn cringles with the ring sewn into a wide area of cloth spreading the load. A stainless-steel clew ring flogging around in the air might knock you out if it hits you just right when you are working the fore-deck (Fig. 3).

Patches at the reefing tacks and clews of your cruising sails should be almost as large and strong as those for an unreefed sail. The forces on the corner patches are about the same reefed or not.

I like heavy taped leeches on my working sails. This takes the strain off the panel stitching and makes it almost impossible to split a seam horizontally from the leech forward.

All cruising headsails should have a hollow leech and foot to prevent flutter and flogging. Your main can also have a hollow leech, like a genoa, without battens or headboard. Torn or chafed batten pockets, incidentally, are the commonest repairs in a sail loft. Having a battenless mainsail allows small boats to raise and lower their mainsails on any point without fouling the shrouds. The original bermuda or leg-of-mutton sails were cut this way for ease of handling. Battens and head-boards were only added later to beat the racing rules.

Nothing is more impractical on a cruising boat than a maximum luff, deck-sweeping, large, overlapping genoa. It chafes against the pulpit, life-lines, blocks and spreaders. A large portion of your field of vision is blocked. It's difficult to tack with because of its long foot. With high cut, small overlap jibs you have less chafe and you can see steamer lights. If your running lights are on the shrouds or cabin sides they will not be obscured by the foot of the sail. The foot of the jib won't scoop up water when you're going to windward. Only racing men put up with all these unseamanlike disadvantages. I know, I've done it racing but it isn't comforting to me to be on watch alone and not have 360-degree visibility.

Space inside 24-foot *Seraffyn* is at a premium and anything we don't have to store below gives us more living or storage space. So first we eliminated a working jib, storm trysail and storm main by adding reef points. We also furl and cover our main on the boom. The staysail is bagged on its stay. We don't use a staysail boom as it clutters up the foredeck too much, makes it harder to handle the anchor gear, the sail rarely sets perfectly on a self-tend-ing boom, and the boom and its gear all cost extra money. Our lapper is re-moved from the bowsprit and stored in a bag on deck. That way our three working sails are kept out of our living space and are right at hand in case we want to go for a short day sail, or we have to move to a new anchorage quickly.

All bags and the sail covers are wa-terproof PVC-covered Dacron fabric which keeps the water and most impor-tant the sun, off our sails. My first main-sail was 3½ years old and looked as though it was in perfect condition, but you could poke your finger through the two lower panels. We had been furling the sail on the boom without a cover and the foot had been exposed to the constant tropical sun. The ultra-violet rays had done their dirty work. Now we take the two or three minutes extra to put on a cover or bag our headsails every time we take them down. We use these three working sails 80 to 90 percent of the time. It's only in winds of Force 3 or less that we have to go below for our light sails.

We sail *Seraffyn* with no engine and only three working sails, a light-weather genoa, drifter and spinnaker, six sails in all. These are more than adequate for simple cruising. And we don't seem to have any serious gaps when we are invited for the occasional informal cruiser race. A small part of the money we saved by having only six sails instead of nine or 10 was spent on having those sails made to extra strong, longer-lasting ocean-cruising specifications.

The next time you see an old photo of a commercial schooner or skipjack from around the turn of the century, notice the area in the large working sail-plan. Note the multiple reefs in the non-overlapping headsails, reefs in the foresails and multiple reefs in the mainsail. The old timers didn't waste their time sewing together three jibs when one with two sets of reefs points, strongly made, would do the job. Try it, it's simple, well proven and in these inflationary times, gratefully cheap.

Save That Sail

Ways to prolong sail life

Glenn Housley

Sails are the most expensive items a boat owner must buy. Moreover, sails deteriorate and the average boat may be outfitted with new sails several times in its lifetime.

How long sails last depends on how they are used — and how little they are abused. There are many things a boat owner can do to prolong their life. The most important, though, is annually to take all the sails to a sailmaker and to discuss with him what he can do to make sails last and hence save money.

For instance, if a boat is equipped with roller-reefing gear, the mainsail takes a beating every time a reef is rolled in. Roller reefing, apart from causing the mainsail to take a poor shape when reefed, often causes punctures along the foot of the sail where the slides are fastened, chafes the luff at the jackline, and exerts a tremendous strain on the sail especially along the leech, strain that stretches and weakens the mainsail.

Slab reefing alleviates all these problems. Essentially a return to the method of reducing canvas popular before roller reefing, slab or jiffy reefing is the method by which, when the halyard is slacked, the sail is drawn down to the boom by prereeved lines running through secondary tack and clew cringles in the sail (SAIL, September 1971).

The system is simple, quick, and, most important, gentle to a properly reinforced sail. Moreover, the funds expended for jiffy reefing will be more than returned in the form of reduced repair bills, and a better setting and longer lasting mainsail.

When arranging for reefing patches and cringles to be installed in a sail, an owner should check with his sailmaker concerning the hardware to buy and where to place the hardware on the boom. Likely the sailmaker has handled a number of such alterations and probably has helpful ideas about a proper installation that will be the best for a particular mainsail.

For the sailor who uses his boat strictly for cruising, there is a simple and inexpensive method to facilitate mainsail handling, reduce repair costs and extend the life of the mainsail. Nearly two thirds of the mainsails we repair have torn batten pockets. By cutting a slight hollow into the leech of a mainsail, the roach and therefore the need for battens is eliminated (Fig. 1). Without battens the sail can be raised or lowered downwind, a maneuver which, with battens, is virtually impossible with-

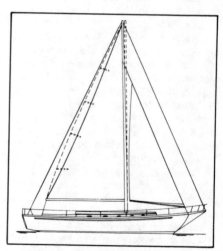

Figure 1: By hollowing cruising mainsail leech a little, area is sacrificed but battens can be eliminated. Rake mast slightly aft to compensate for change of balance

out fouling the spreaders or shrouds and breaking a batten with the subsequent risk of tearing the batten pocket.

Although the roach provides better performance, after several seasons of use it tends to move towards the body of the sail. The result is a sail that has the draft too far aft and is characterized as "blown out."

A hollowed leech resists the tendency of the roach to move forward and the draft aft and hence it can prolong the shape-holding ability of the sail.

For those sailors who cry that with a hollow leech their mainsails would lose performance and a lee helm might result, let me suggest that raking the mast aft a bit probably will compensate for the change of balance and the boat will have reduced heeling moment and thus be more comfortable in stronger winds.

While discussing with a sailmaker ways to extend the life of the mainsail, ask him to look over the places on the sail where chafe is likely. It is best to sew on a patch of sailcloth where the sail is prone to being pinched between the boom and the shrouds or where it rubs on the spreader tips before the sail wears through, rather than to have to patch a hole later.

Likewise, before wear becomes acute is the time for a sailmaker to replace leather or Dacron chafe protection where the sail rubs at the tack and clew fittings and against the mast at the headboard.

Headsails are too often discarded when they are stretched out of shape, not when the cloth has become weak. By re-tensioning the luff and hollowing the leech a sailmaker can prolong the usefulness of a stretched genoa as long as the cloth remains strong (Fig. 2).

Hollowing the leech is a relatively simple operation for a sailmaker, but re-tensioning the luff can prove difficult. Stretchy luff genoa jibs not already fitted with cunningham cringles only may need to have an extra ring sewn in a foot or so above the

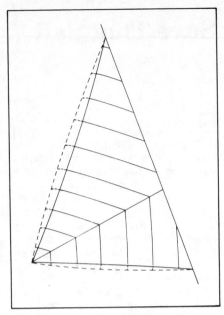

Figure 2: A genoa jib with leech or foot that has stretched can be re-cut with hollow roach and foot

tack to provide a means of varying luff tension and restoring a better shape.

Blown-out jibs with conventional wire sewn into the luff present a more sticky task. Normally, such a sail is cut to permit the luff to stretch to within a few inches of the extreme length of the luff wire. If the sail has not fully stretched to the limit of the wire, a sailmaker can cut the lacing at the head ring and thimble and re-tension the cloth. However, if the sail has stretched the full length of the luff wire then some recutting may be required.

Sailmakers perform these operations frequently and will quickly recognize the problem and can give an estimate for the cost. Although the alteration may seem expensive, the expenditure is worthwhile if the cloth is sound and saves the cost of a new sail.

Roller-furling headsails for cruising have certainly gained a number of proponents in recent years. Although there are perhaps better ways to handle a large headsail, roller furling has several attractive features and more and more cruising sailors are ordering such sails from their sailmakers.

Remaking a conventional jib into a roller-furling sail is an expensive operation and the price difference of such a conversion versus a whole new sail should be a matter of discussion with sailmakers.

If the boat is already equipped with a roller-furled headsail, it should have the special attention of a sailmaker to prolong its life. A well-built roller-furled sail has a taped and marline-hitched 1x19 luff wire with hand stitching the length of the luff. Without this secure method of attaching the cloth of the sail to the luff wire, the wire can twist independently of the sail when being furled. Eventually the system will fail, probably at the time of maximum loading such as during heavy weather.

Let a sailmaker examine your roller-furled headsail for any signs of independent twist and let him restitch the luff wire to the cloth if twist is occurring.

Ultra-violet rays from the sun attack Dacron, and any sail that is left rigged must be protected with either a cover or a strip of cloth that can be replaced easily (Fig. 3). Of course, lowering and stowing a roller-furled jib when it is not being used will protect it from exposure and chafe, but the task may be difficult and all but eliminates the advantage of a handily-furled jib.

If the leech of a roller-furled jib already shows signs of deterioration, a sailmaker can cut down the sail to make a number two genoa or a lapper as the cloth in the body of the sail may still be in excellent shape.

In the meantime, the frugal owner should ask his sailmaker about sewing on leech strips or making up a sleeve that can be hoisted over the headsail when it is not in use.

There are other methods of extending the life of sails by preventive maintenance. Restitching is best done before a seam parts and reseizing before a slide comes loose. Cheap battens break and tear pockets, so use good ones and replace split or warped ones before they do any damage to the sail.

A short tack pennant on a jib can prevent the foot of the jib's chafing on lifelines and the bow pulpit; rollers on shrouds reduce wear on a

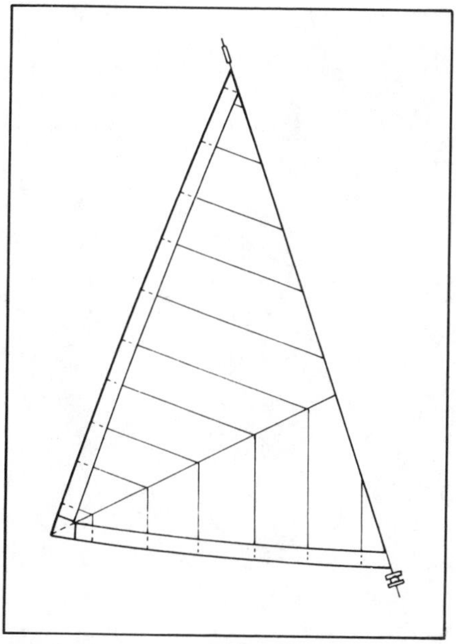

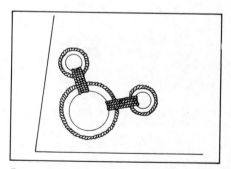

Figure 3: Strips of sailcloth sewn on leech and foot protect cloth in the sail itself from effects of sunlight and chafe

Figure 4: Anchor cringles help prevent clew cringle from distorting

jib as it crosses them during tacking; tape or boots on turnbuckles cut down the chances of a sail's hanging up and tearing on a cotter pin; and an anchor ring sewn in and laced to the clew ring of the mainsail prevents distortion and ultimate failure of the clew ring (Fig. 4).

While any sailmaker is anxious to make a new sail, he realizes that servicing existing sails is a vital part of his business. Also he knows that if he gives an owner good service he will be in line for getting an order for future sails. Thus it is worthwhile to solicit his advice. Remember, though, at times he is apt to be very busy; and the best time both to have a discussion with him and to have him do the best work on your sails is during his slack periods.

The Right Cruising Sails

Choosing proper cloth and construction   Mike Saunders

Contrary to **popular** supposition the wind is not free. It blows for nothing but to catch it costs money. Sometimes a lot of money.

This fact is only too obvious to those of us who have recently bought sails. But once we have bought them, to catch the wind you might say, then surely it is free. You could cheer yourself up by thinking of the powerboat men at the mercy of costly machinery and rising fuel costs; but your cheer though not altogether false would not be altogether true either because gear and especially sails, do wear out.

So because the wind is not entirely free, one has to think carefully about the requirements for cruising sails. The principles, of course, are quite clear: reliability, durability, and practicability. Solid uninteresting principles but ones designed to keep you sailing. The last one is not always compatible with the others but we can go a long way by discarding all that is gimmicky and purely fashionable. I am all for innovation but it must be an improvement and not just a means of keeping up with the Tabarlys.

What then should one look for in a cruising sail? There are three things: materials, construction and shape. Let's look at them separately.

Materials

Polyester filament fiber (Dacron) has gained universal acceptance as a sailcloth simply because it is the best all-round material available. Of its many superior properties its high strength and immunity from damp rot are the most important.

Dacron is, however, far from rot proof. Ultraviolet light breaks down the chemical structure and eventually the material falls apart. Expensive trials have been made all over the world in an effort to determine the rate of decay and the conclusion seems to be that there are so many variables in the light and in the atmosphere that the life of such material is virtually unpredictable. My own experience and that of some other cruising folk suggests something vaguely in the region of 5,000 hours of sunlight, i.e., a year or two of continuous sailing, or about 10 years of weekend sailing.

However the most important thing to look at is the finished cloth rather than the raw fiber. After sailcloth has been woven, it is subject to mystic finishing processes involving resinating. This makes it stretch resistant, glossy, and stiff. A cloth that has been overtreated often makes a poor cruising sail. It can be very stiff and will not set well. It will not handle easily, it will not stow properly and it seems to wear out more quickly, especially along the seams.

Sailmakers do offer different grades of finish including soft, resin-free cloth which is very tightly woven. It can be more expensive, but it lasts longer and I am convinced that, in the long run, a soft, resin-free or slightly resinated film saves money.

Once I had a lightweight genoa of soft cloth that took dreadful abuse, up to Force 7 for thousands of miles, before giving any trouble and then only the stitching disintegrated. Later, when the fabric itself became tired, the whole clew ripped out. But even then it needed a wave jumping over the bows and landing smack in the sail, to do the damage.

As for material weights, the tendency is for cruising sails to be made of cloth that is too heavy. This displays the same vices as cloth that is too stiff. Eric Hiscock in *Cruising Under Sail* (Oxford University Press) gives a table of sail weights which represents average practice. A 300-square-foot main, for instance, is 8.9 ozs/American yd, and a working headsail of the same size is 8.7 ozs/yd. I personally would specify sailcloths about 1½ numbers lighter.

It is interesting that Bernard Moitessier who sailed in the 1968 solo Round-the-World Race tested a 161-square-foot jib of only four-ounce Tergal (like Dacron) compared with the usual six- or seven-ounce weight; the cloth was also of the soft variety. The jib survived more than a circumnavigation in the Southern Ocean and Moitessier found it delightfully easy to use and remarked how well it shaped.

Exactly the same arguments for lightweight working sails apply to storm sails, which are often as stiff as plywood and apparently designed to stand on edge without the assistance of either mast or rigging. In general, I feel storm sails (both headsail and trysail) should be about the same weight as working sails, though they must be carefully reinforced.

The secret of light sails is not only to use good cloth but to reinforce them extensively. And that is the next point.

Construction

When a Dacron sail rips, it nearly always is along a seam. In fact, a sail frequently requires complete re-stitching several times during its life, and this I feel is the weak link in sail construction.

The reason for this weakness can be found in the nature of the cloth itself. Even the softest Dacron cloth is hard and slippery compared with cotton. The stitching holds the pieces together rather like staples hold two sheets of plastic. Any movement between the pieces tends to chafe across the thread and, in effect, the sail becomes self-chafing.

While there is no elegant solution to this problem, all cruising sail seams *must* be triple-stitched (three rows of

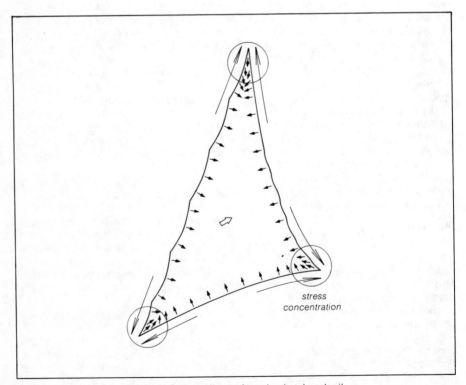

stress concentration

Figure 1: General lines of tension in a headsail

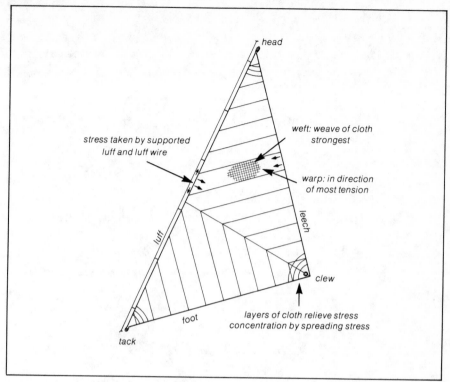

Figure 2: One way of construction that withstands stress

Labels within the figure:
- head
- weft: weave of cloth strongest
- stress taken by supported luff and luff wire
- warp: in direction of most tension
- leech
- luff
- clew
- foot
- layers of cloth relieve stress concentration by spreading stress
- tack

stitching) with the heaviest thread. This greatly reduces the chafe but does not eliminate it. Some feel that because stitching stands clear of the Dacron cloth, hand stitching which beds the thread, should be used for the third row.

I very much doubt whether the extra cost is justified. One answer is to glue or weld in addition to stitching, but unfortunately neither technique is developed enough to be in widespread use. Some sailmakers will glue, and anyone ordering a new sail should ask for a quotation and judge whether the extra expense is worthwhile.

Apart from the seams, the sail should be very well reinforced at every stress point. Figures 1, 2 and 3 help illustrate the problems and try to give some of the solutions in the case of a headsail.

Figure 1 shows how a triangular piece of cloth distorts under the pressure of wind, and shows the stresses created. In Figure 2 we see how a

sailmaker generally constructs the sail to withstand the stresses and retain its shape.

Much more than this is required, however, in a good cruising sail. Every stress point, even minor ones, must be considered, for over a long period heavy loads, fluctuating loads, flogging, etc., will exploit a weakness and endanger the whole sail.

Figure 3 illustrates the reinforcing required at four common points of weakness. Some of the severest stresses concentrate at the clew, and an eyelet bedded in concentric layers of cloth will pull out eventually because it cannot spread the load far enough. Fig 3A shows one way to spread the load more evenly. Similar problems are encountered at the head and the tack, but because of the luff rope which takes the load in one direction perfectly, a slightly different technique is required (Fig. 3B).

The ends of seams invariably give

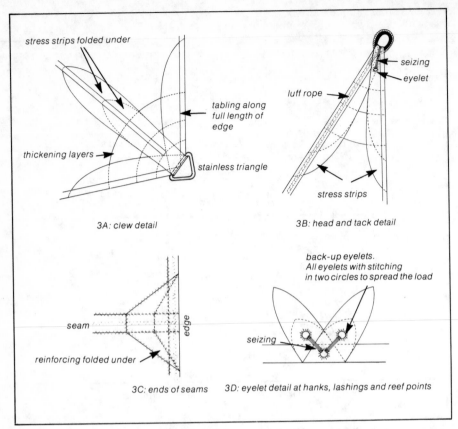

3A: clew detail

3B: head and tack detail

3C: ends of seams

3D: eyelet detail at hanks, lashings and reef points

Figure 3: Reinforcement details

trouble unless reinforced, and Figure 3C shows how this can be done. Eyelets must also be reinforced and a good way of spreading the load from an eyelet to the cloth is with two concentric circles of stitching, as shown in Fig. 3D. Incidentally, this is nothing new. On H.M.S. *Victory*, Nelson's flagship in the battle of Trafalgar and still the flagship of the Royal Navy, this same technique was used.

One edge presents a particular problem, and that is the luff of a foresail. In my own experience, a luff wire is a nuisance. It chafes through at piston hanks and other points, it makes the sail more difficult to handle, and if not made of the correct grade of stainless steel it can either corrode or attack the cloth. Galvanized wire, plastic covered or otherwise, is poor because salt water is trapped in the cloth and in the

splices and corrodes the wire.

On the other hand, I have had good performance out of prestretched Dacron rope luffs, and would certainly use them again for longevity and ease of handling. But they do sag to leeward and can affect windward performance a little.

One source of irritation is the failure of brass eyelets through corrosion, aided by chafe. It is possible to side-step the problem at head and tack by using stainless thimbles, and at the clew by using a stainless triangle. But at other places you have to grin and bear it unless you can get bronze eyelets, which are quite difficult to obtain.

Finally, there is what I feel is indifferent performance of the many bronze piston hanks, which flog free and simply do not last the life of the sail. Stainless ones are claimed to be better and certainly seem so. And then there are any number of grooved headsail systems which are specialized and good. But if you use hanks, they should be seized *solidly* to the sail with a square lashing and not allowed to swivel (and chafe) as is often the case.

Shape

The outline dimensions of the sail usually are determined by the design, but there is a certain amount of flexibility in the things you can (and should) decide for yourself.

The most important is camber, or curvature, of the sail. As shown in Figure 4, this is expressed as the ratio of cord to depth, and typically this can vary from 1/7 to 1/25. C. A. Marchaj in his book *Sailing Theory and Practice* (Adlard Coles) treats the effects of camber on performance at some length, but his results boil down to this: the greater the camber, the greater the driving force of the sail, but at the same time the side force (heeling force) rises even faster. So when going to windward in strong winds you want flat sails. But in light winds, when heeling is not critical, more curvature is advantageous. Off the wind, where heeling does not matter so much, greater curvature is more effective. Marchaj concludes that a racing boat should have sails of different cuts for different conditions.

On a cruising boat this will not do. Here you want a suit of sails that can serve as jack-of-all-trades, and here not only performance but also ease of handling is important. Flat sails are easier to handle in strong winds, and easier to set in all winds. A flat main also seems to reef down better. Also, minimum heeling for maximum driving force is the most important single consideration in strong winds.

For cruising, therefore, I think that moderately flat sails with a camber of about 1/15 are best. A possible exception might be light-weather sails which could be about 1/9. A good sailmaker, incidentally, will want to know how your boat is rigged as this can also affect the camber of the headsails.

Battens are another important point. I have passed through the whole gamut of batten experience, from a trimaran I once built which had a fully-battened main with a roach that stood out like a gleaming, siliconed bust, to a completely flat-chested job, battenless and roach-free. I am sorry to say the flat-chested sail was best for cruising. The reason is that battens are arch promoters of chafe. Not only do they eventually chafe through their pockets, but they break, get lost, and get in the way when you are reefing and furling. They also have a nasty habit of snagging in the shrouds when you are hoisting sail off the wind.

Designers, of course, like a battened-out roach because, aerody-

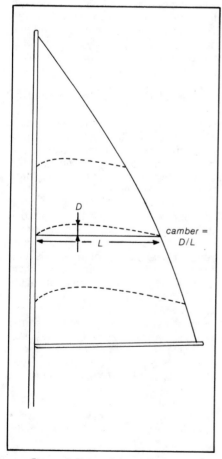

Figure 4: Determining sail camber

camber = D/L

63

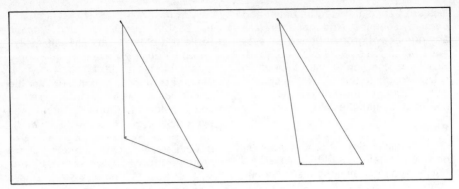

Figure 5: Headsail shape

namically, it is more efficient. But designers do not have the problem of repairing a sail in St. Helena, for example, where the only heavy sewing machine on the island used to belong to a gnarled old barman, who was also a part-time shoe-mender. The difficulty of cranking the machine into action was only exceeded by the difficulty of cranking the barman into action, and the result of both efforts was more like a crippled shoe than a batten pocket. So in the teeth of the most convincing aerodynamic evidence, my own option is for a straight and sturdy leech without battens.

The other thing designers like is a high aspect ratio, again for sound aerodynamic reasons. The problem here for the cruising man is one of both ease of handling and more especially, wear. One of the congenital defects of any marconi sail is its tendency to twist. Twist affects performance and is also a great nuisance off the wind, when the sail tends to bear up against shrouds and spreaders.

The only way to reduce twist on a marconi main is to tension the leech by hauling down on the boom with sheets, guy and kicking strap. The higher the aspect ratio, the greater must be the tension, and the more quickly the sail and gear wears out. Clearly there is no hard and fast rule here but personally I would be reluctant to have a luff more than 2.5 times the length of the foot, and would prefer a figure closer to 2.2.

The dimensions of the main are very often fixed, but headsails generally allow some choice. Twist again is a source of annoyance, but with headsails this can be dealt with by selecting the correct shape. Look at Figure 5 and you will see two sails; the left-hand one obviously will set easily without twist, the other will not. Yet both sails have the same area and the same length of luff.

Headsails take the greatest punishment, particularly from the seas breaking on the bow. A smaller heavy-duty sail should have the foot cut well up to avoid the waves. This is especially important with bowsprits, which tend to expose their headsails to the full force of a breaking wave.

So if you are interested in new sails, a round-robin request for quotations accompanied by a thumbnail sketch, will merely result in a range of prices reflecting a variety of materials and techniques which will be impossible to compare. You must specify right at the start, and as fully as you are able, exactly what it is you want. If you are unsure of certain points, specify something anyway because the first objective is to get comparable quotations. Once you have a sailmaker, you can draw on his expertise to settle any final details.

Remember that what you really want is a sail that will not let you down when you get involved with whatever you are planning to get involved in!

Essentials of Furling Gear

Roller systems for shorthanding

Chet Swenson

Contrary to popular thought, not all singlehanded sailing involves crossing great oceans. Nor to my mind does it involve sailing alone. It does, however, imply being able to sail the ship by one's self as an alternative to going forward (in a breeze for example) where even brawn and great experience would prefer not to tread. This is where the virtues of rigging a boat for singlehanded sailing lie; so that all sail may be trimmed, set, reefed and handed with the crew safe and secure in the cockpit.

One of today's most serviceable pieces of singlehanded gear is the modern furling system. One kind of standard furling gear consists of a furling drum, furling swivel and furling sheet that controls the setting and furling of the sail (Fig. 1). Despite the growing use of furling gear among cruising sailors however, the advantages of a properly rigged furling system frequently are lost because of an inadequate understanding of furling gear, its application, and the requirements for proper rigging.

While furling gear can control any sail whether that sail is set flying, on a stay, or on a spar, the problems of each application require significantly different solutions.

Before we discuss rigging furling gear let's look at the sail. To begin with, any sail with furling gear must be set flying so the luff of the sail is free to rotate and gather in the body of the sail as the sail furls itself around its rotating luff. In order to accommodate this furling action, a sail cannot have any battens.

Therefore, if a furling sail such as a main or mizzen is set to a spar it will have to be recut to eliminate the battens. And any roach that may have been cut into the sail will have to be removed to assure that the leech will stand without the support given by the battens. Of course the sail must also be loose footed so that it can furl freely and fairly about its luff. This, as we shall see, does not mean that the sail cannot be set to a boom or club. It only means that we must satisfy some requirements that are unique to the rigging of furling gear so that the sail sets properly and the furling gear operates with complete ease and dependability.

After a sail has been cut, or recut, for roller furling, the gear can be rigged to the sail. Let's clearly establish our terminology, especially with respect to the difference between *roller furling* and *roller reefing*. Roller furling is what I am talking about in this article and it is a method of furling a sail by wrapping it about its own luff as I have already explained.

Roller reefing is a way to reduce or reef a sail by wrapping it around a boom. A sail can be reduced and stowed by completely wrapping it

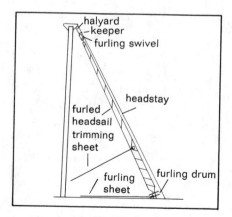

Figure 1

(labels in figure: halyard, keeper, furling swivel, headstay, furled headsail trimming sheet, furling sheet, furling drum)

around the boom until the entire sail is furled on the boom, but this is rarely done, and roller reefing usually is only used to shorten sail.

Roller furling also may be used to shorten sail by only partially wrapping it until only the desired amount of sail remains flying, but this application requires special attention to the sail's luff.

If you are rigging any furling gear to a headsail that will be set independent of the headstay, jibstay or forestay, your first consideration must be to choose a suitable location behind the stay to set the sail. Do not use the sail's luff wire as a substitute for the headstay. Leave the headstay in place to serve the important function of giving additional longitudinal support to the mast.

If you always have the headstay in place there never is any question of your ability to lower your furling headsail as long as you have a headstay to support the mast. In addition, the presence of a permanent headstay allows a convenient way to rig the swivel keeper as a means of preventing the swivel from rotating (Fig. 2).

The singlehander also may want to explore other available furling systems. Some have specialized application such as downwind rigs, others are useful for all points of sailing. Many of these rigs do provide an integral system for combining the luff and swivel furling features of the rig with a single headstay, and they are capable of providing luff tensions to meet the demands of the most experienced offshore sailor.

When you are rigging any standard furling gear, the drum should rotate as the luff of the sail revolves. The upper swivel however, must allow the top of the sail to rotate but the body of the swivel must stand fast. If it doesn't, the swivel will twist the halyard. I was vividly reminded of this once when someone forgot to attach the swivel keeper to the headstay before the sail was hoisted. When the sail was broken out the 1/4" 7x19 stainless steel halyard

parted just as though it was a pinched noodle. The resulting crash of the swivel could have been serious if the foredeck had not been clear of hands.

The furling drum must always be set on deck and must be placed far enough behind the headstay to assure that the sail, when it is fully furled, clears the headstay and does not bind or rub against it. In addition, a backup plate should be used beneath the deck to spread the drum load once the sail is set up. The backup plate should be at least equal in area to the size of the furling gear's base plate. If your boat is rigged with lifelines (and what knowledgeable singlehander would have it otherwise) you will have to use a tack pennant to allow your headsail to "clear the rail" unless it is cut unusually high (Fig. 3). And here we come to my pet peeve: the incompatibility of swaged fittings in any given size with the corresponding marine eyes and their corresponding sized jaws! Roller furling sails are made up with

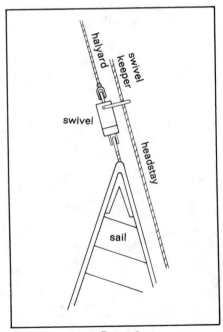

Figure 2

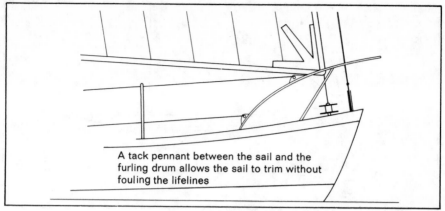

A tack pennant between the sail and the furling drum allows the sail to trim without fouling the lifelines

Figure 3

a wire rope luff that terminates in a marine eye. If your headsail will clear your lifelines when the tack is run directly into the jaws of the furling drum located on deck, you are in good shape.

But if, as is usually the case, your sail is too low at the clew, then you must use a tack pennant to raise the tack of the sail to a point where it will clear the lifelines. The best way to do this is to have a pennant made up of a length of 1x19 stainless-steel wire rope with a jaw at one end and an eye at the other. The eye can then be let into the jaws on the furling drum and the jaw end of the pennant can be let into the eye at the tack of the sail; that is if the eye will fit the jaw. But unfortunately they don't make them like that. You'll usually find the marine eye is too large for the jaw.

The answer is either to make up the pennant with an eye, and then rig two plates to be bolted to each side of the eye (you can't use a shackle to join them for you can't pass the body of the shackle through the eye). Or you can have the sail made up with a jaw for a tack fitting and use a single plate to join the pennant to the sail (Fig. 4).

The *furling sheet* is what you use to furl the sail. When a sail is fully furled, there should be eight to ten turns of the furling sheet around the furling drum. This is an important allowance for the number of turns required to furl the sail will vary with the strength of the wind. When the wind blows hardest, the sail is wrapped tightest and the amount of sheet required to furl the sail is greatest. The sail, of course, is unfurled by casting off the furling sheet and taking in on the trimming sheet (Fig. 1).

However, you should keep a small

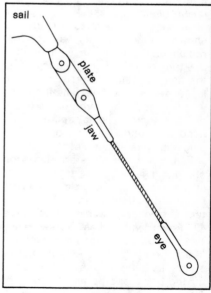

Figure 4

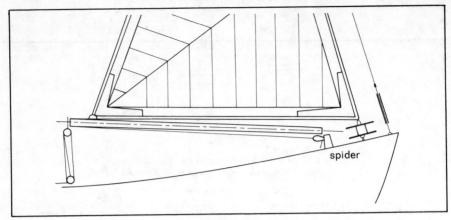

Figure 5

amount of tension on the furling sheet at the same time as you trim in. If you do not, the furling sheet will not rewind smoothly and fairly around the furling drum. Similarly, when you are furling the sail on a windless or light air day, keep a little tension on the trimming sheet to put a little load on the furling drum. If you do not, the sail will wrap so loosely about itself that you may run out of furling sheet before the sail is fully furled.

There is one very good way to rig a furling headsail to a boom to make it self-trimming. The task is best done by tacking the boom to a spider as shown in Figure 5. This way, the trim radius of the boom is smaller than the trim radius of the headsail and the sail will tend to get fuller when it is eased, and will become flat when it is trimmed. This overcomes a key disadvantage to regular self-trimming headsails and makes for a fine singlehanded arrangement.

Figure 6 shows a preferred method of rigging furling gear to a main or mizzen and it is especially suitable for coastal singlehanding. The system shown here was devised for a 47' ketch and it has worked well. The method overcomes my chief dislike for rigging roller furling gear to spar sails by getting the furling drum off the boom and putting the tack of the sail down where it belongs in-stead of placing it in an elevated position above the boom.

The gooseneck pedestals that support both the boom and the furling drum are readily fabricated and can either be bolted or welded in place. The sail is joined to the furling drum through a tack pennant lead through a heavy-walled PVC sleeve. This makes a fine bearing surface and will work well as long as the tack of

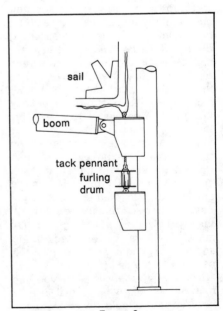

Figure 6

the sail is kept close to the intersection of the mast and boom. The arrangement provides for a far better setting sail and it furls much more smoothly than its boom-mounted-furling-drum counterpart. It looks better too!

The secret to any spar-mounted furling gear is to have an effective system for keeping the swivel from pinching off the halyard or, at best, binding the system so that it cannot be furled in anything but light going. This problem can be nicely resolved by using a wire topping lift (preferably a fixed lift of 1x19 stainless steel) and attaching the swivel keeper to it. The weight of the boom is sufficient to keep the topping lift in some degree of tension. This fact, together with the relatively short distance between the keeper and the point where the topping lift is attached to the spar cap, assures sufficient tension to load the top of the swivel and keep the halyard from rotating.

Always be sure that any furling drum is set up so that the furling sheet rotates the drum in a direction *that is consistent with the lay* of the wire rope luff and tack pennant. If you don't pay attention to this, you can count on losing your sail and/or pennant in a brisk breeze by unlaying it as you try to furl the sail. If the drum rotates against the lay of the wire rope, the furling resistance in a breeze will unlay the wire. Contrary to flexible wire rope (7x19 construction) that always is right-hand layed, you will find that 1x19 construction comes in both left and right-hand lay. You *must* furl so that the furling drum rotates with the lay of the wire rope, for this tends to tighten the lay. Not looking for this potential problem is a mistake that has been made so often by both professional and amateur alike that it is worth asking your own sailmaker to save you a hunk of your coated luff wire just so you can be sure of the lay of your bolt rope. Whatever it is, make the tack pennant just like it and rig the drum so that it rotates accordingly.

After you've rigged your furling gear, lead all the halyards and sheets aft to the cockpit. When you have finished you will be amazed at the ease with which even a relatively large vessel can set and take in sail under a wide range of conditions and situations without having any "uncalloused" hand go forward.

Handy Headsail Dousing

How to set up a jib downhaul   Larry Pardey

For easier headsail handling when cruising, try using a jib downhaul. With or without a bowsprit, this is a good piece of gear for single or shorthanded sailing.

I first used a jib downhaul on a 120-ton gaff-rigged schooner I was sailing aboard as we ran from Los Angeles to Honolulu (and back). One crewman could ease the jib sheets,

then with the halyard tail secured, he could haul the jib down the forestay without going forward of the mast area. Going forward alone to pull the luff down the headstay on a boat that size could be dangerous.

Then, when the sail was down, he could muzzle the large headsail into the jib net and work out on the bowsprit to secure the sail with gaskets

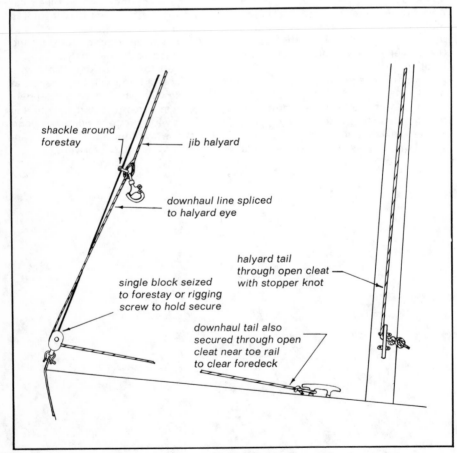

shackle around forestay — jib halyard

downhaul line spliced to halyard eye

halyard tail through open cleat with stopper knot

single block seized to forestay or rigging screw to hold secure

downhaul tail also secured through open cleat near toe rail to clear foredeck

Jib Downhaul

(sail-stops) that were permanently attached to the top of the spar.

A jib downhaul can be just as useful on any shorthanded cruising yacht no matter what size. To rig a jib downhaul, you splice a light line through the eye of the halyard shackle (Fig. 1). This line should be a small diameter, soft lay, three-strand nylon or Dacron so that it will not jam or kink when hoisting the sail. It should lead down to and through a single block at the tack, then back along the deck to a handy open cleat near the mast.

The bitter end of the downhaul line should be secured through the open cleat with a figure-eight knot or a bowline tied around a leg of the cleat. The end of the jib halyard, of course, also should be secured in this way.

A shackle put through the eye-splice of the halyard and around the forestay permits you to leave the downhaul, and halyard snap shackle in position at the lower end of the forestay. If you have a rod head-stay you might have to modify the snap-shackle arrangement some-what because of the nicking prob-lems. Check with the headstay manufacturer to be sure your rig is satisfactory.

When the downhaul line is tight-ened and secured, it holds the sail down and keeps the head of the jib, with its heavy shackle, from swing-ing around and whacking you on the head while you are working on the foredeck.

When you are ready to hoist your jib, uncleat the downhaul line and coil it on deck ahead of time so it runs free. It may take a bit of time to work all the kinks out of a new piece of line so be patient and watch it carefully when you are pulling on the halyard. If your jib has a wire luff and the hanks are of minimum size the bending of the luff wire can cause the hanks to twist and jam on the head-stay. Larger hanks will usually solve this hang-up. Rope luff or stretchy luff sails are better and downhaul like a dream.

Other advantages of the down-haul shackled to the forestay are that the halyard cannot be lost acci-dentally half way up the mast; you simply pull it back with the down-haul line. Your downhaul also can double as a stowing pennant to keep the halyard from banging against the mast. Finally, this inexpensive piece of gear also allows you to send the anchor light aloft easily and quickly. And you can get it down again as well.

The next time you take your jib down alone, think about how much safer and more convenient it might be if you eased the halyard, then pulled the jib down to the deck or jib net while you stood safely back near the mast.

Vane Steering

Choosing the right installation   John S. Letcher

Windvane steering seems finally to be catching on among cruising sailors in the United States. US sailors are really far behind Europe's in recognition and acceptance of vane gears for cruising boats. After all, they were invented and first commercially developed in France and England. For many years practically the only ones seen in the United States were aboard the yachts they had helped to steer across an ocean; they were thought of as ocean-crossing hardware, not cruising equipment.

Gradually, with increased understanding of how vane-steering works, with the commercial availability of more and more reliable, adaptable and sea-tested models, and with an exploding interest in cruising under sail, the vane gear has been winning acceptance. I saw more of them while I was cruising in Maine waters last summer than in the previous four summers put together. Vigorous demand has made America a principal market for some European manufacturers, and a growing number of US manufacturers are entering the competition. More and more sailors are seeing the advantages of the device in their own kind of cruising—the need for fewer crew members, more comfort, more time to navigate—and are giving serious thought to buying one.

This thinking, though, is affected by a great deal of confusion and uncertainty on the subject. First, the prices of most commercial models are enough to make most sailors stop and think for quite a while. Moreover, the variety of models available, many of them working by different principles, makes choosing the "right" vane a dilemma. Then there are those complex and delicate moving parts that seem so out of place and vulnerable beside the usual simple, robust, time-tested gear of a cruising boat. Then, too, sailors have heard dozens of well-publicized accounts of mechanical failures or, worse, vane gears that simply refused to steer a steady course from the beginning.

How can you be confident that, after spending many hundreds or even a couple thousand dollars on a vane gear, you will get something that works? No vane gear I know of is sold with a warranty that says if it doesn't steer your boat properly, you get your money back. With all these factors affecting a decision, there is good reason for hesitation. But let's try to throw some light on the basic problem.

First, back to the principles. The zero-order theory of windvane steering is easy enough to explain. The *windvane* is an airfoil aligned with the apparent wind, according to the desired course relative to the wind. If the boat goes off course, the apparent wind direction changes; and the vane senses this different angle of attack and develops a torque. The torque is transmitted through some form of mechanical *linkage* to one or more rudder-like underwater foils (the *control*) that are capable of steering the boat. The linkage is arranged so the control turns in the right direction to return the boat to course, correcting the original error. As long as the true wind stays in the same direction and strength, the boat holds the course true.

This simple theory is complicated by a whole raft of factors. The true wind is never steady, because the natural state of the atmosphere is turbulent. The apparent wind direction may change by much more or much less than the change in course. The inertia of the boat and of the vane gear components means neither can respond instantly, and both have natural oscillatory modes. The boat's rolling, pitching and

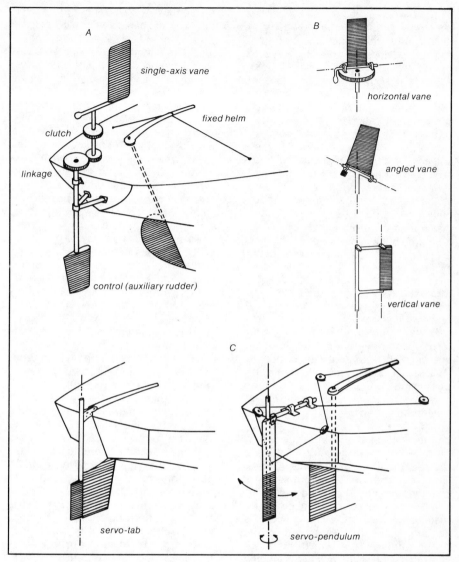

Figure 1: The basic design of a vane self steering system (A) with three dual-axis vane configurations (B) and principles of servo-tab and servo-pendulum controls (C)

yawing all cause apparent motions of wind and water at the vane and control, affecting their dynamic responses. The sail plan, the hull profile and the longitudinal weight distribution of the boat, as well as the areas, positions and interconnections of the vane and control, have crucial effects on the overall behavior of the system. I've been instrumental in developing a "first-order" vane-gear theory that takes many of these factors into account, but it doesn't give all the answers. One certain conclusion is: *the response of the boat depends on a lot of factors besides the vane gear.*

Thus there is a major problem in selecting a suitable vane gear— matching its characteristics to those of the boat so that steady, reliable course-keeping results. The theory does offer encouragement by guaranteeing that such a match is possible for *any* boat, and it suggests ways to assess the relevant stability of the boat.

Figure 1 shows the basic types of vanes and controls which can be applied in any combination. A "servo" control is one that generates an amplification of power by the flow of water past a foil. The linkage between vane and control can take many forms: lines or cables running over quadrants and sheaves, gears, rotating or sliding shafts, levers, and bell cranks. "Feedback" is a subtle feature of a linkage that transmits information about rudder angle back to the windvane setting in order to stabilize the operation of the system.

The principal aspects of system performance that are governed by the type and size of the vane and control are *power* and *stability*.

Power tells how much steering torque is developed per degree change of the apparent wind direction. Power is a characteristic of the vane gear itself, so it is a factor very much under the manufacturer's control. He presumably has tested his gear on boats of different sizes, and can recommend a suitable size range (often modified somewhat by the vessel's displacement) for each of his models. This experience and subsequent recommendation should be a fairly reliable indication of adequate power for installation on comparable boats. He certainly doesn't want you going around telling the world his gear doesn't have enough power to steer the size of boat he sells it for. However, there is room for argument about the upper range of wind and sea conditions the gear should be able to cope with. Certainly as winds and seas increase, unless sail is reduced, steering eventually becomes difficult or impossible even for a human helmsman who can anticipate the seas, read the compass and feel the roll of the boat, using a lot of information not available to a vane gear. So we shouldn't expect too much. When a manufacturer specifies the limits of his gear, he is apt to be thinking of moderate-to-fresh conditions. Nevertheless, when a boat is balanced out to steer easily under reduced sail, a vane gear may well be able to cope with gale conditions.

Stability refers to the character of the boat's response following a specific disturbance such as a 10-degree wind shift. A stable boat quickly settles down to a steady course on a new heading at the same apparent wind angle; a marginally stable boat will oversteer, swinging past the proper new course many times in a weaving mode; and an unstable boat will oversteer more wildly on each cycle until she tacks or gybes herself. These yawing oscillations are opposed by a combination of the boat's inherent "yaw resistance" and synthetic "yaw damping" supplied by the vane gear. Because of apparent wind effects, instability is much more likely and common on downwind courses.

Stability, dependent as it is on both the vane gear and the boat, is somewhat outside the manufacturer's control. He may indeed have tested his gear on one or more boats and found a comfortably stable response. He may also be unaware that that stable response doesn't guarantee satisfactory performance on another, even an outwardly similar, boat. The inability to assure stability of a particular steering system to be used on a particular boat is the big problem, both for the prospective purchaser and for the manufacturer who wants to make a product suitable for a wide range of boats.

One happy side to the picture is that there is *little harm in providing more yaw damping than is necessary* for stable operation. This means it is safe to err on the side of too much damping, and this fact is a big help to both the boat owner and the gear manufacturer. An overdamped system is slower to respond to wind shifts, slower to settle down after a change of course, but these faults are insignificant in practice, especially as compared with the

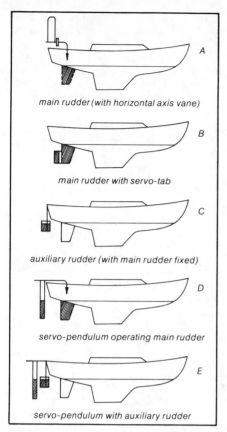

main rudder (with horizontal axis vane)

main rudder with servo-tab

auxiliary rudder (with main rudder fixed)

servo-pendulum operating main rudder

servo-pendulum with auxiliary rudder

Figure 2: Types of control surfaces used in vane steering in order of increasing yaw-dampening effectiveness

opposite symptoms of wild oversteering. The only trouble is that, so far, high yaw damping seems to be more or less tied in with more complex, therefore more expensive and/or unreliable, mechanisms.

The possibilities of effective yaw damping are least when the boat's own rudder is used as the sole control. Thus, the simplest and by far the least expensive system, a *horizontal-axis vane connected to the tiller or wheel by a running-line linkage* (Fig. 2A), is also the system that provides the least yaw damping; less, in fact, than the helm-free yaw resistance of the boat itself. According to advertising this system has been used on a very large number of boats, but I would expect that a fairly small proportion of them have found it

satisfactory except in a narrow range of ideal wind and sea conditions.

Likewise, *a servo-tab on the main rudder* (Fig. 2B) is quite limited in yaw damping. If it is used with a feedback linkage and a relatively large vertical-axis vane, it can approach the helm-*fixed* yaw damping of the boat itself. In my experience, the world of sailing craft seems about evenly divided between positive and negative helm-fixed yaw resistance. Therefore, the half that are positive might do all right with a servo-tab, and the others wouldn't. This 50-50 chance of success, aside from the problems of connecting a tab to a through-hull rudder and adapting it to various rudder designs and positions, has considerably limited the commercial success of servo-tab systems using the main rudder for steering.

More expensive, larger, but often mechanically simpler than a tab is the *auxiliary rudder control* (Fig. 2C). This has a substantial capability of augmenting the helm-fixed yaw damping of the bare boat—to a degree proportional to the auxiliary rudder area times its distance from the hydrodynamic center of the hull. The possibility of building a single version of a transom-mounted auxiliary rudder adaptable to a wide variety of boats has made this an attractive commercial system, so a number of manufactured gears are based on it. Some drive the auxiliary rudder directly from the vane through a geared-down reversing linkage, as shown in Figure 1, while others use a servo-tab or servo-pendulum with an auxiliary rudder.

Whether the full yaw damping capability of the auxiliary rudder is actually realized depends on several factors: its degree of hydrodynamic balance; the type of windvane connected to it; and details of the linkage, especially when a servo-tab is involved. At one extreme, an unbalanced auxiliary rudder driven from a horizontal-axis vane without feedback, the vane gear contributes no yaw damping at all; however, if the auxiliary rudder is fully balanced, its full yaw damping capability is realized in any system.

The ultimate level in complexity and cost—and also offering the greatest assurance of stable operation through yaw damping—is *the servo-pendulum* (Fig. 2D). This control is a foil that turns on a vertical axis, serving as an auxiliary rudder (and lifting in the correct way to return the boat to course) and at the same time rotates about a horizontal axis which is coupled with a high mechanical advantage to a much larger rudder, usually the yacht's main rudder. This combination possesses the yaw-damping characteristics of an auxiliary rudder having the area of the pendulum blade but *multiplied* several times over by the coupling with the main rudder.

The servo-pendulum is a strongly stabilizing device as it is highly sensitive to any yawing rotation of the boat and acts instantly and powerfully to counteract it. Despite its inherent complexity, it has been the choice for the most successful and widely accepted commercial vane gears, and I think its success rests largely on providing strong yaw damping, sufficient to stabilize any boat. I have not personally heard of any case where a boat with a pendulum-type vane gear exhibited divergent oscillations, although I can picture some special circumstances in which this would occur. (In particular, if the primary rudder operated by the pendulum is hydrodynamically balanced, feedback has to be designed into the system to prevent the pendulum from overpowering the rudder, causing excessively strong corrections.)

The alternatives seem to be: (1) buy a pendulum gear, with high confidence of stable operation; or (2) buy an auxiliary rudder gear, with attention to some rather subtle details, with a good chance of stable operation; or (3) follow the directions for the "sailing test for yaw resistance" given in my previous article or my book to assess the yaw damping characteristics of your own boat, and select or build an appropriate type of vane gear suited to those characteristics. I naturally recommend option (3) as being the most elegant and satisfying solution.

In addition to performance, the mechanical strength, durability and protection against accidents to the gear should also be high on the list of concerns in selecting a vane gear. These qualities can be hard to judge. I think most cruising sailors can look at a piece of gear and tell the difference between genuine cruising equipment and junk, but there are a lot of shades of gray in between and you see them all represented in vane gears.

As an aid to judging quality, check the following:

Materials Reinforced plastics are among the most suitable marine materials; they are often used for underwater parts of controls and for bearings, but they could be applied in many other areas. However, metal parts are unavoidable, and a variety of metals are typically employed, with numerous possibilities for corrosion. Aluminum must be heavily anodized and should be further protected by plastic coatings. Stainless steel is popular but is always susceptible to stress-corrosion cracking when used around sea water. Contact with non-anodized aluminum parts will help protect the stainless, but then the aluminum will corrode. Monel and the bronzes remain the best alloys for almost any marine application. Galvanized steel can also make very good, durable marine hardware.

Design Mechanical parts should show a balance of strength suitable to the highest loads that they may have to carry, efficient use of the materials, and good machining and assembly practices. Judging this is really a job for an engineer, but you can see if the parts look finished and if they fit together as they should, and if everything seems really strong. The forces exerted by wave action can be really tremendous despite the wishful thinking evidenced by a number of vane-gear designs. Often a shear-pin or weakest-link design is essential to guard against overloading of critical parts.

Accidents The foremost accidental loading that so many vane gears are susceptible to is snagging on floating or underwater obstructions. It may be because I have a spade rudder and sail in lobster-trapping waters that I am so acutely conscious of the eventuality, but it is almost inevitable that a boat will someday run over a mooring or a cable or a floating timber and simply wipe out a control that does not have a kick-up or shear-pin feature. The other likely accident is a crewmember's lurching against the vane or climbing aboard over the stern by way of the control and linkage. Gear components have to be really tough, or hinged so they will get out of the way by themselves.

Good materials, workmanship and design are all expensive. Strong parts mean more material, more machining, more careful design. But also they can mean the gear will do its job for years rather than days, and so they can pay for themselves many times over.

What does the future hold for wind-vane self-steering? I expect to see many more vane gears on boats that never go out of sight of land. I also ex-pect that as manufacturing volume increases and more competitors enter the field, prices will go down, although perhaps not dramatically. Remember, the prices we see today have been determined primarily by competition in Europe where a large market for vane gears has been active for quite a few years.

Many of the new commercial models will continue to represent development of the same basic vanes and controls in use today. There seems little chance for a breakthrough in terms of a new type of vane or control that might allow a really superior new gear to be marketed at a lower price—but then breakthroughs are never foreseen, are they? Certainly none of the vane gears now available is a final and universal solution to self-steering, so there are going to be plenty of inventive people hard at work on the problem. The results are sure to be interesting.

Navigation

The Navigation Package

Publications and equipment for safe passagemaking　　　　James B. Kane

Frequently **I hear** sailors ask, "What equipment should I have aboard my boat for navigating? What books and charts do I need? Where can I get all this gear and how do I keep this material up-to-date?"

To give an absolute and precise answer is impossible, for needs vary among daysailers, ocean cruisers and coastal cruisers.

Nowadays some daysailers will sail almost anywhere. So, before considering your boat's needs, bear in mind that any boat, no matter how small, that sails out of the sight of land or sails in unfamiliar waters will need all the gear, charts, and books ordinarily found aboard ocean or coastwise cruisers.

On the other hand, a daysailer might be able to get by with little or no navigation gear at all *providing* the boat stays within close sight of buoys, lighthouses or familiar landmarks. But many times the visibility drops while you're far from your mooring, and you had better be prepared.

A daysailer's navigation package therefore, always should include at least a good compass, a hand lead for taking soundings, and a chart of the area.

Before looking over any list of gear you might need, let's see what printed matter you ought to have, where you can get it and how you update it.

Your publication needs will differ depending on the standard of accuracy of piloting you want. The following table is a list of printed material used by navigators that is put out by several government agencies. Unfortunately no single government office can supply the navigator with all his needs for charts and books so this list also gives you the source of the material. By going over the list and considering

what waters you'll be sailing on, you yourself can judge what you'll need (Table I).

Material published by DMAHC formerly was published by the US Naval Oceanographic Office. To obtain DMAHC charts and books or a catalog

Nautical Charts	Source
Coasts of the United States and its territories and possessions	National Ocean Survey (formerly the Coast and Geodetic Survey) and its authorized sales agents
Mississippi River from the Head of Passes to Cairo, Ill.	Mississippi River Commission, Vicksburg, Miss.
Illinois waterway system (Great Lakes to Gulf of Mexico)	District Engineer, Chicago District, Chicago, Ill.
Great Lakes, Lake Champlain, and the St. Lawrence River above St. Regis and Cornwall, Canada	US Lake Survey, Detroit, Mich., and District Engineer, Buffalo, NY
New York State canals	US Lake Survey, Detroit, Mich.; Superintendent of Public Works Albany, NY; and District Engineer, Buffalo District, Buffalo, NY
Coasts of foreign countries	Defense Mapping Agency Hydrographic Center (DMAHC) and its sales agents
Great Circle Charts	DMAHC and its agents
Plotting Sheets	DMAHC and its agents
Pilot Charts of the oceans	DMAHC and its agents
Current Charts of oceans	DMAHC and its agents

Table I

Item	Source
Tide Tables (printed in four volumes): Europe and the West Coast of Africa (including the Mediterranean Sea); East Coast of North & South America; West Coast of North & South America (including the Hawaiian Islands); Central & Western Pacific Ocean and Indian Ocean	National Ocean Survey and sales agents
Tidal Current Tables Atlantic Coast of North America, Tidal Current Tables, Pacific Coast of North America and Asia	National Ocean Survey and sales agents National Ocean Survey and sales agents
Tidal Current Charts (sold separately for: NY Harbor, Boston, San Francisco Bay, Long Island Sound, Narragansett Bay to Nantucket Sound, Delaware Bay & River and Puget Sound)	National Ocean Survey and sales agents
Radio Navigational Aids Publication No. 117	DMAHC
Radio Weather Aids Publication No. 118	DMAHC
Sailing Directions of foreign coasts	DMAHC
Light Lists of foreign coasts (six volumes)	DMAHC
Loran Tables (there is a loran table for each rate, that is 1H4,2L6 etc.)	DMAHC
Light List, US waters (describes aids to Navigation, lights, fog signals, buoys and electronic aids)	Published by the US Coast Guard Distributed by the Superintendent of Documents and sales agents
Azimuth Tables of the Sun: Publication No. 71	DMAHC
Azimuth Tables of Bodies Whose Declinations Range from 24° to 70°	DMAHC

Item	Source
Publication 120 The Nautical Almanac (Issued each year)	Published by the US Naval Observatory, distributed by Superintendent of Documents
Aids to Marine Navigation of the United States (DG-193)	Published by the US Coast Guard, distributed by Superintendent of Documents
International Code of Signals, Vol. I Visual; Vol. II Radio	DMAHC
Official US Coast Guard Recreational Boating Guide (CG-340)	Published by the US Coast Guard, distributed by Superintendent of Documents

Table II

write the Superintendent of Documents, US Government Printing Office, Washington, DC.

National Ocean Survey, Distribution Division (C44), 6501 Lafayette Ave., Riverdale, Maryland, 20840 issues (free) a list of their authorized sales agents and a catalog of their material. If you are buying directly from NOS, make checks or money orders payable to NOS, Department of Commerce.

On any navigation chart, underneath the border, you'll find the edition date. The most recent correction date to the chart plates is printed in the lower left side below the border. Table 2 gives you details on other printed matter.

The National Ocean Survey also puts out the Coast Pilots and these Coast Pilots contain information which the National Ocean Survey is unable to show graphically on nautical charts such as navigation regulations, outstanding land marks, channel and anchorage pecularities, dangers, weather, ice, freshets, routes, and port facilities.

The National Ocean Survey now shows Loran Lines on their general charts of the United States coasts.

To keep your charts and publications up-to-date, you should correct them by using the *Notice to Mariners*. The DMAHC issues this pamphlet weekly and it covers the world. You can look at Notices to Mariners at Coast Guard District Offices, National Ocean Survey Field Offices, US Naval Oceanographic Branch and Distribution Offices, most local marine facilities as well as sales agents handling charts and publications.

Beside the Notice to Mariners, all Coast Guard Districts issue a Local Notice to Mariners. You should consult the Local Notice to Mariners for reports pertaining to the Intracoastal Waterway and other waterways and harbors within the United States that ocean-going vessels usually don't use.

Because the waters where you normally sail your boat interest you most, you're usually better off using the Local Notice to Mariners. Anytime you correct a chart, you should put the date and Notice to Mariners number on the lower left side of the chart underneath the border.

If you're going to navigate with the sun and stars, you'll need tables to solve the navigational triangle. The US Naval Oceanographic Office puts out several tables. Today, the newest and best table is Publication 229, Sight Reduction Tables for Marine Navigation. Every 15 degrees of latitude has a volume and each volume is about $10. If you consider it takes six volumes to cover all latitudes, the price seems high. But you only need to buy the volumes for the latitudes you'll be sailing in.

Publication 214 is also another easy table to use for celestial navigation, though this table, as does Publication 229, takes up a great deal of room. Table 208 (Dreisonstok) is contained in one small book, is inexpensive, and you can say the same for table 211 (Ageton). However both 208 and 211 require more figures to arrive at an answer. Using more figures means more work, more time, and more chance of making errors.

When buying any type of navigation tables, you ought to consider price, the space the table takes up and its sim-

plicity. Of course you can use any of these tables to take the place of azimuth tables when finding the true bearing of the sun.

There are any number of books on the subject of navigation and every serious sailor usually has one or more on his book shelf. Among them is Bowditch (HO9) which has just been revised and reissued. There are also any number of instructional texts on navigation; you can and ought to find one you like and stick with it. It should be aboard as well.

Now that you're set with the printed matter, what kind of navigation instruments should you have? I've made a list of navigational instruments and checked off in the columns the instruments a particular category of boat might need.

Table 3 itemizes a basic list of instruments you ought to think about having, though I admit it is a matter of personal taste whether you should carry everything. For example, boats

Items	day-sailer	coastal cruiser	ocean cruiser
Compass	x	x	x
Binoculars	x	x	x
Hand lead	x	x	x
Depth finder	•	x	x
Dividers	x	x	x
Parallel rulers	x	x	x
Pelorus	•	x	x
Azimuth circle	An azimuth circle which fits over the top of some of the larger compasses takes the place of a pelorus		
Radio receiver	x	x	x
Radio direction finder	•	x	x
Log	•	x	x
Barometer	•	x	x
Hygrometer	•	x	x
Anemometer (Wind Speed Ind.)	•	x	x
Chronometer		•	x
Sextant		•	x
Stopwatch		•	x
Radar		•	x
Pad of radar plotting sheets (Publication 4665-10)		•	•
Omni		•	•
Omega			•
Radio transmitter	•	x	x
Calculator	•	•	•

x instruments that should be aboard
• instruments that might be considered

Table III

sailed for years before the arrival of radar and loran. You therefore, can get by without them as well. But with them you do improve your safety and accuracy as well as simplify the navigation problem. Obviously, you have to look into the power sources and so forth aboard your own boat before you finalize your thoughts. But you should never sacrifice safety just for the sake of economy. If you think you would be happier with a particular piece of gear aboard, you should get it. Chances are you will put the equipment to good use over the long run.

When taking a sight with a sextant, you certainly can eliminate the need for a chronometer by using a stopwatch with a radio receiver that has a time-tick capability. Stations WWV, WWVH and CHU broadcast coordinated Universal Time signals continuously on frequencies of 2.5, 5, 10, 15 and 20 MHz. If your radio cannot receive the signal or becomes damaged, you will be hard pressed to get an accurate tick. So you are back to having a chronometer again.

Your shipboard radio should be able to pick up weather and warnings of approaching storms. The National Weather Service broadcasts continually on FM usually on 162.55 MHz and you can receive this signal out to about 40 miles from the station.

Some boats use only loran instead of carrying a sextant. This is OK but if your loran set breaks down, or if your power fails, you're in trouble again.

You can buy many of these items in nautical supply stores and marine electronics stores sell those radios, lorans, radars, and omegas.

By looking through catalogs and magazines you will spot many of the instruments listed above, as well as some other specialty items which are also nice to have.

To feel safe and confident, the next time you cast off from your mooring you should have all the necessary books and gear aboard. It will pay off by making your sailing more safe and enjoyable.

Keep It Simple

Dangers of overprecise piloting

John Mellor

One of the most common sources of error in the navigation of small boats is the temptation to try to be too accurate. If that sounds like a contradiction, just consider for a moment the inherent differences between navigating a large ocean liner and a 25-foot sailing cruiser. Consider first the difference in their capabilities for being accurately steered. In virtually any conditions short of a hurricane in mid-Atlantic the ocean liner can steer, and maintain accurately, a course to within half a degree. The average sailor in a small sailing boat will do well to keep within five degrees of the course he wants; in any kind of heavy weather it is likely to be nearer 10 or more.

So right away you have a situation in which the average small boat does not carve a neat furrow through the seas, as many a chart plot would have us believe, but instead meanders somewhat casually back and forth like a foxhound casting for a scent, and hopes thereby to average out a course somewhere in the region of the one the skipper wants. If you can appreciate this, it is but one step further to realize that a neat and accurately-plotted course on the chart, based on log readings and compass courses alone, will not only be most likely inaccurate, but also misleading. And this is where the danger lies.

Once you understand how approximate the navigation of a small sailing boat actually is, you are half way to coping with it. If, however, you draw neat little lines on the chart, then fondly imagine you are sailing along them, you may be headed for trouble. I'm not suggesting for a minute that you shouldn't be as accurate with your navigation as you possibly can be at all times. And that, of course, includes accurate and precise plotting. But if you are navigating by yourself as well as

sailing the boat — in short you don't have a full-time navigator aboard as is the case with a larger racing boat — you do create opportunities for introducing errors (and further risk) if you get "too complicated" in your plotting. So let us take a look at these unavoidable errors that cause our navigating, however carefully carried out, essentially to be rather approximate.

The first error, as I have already mentioned, is the fact that a small sailing boat will steer a somewhat meandering course. Thus the course we plot on the chart as having been steered is only an *estimated* average. And, although with experience you can estimate it fairly accurately, especially in calm weather, there is no way you can define it precisely, certainly not to within the limits possible for a big ship. Consequently, to assume that you have steered that precise course is to invite trouble.

You must always bear in mind that you could have averaged a couple of degrees (or more) to one side or the other of the plotted course, and you will find this very much easier if you always steer courses that are clearly marked on the compass even if they don't lead on the chart to precisely where you want to go. You can always put in a dogleg. For example, imagine the course you want on the chart is 181½ degrees. Now, if you steer 181½ degrees, which would be extremely difficult to do with a small compass bouncing around in a small boat, you stand a very good chance of deluding yourself that you have averaged 181½ degrees which would be most unlikely. If, however, you steer due south (180), not only will it be more accurate (for it is easier to steer), but you will also find yourself thinking in terms of having averaged around south. And that will be just about what you will have done

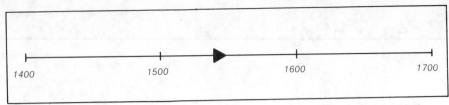

Figure 1: When simple plotting like this is used, very often mistakes can be avoided. When you get to 1700 in this diagram it is appropriate to say you are "somewhere" around the position indicated

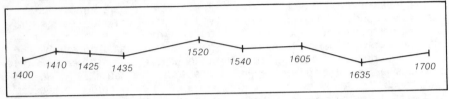

Figure 2: A more accurately-plotted course could actually be less precise because of the possibility of more chances for error

whether you try to steer 181½ or 180.

What you do on the chart is take a sharp pencil and draw a bold line due south from your departure fix, write 180 alongside it and draw a bold arrowhead to indicate the direction. Then every hour (on the hour, as it is easy to remember) read the log and plot the distance run along that line. When you get to 1700 (Fig. 1) you can say that you are somewhere *around* the position indicated, and you won't be that far out.

If, however, you try to be ultra-accurate you will wind up replotting your course continually every time you *think* it has changed slightly, and you will end up with a plot like the one in Figure 2. On the face of it, it would seem that it should be more accurate than the rather casually-plotted one in Figure 1. But is it? In practice, if it is plotted carefully and accurately, the difference in the two positions at 1700 will be negligible. However, considerably more plotting and concentration has gone into the plot in Figure 2; more log readings, more course estimates, more lines drawn, more distances measured, and many more opportunities created for mistakes.

What you actually find is that the more accurately-plotted course stands a far greater chance of being inaccurate than the one that is plotted simply.

And it can be inaccurate by a possibly large (and dangerous) amount, if a big error is plotted in somewhere along the line. And the longer you sail, the greater will be the chance of a large error in the accurately-plotted course.

And it gets worse. All those nice little distances run that you keep neatly marking on your plot—how accurate are they? Even assuming an accurate log (when did you last check yours?), you have a built-in error caused by the meandering nature of the sailing boat. Have a look at Figure 3. In a form exaggerated for clarity, you see how the distance measured by the log actually is the distance along all the meanderings and not the distance along the straight line drawn on the chart. Negligible perhaps in calm weather, it is important that you be aware of it. It is one more factor contributing to the generally approximate nature of the DR plot, one more factor that cannot be measured and applied to the ultra-accurate plot shown in Figure 2.

Leeway is another. If you have a lot of experience on the same boat, generally you can judge your leeway reasonably accurately. Still it is one more thing that is no more than a shrewd approximation. And when you add to these the very real difficulty of reading a compass accurately in a small, rolling, lurching boat, and the loss of con-

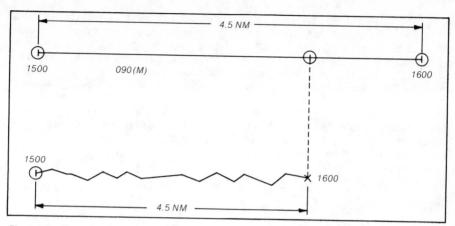

Figure 3: Course alterations included in summary of log reading may make substantial difference between two estimated positions. It is important to be aware of this

centration caused by tiredness and seasickness, the optimistic nature of the average helmsman who will tend to report having steered the course ordered regardless of what he actually did steer, you can begin to see the grave danger inherent in trying to construct a highly accurate and complex plot.

Actually, the dangers are twofold. First the danger of making an error in calculation or plotting increases the more information you try to assess and plot. Second, and rather more insidious, is the temptation to assume that, because the plot *looks* complicated and accurate, it is. As we have seen, it can never be that accurate. But the problem can be solved quite easily with some relaxed confidence and a good pencil. Stick to simple, easily-remembered, easily-steered, and easily-plotted courses such as 180, 185, 190, etc.; the cardinal points themselves are best of all if your compass has them. Whatever you do, avoid 181½ and the like. And always start with an accurate departure fix—the one thing many otherwise fanatically accurate navigators don't bother with too much. Draw a bold course line on the course you want to make good, then steer the course you have calculated you must steer and write this in the log, *not on the chart*. That way the chart is kept simple and uncluttered, an excellent way of avoiding mistakes.

Still talking about the chart, I wish I had a dollar for every time I have seen variation plotted the wrong way round! And not just by the inexperienced, but by the tired and seasick. I spent a very cheerless windy night once heading for America instead of Ireland (where we wanted to go) because a very experienced navigator had done just that thing. And yet the solution is so simple. *Never* try to work with true courses and bearings. Always use the magnetic compass rose on the chart and take your courses and bearings directly from it. If the chart is very old and the variation has changed, then simply draw in the new direction of magnetic north and apply the correction each time. The drawing will tell you which way to apply it and there is far less chance of making a mistake than there is with applying variation.

The chart is not the only place you can apply simplified techniques in order to reduce the chances of mistakes. It is very often quicker, easier, and perhaps even more accurate to take bearings simply by sighting over the main compass than by using a handbearing one because of the inherent greater accuracy of the former and its better damping. There's also less chance of its being affected by extraneous metal. In very rough weather, when it can be very difficult to keep a handbearer sufficiently still to get a reasonable bearing, one of the best methods of all is simply to point the boat at the object you want a bearing to and read off the ship's heading on the main compass.

I'm not suggesting that you ever should be less precise than you can be when you are navigating a small boat. But you should be aware that errors can and do creep in when the boat is moving around in a seaway and you may be wet and tired. And it is in this kind of situation that you ought to at least consider keeping your calculations and plotting to an absolute minimum. If you do have to calculate, do so very carefully. You might even approximate—and then add in a good margin of safety. If you do, you will be as confident as you can be of your estimated position and can maneuver accordingly.

Keep Your Compass Corrected

Do-it-yourself accounting for errors

James B. Kane

You **probably know** the earth's *magnetic* North Pole differs from the *true* geographic North Pole and this difference, expressed in degrees and minutes, is called *variation*. Variation can be either East or West, depending upon which side of true North magnetic North lies. Variation depends upon the location of your boat, and you really have no control over it. Variation remains a constant on every heading, and you should not attempt to eliminate variation from your compass.

Because most coastal charts do have magnetic compass roses printed on them, you might wonder why worry about variation at all? Well for one thing, the *current tables, light lists* and *sailing directions* all use only true bearings. This means there

well could be an instance when you want to convert a bearing or course to true degrees, or vice versa.

When you first install a magnetic compass aboard a boat, and nothing affects it other than the existing local variation, all the magnetic courses and bearings taken with the compass should be "properly" magnetic. But in almost all cases, the boat's own magnetic field will cause the compass card to deflect from magnetic North, and this divergence, caused by the boat and the gear aboard, is called *deviation*. Deviation will be either East or West just as it is with variation. Deviation, added together with any variation, comprises what is called *compass error*.

You always should eliminate as much deviation as possible, and to

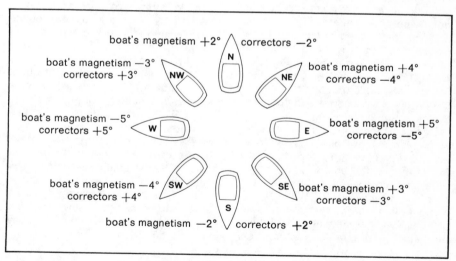

Figure 1
Correctors eliminate your boat's
deviation by setting up a magnetic field
equal and opposite to your boat's
polarity.

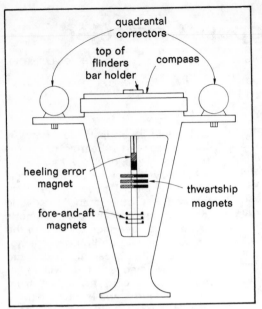

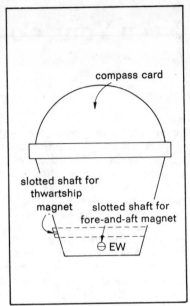

Figure 2
After end of binnacle with door
removed providing a view of fore-and-
aft as well as thwartships magnets.
Heeling error magnet is hanging
in its tube by a small chain.

Figure 3
Compass with slotted shafts.

do this you set up around your compass a magnetic field that is equal
in strength but opposite to the boat's
polarity. In a large compass this is
done with bar magnets (Fig. 1). With
a binnacle-mounted compass, these
magnets lie in trays and you can
raise or lower them inside the binnacle (Fig. 2). Smaller compasses
usually have slotted shafts on the
bottom of the compass instead of
the bar magnets (Fig. 3).

Besides these smaller *correctors*,
some large compass installations
have quadrantal correctors consist-
ing of two soft iron balls, or cylinders that compensate for a boat's
soft iron effect (Fig. 2). While there
is no real need for them aboard a
small sailboat, some sailors feel they
do need quadrantal correctors because of engine, winches, steel rigging and other metal installations
that might be aboard. It's strictly a
personal choice, but if your compass
does have these correctors, by all
means use them.

All standing binnacles have a
metal tube for a heeling magnet: a
bar magnet that stands vertically
and corrects for any deviation
caused by list. It also can reduce
the swinging of the compass card
when the boat is rolling and pitching (Fig. 2).

At this point let's talk a bit about
flinders bars. A binnacle may have a
flinders bar holder, but any boat that
stays within a few degrees latitude
of where its compass was adjusted
really doesn't need one. Most small
boat compasses have no flinders bar
and we'll omit using one in the compass adjustment calculations below.

The first thing you should do every
year is to recheck the amount of deviation your compass has. One easy
way to do this is to cross a range
headed on cardinal and intercardinal
points: North, Northeast, East, etc.,
and take a bearing on the range at
each crossing.

One good way to obtain a range
is to draw a line between any two

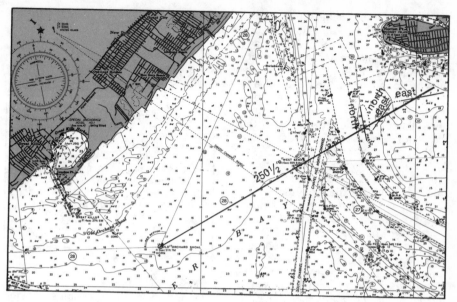

Figure 4

conspicuous objects on your chart (Fig. 4). Extend this (range) line out to the area you will be maneuvering in. Then, take your parallel rulers or triangles, and transfer the range line to the compass rose and read the *magnetic* direction of the range. Once you know the magnetic direction of the range, you simply take the difference between the range and your own compass bearing of the range each time you cross it. The *difference* will be the amount of deviation in the compass. Obviously it is essential you take your bearing the instant the two range objects are precisely in line.

In Figure 4, note that the range made by Old Orchard, and West Bank Lighthouses, is 250.5° magnetic. Now cross this range while you're headed on the listed compass headings. We'll assume the bearings appear as follows:

Compass Heading	Actual Magnetic Bearing of Range	Compass Bearing of Range	Deviation
000	250.5	240	10.5 E
045	250.5	245	5.5 E
090	250.5	245	5.5 E
135	250.5	249	1.5 E
180	250.5	255	4.5 W
225	250.5	260	9.5 W
270	250.5	255	4.5 W
315	250.5	250	0.5 E

Always add easterly deviation to your compass headings or bearings to get your magnetic headings or bearings. Do the opposite if you have westerly deviation. An easy way to remember this when correcting your compass heading to a magnetic heading is, *"Magnetic to the left: Deviation is West. Magnetic to the right: Deviation is East."*

Though you probably should use a professional adjuster to reduce or eliminate this deviation, you can do it yourself by using the following guide. Where fore-and-aft or thwartship magnets are specified, either the magnet trays in binnacles, or the slotted shafts in other compasses are what is being referred to.

First head East, and with the fore-and-aft magnets, remove all deviation.

Then head South, and with the thwartship magnets, remove all deviation.

Head West, and with the fore-and-aft magnets remove half of any remaining deviation.

Next head North, and with the thwartship magnets, remove half of any remaining deviation.

You now must make a new deviation table for any deviation that is left in your compass. While many navigators make their table for every 15°, your table should show the deviation for at least the cardinal and intercardinal headings. A deviation table is simply a card with the headings listed in one column and the deviation, either East or West, listed in the opposite column.

Even if your compass is already adjusted, it's a good idea to make a new deviation card every year.

To use a deviation card in piloting, take your compass heading and read from the card what the correct amount of deviation is in degrees. Then apply this amount to your compass heading to get the correct magnetic heading; either add the deviation if it's East or subtract if it's West.

Deviation must also be applied to any bearing you take with your compass. But remember the amount of deviation depends on your boat's heading and *not* the amount that exists on the bearing.

A word of warning: if your compass has something seriously wrong with it such as a bad pivot, a damaged compass card or a bubble that indicates the compass needs fluid, always get a professional compass adjuster. This is no repair job for an amateur.

A few other points. Be aware of local magnetic disturbances. Notes on a chart will warn you of such disturbances (Fig. 5).

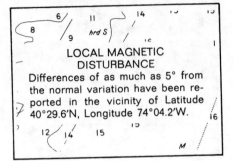

Figure 5

Keep in mind local sources of magnetism such as engines, electronic equipment, fire extinguishers, keys, flashlights and knives. Never put photoelectric light meters or a transistor radio near your compass.

Remember it's the lubbers line that is moving, not the compass card.

Keep clear of channels when adjusting your compass.

And finally, a compass with unknown deviation is a real danger, *not* an asset. So always check it, and if possible, adjust it at least once a year.

Caring for Your Sextant

Proper treatment and adjustment

Paul Dodson

One of the oldest rules of the sea is that there be a place for everything, and everything stowed properly. This is especially important with the sextant, a delicate precisely made optical instrument. When you're not actually using your sextant, it should be secure in its case, and the case well fastened down in an accessible spot.

I like to fasten the sextant case (preferably with shock absorbing mounts) vertically to the bulkhead at the head of a quarterberth. The top of the case is then like a cabinet door, the instrument is out of the way of heavy-handed and heavy-footed crew, can't tumble about in a seaway, and yet is easy to reach for a quick sun sight when you see a break in the clouds.

If a sextant is dropped, it will almost certainly be irreparably damaged. So think twice before you ask the literally butter-fingered cook to pass your sextant out to you, or before you set it down on the chart table "just for a second" while you go to the head.

No sextant on a sailboat should be without a lanyard — one end spliced into the sextant handle and the other around your neck at all times when the sextant is out of its case. This lanyard will save you from the awful choice between losing your sextant and losing your life if all of a sudden you need two free hands to keep yourself on board.

In foul weather keep the sextant dry in a plastic bag when you're not actually taking a sight. For rough seas, have a short-scope safety line ready to secure yourself to the rigging, so that you can stand upright, well braced, and concentrate on taking a good sight.

Sextants invariably get wet at sea from rain, spray or condensation. It is most important to see that moisture and salt are removed from the mirrors and the arc. The best way to remove moisture is by wiping down the mirrors, telescope lenses and arc with a fresh sheet of plain lens paper, available at any camera store. Clean linen cloth is also good but it tends to collect abrasive dust that will scratch the mirrors and lenses.

Lens paper dampened with fresh water should first be used to remove salt deposits. The tangent screw and teeth of the limb should be kept clean and lightly oiled, as should the other moving parts. A small bag of silica gel kept in the sextant case will greatly reduce corrosion and protect the mirror silvering.

Even when you use the utmost care, your sextant will occasionally get bumped at sea in a sailboat, so it's necessary to know how to detect errors and misalignment.

Sextant errors fall into two categories: adjustable and nonadjustable. The nonadjustable errors are built in at the factory (or caused by dropping the sextant) and there is nothing you can do about removing them. Some sources of nonadjustable errors are warped frame, prismatic effect in shade glasses and mirrors, graduation errors on the arc, vernier or micrometer drum, and eccentricity of the arc caused by the index arm not pivoting in the exact center of the arc.

The amount of nonadjustable error in a sextant is of course directly related to the quality of the sextant. Very few sextants are perfect, and errors inherent to each particular sextant are measured by the manufacturer or a testing laboratory and listed on the certificate which is pasted to the inside of the sextant case. In good sextants these residual errors are negligible for sailboat navigation.

Adjustable errors are an entirely different matter. Although they can be readily rectified, they can also be easily introduced by wear and tear or mishandling. These errors are (1) Index error, caused by the index mirror and the horizon glass not being parallel when the index arm is set exactly at zero degrees; (2) Nonperpendicularity of the index mirror to the frame of the sextant; (3) Nonperpendicularity of the horizon glass to the frame of the sextant (side error), and (4) Collimation error, caused by the telescope axis not being parallel to the frame of the sextant. Since all these adjustments are very sensitive, you now know why a navigator fiercely guards his sextant.

Of these four adjustable errors, the one which is by far the most important to know is the index error. Index error directly affects the accuracy of the sight, and therefore the line of position drawn, and the fix position. *Index error need not be*

removed as long as it is accurately known.

If a star were exactly on the horizon and its altitude could be measured by a sextant, the sextant should read exactly zero. When there is index error present the sextant either reads above or below zero. If the zero of the index arm is on the arc to the left of zero, the index error is subtracted from the observed altitude; if it is off to the right of the zero of the arc, the correction is added. From this fact we have the nonsensical but helpful adage: "When it's on, it's off; and when it's off, it's on."

Always, but *always*, check your sextant to determine index error either before or after every set of altitude observations. The horizon is the reference to be used to check for zero reading (index) error, and it is most distinct after morning stars, and before evening stars.

Check the index error by bringing the direct and reflected images of the horizon into coincidence. This should be done by approaching coincidence from both above and below. If two different index errors are determined this way, your

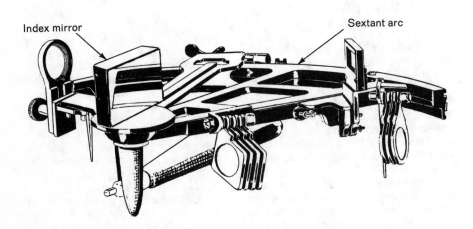

Figure 1. Drawing shows non-perpendicular index mirror requiring adjustment of mirror mounting screws.

sextant evidently has some backlash in the tangent screw, and you won't be able to correct the problem, but at least you can compensate for it.

If the index error becomes excessive (more than two minutes), it can be reduced by adjusting the two screws on the horizon glass which control parallelism with the index mirror. Use the small screwdriver or key provided with the sextant. This adjustment must be done carefully — always back out one screw a little before screwing in the other — or you may be out of business with a broken horizon glass!

The other three adjustable errors won't be too troublesome as long as they are not great in size. Nonperpendicularity of the index mirror is detected by setting the index arm of the sextant at about the middle of the arc (40°-60°). Hold the sextant with the index mirror "up" and towards your eye. Observe both the direct and reflected views of the sextant arc, as in figure 1; if the two views do not appear to be a continuously straight line, the index mirror is not perpendicular to the frame. Perpendicularity can be restored by adjusting the mirror mounting screws carefully, as before. (Remember — this adjustment will probably change your index error.)

Nonperpendicularity of the horizon glass (side error) is also easily detected. If you set your sextant index at zero, sight at a star, and then see two stars side by side in the horizon glass, you've got side error. You will also detect this error when you sight at a vertical line, such as a mast or flagstaff. If the direct and reflected images do not coincide the horizon glass is not perpendicular.

Another test is to sight the horizon with the sextant tilted. If the direct and reflected views (see figure 2) do not coincide, side error exists.

When the horizon glass is adjusted exactly perpendicular to the frame, the direct and reflected views of the star, flagstaff, or horizon will exactly coincide as you rotate the micrometer drum back and forth past zero

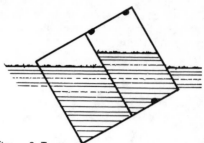

Figure 2. Testing perpendicularity of horizon glass.

on the arc. Adjustment is made in the same way as before, using the other pair of screws to restore the horizon glass to perpendicular.

Telescope collimation error (telescope not parallel to the frame) is checked by observing through the telescope the angle between two stars 90° or more apart. Bring the direct view of one star and the reflected view of the other star into coincidence on either the right or left side of the telescope's field of view. Then tilt the sextant to move the stars to the other side of the field of view. If the stars remain in coincidence the telescope is parallel to the frame, if not, the telescope mounting collar must be 'adjusted by the two screws provided for this purpose.

Some authorities recommend that all sextant adjustments be left to professional instrument repair shops. By all means, if there's one available to you and you're not sure of what you're doing, take the sextant to an expert.

For the navigator who's bumped his sextant against the companionway 2,000 miles out at sea, however, there's no other recourse but to repair and adjust as best he can. I would therefore advise offshore navigators to take H.O. 9 (Bowditch, *American Practical Navigator*) along. This volume, which will get you through many difficulties, goes so far as to describe in detail the method used to resilver sextant mirrors at sea, if you feel so inclined.

95

If you know how to properly adjust and care for your sextant, you can hold it with assurance and pride rather than with the fear and awe of the uninitiated. But don't overuse your new skill — frequent adjustment of the mirrors causes wear. It's much better to handle the sextant so carefully that it rarely needs adjustment.

Problem Solving by Logarithm

A foolproof backup to the calculator

William V. Kielhorn

We **read much nowadays** about the remarkable little pocket-sized electronic computers featuring micro-circuitry and light-emitting diodes, and having all sorts of algebraic and trigonometric functions. They really *are* good, and handy, too. But not all of us can afford the better models, and we might think twice about taking one of these excellent and delicate instruments to sea where it is subject to being dropped, soaked in salt water, and otherwise mistreated.

On the other hand, maybe some of us are missing a bet by not making more use of the simple slide rule. A slide rule costs from $1 to about $30, depending upon its size and features. The least expensive has about the same practical accuracy as the most expensive one, and may be even more rugged. You can drop it, kick it, soak it, and do about everything but break it in half, and it still can be made serviceable again without any particular skill.

The slide rule is simply a graphical means of displaying logarithms. Logarithms, as we all know, are an effective mathematical means of frightening schoolchildren into other, more pleasant endeavors—sailing, for example. Yet, now that we no longer have to face the spectre of examinations dealing with mantissas, characteristics, cologarithms, and such things, perhaps we should look at them again to discover how they may be used to make sailing life a little easier for us.

John Napier of Merchison, Scotland, invented logarithms in 1614 in order to simplify the tedium of handling ". . . multiplications, divisions, square and cubical extractions of great numbers . . . ." In 1620, having studied Napier's discovery, Edmund Gunter of London invented a straight logarithmic scale, and effected calculations with it

by using dividers, the same as may be done today using the log scale appearing on our modern small-craft (SC-series) charts. Ten years later William Oughtred, also an Englishman, adapted two Gunter scales to slide along each other. This was the first true slide rule.

Many improvements in slide rules have been made since that time, including folded scales, log-log scales, special purpose scales, etc. The forms of the slide rule have also varied, and have included the circular, spiral, and cylindrical calculators. For our purposes we will need only a simple six-inch, or preferably a 10-inch straight slide rule. My favorite is the Keufel & Esser "Log-Log Duplex Trig" rule, but this includes many more features than you need for the simpler, more common navigational problems.

There are three basic mathematical rules concerning the properties of logarithms, and these are reviewed below in order that you may understand the slide rule functions a little better:

$$\text{I.} \quad \text{Log } AB = \text{Log } A + \text{Log } B$$
$$\text{II.} \quad \text{Log } A/B = \text{Log } A - \text{Log } B$$
$$\text{III.} \quad \text{Log } A^n = n \text{ Log } A$$

Whenever you buy a slide rule, even an inexpensive one, you also get a little booklet of instructions. If you buy a fancy one, such as the Log-Log Duplex Trig, the booklet is practically equal to a college course in mathematics. In either case, with a very little practice you will soon be doing multiplications, divisions, and proportions in a few seconds. I will assume you have practiced enough with the slide rule to become proficient at this level. Now let's take a look at some examples illustrating the utility of the slide rule for the small-boat mariner.

Time, Speed, Distance

These problems comprise the most common and the most important ones in dead-reckoning navigation. They are also the simplest to solve on the slide rule. The basic relationship is this:

$$\text{Distance} = \text{speed} \times \text{time}$$

You can change this around algebraically any way you choose:

$$\text{Time} = \frac{\text{distance}}{\text{speed}}$$

$$\text{Speed} = \frac{\text{distance}}{\text{time}}$$

These are simple and valid relationships. However, you can get into trouble in a hurry if the units aren't kept straight. We can use all manner of units for speed; knots, cm./sec., m.p.h. Or time; days, hours, seconds. Or distance; miles, kilometers, leagues, fathoms, etc. In order to avoid difficulties in using units, just jot down those you are dealing with:

$$\text{Speed (in knots)} = \frac{\text{distance (in n. miles)}}{\text{time (in hours)}}$$

The units here are correct and consistent, for knots are nautical miles per hour. If we wished to have speed expressed in centimeters per second, as oceanographers frequently do in measuring currents, we would use the following units:

$$\text{Speed (cm./sec.)} = \frac{\text{distance (in cm.)}}{\text{time (in sec.)}}$$

Let's look at a few problems in which the slide rule may be used to advantage.

Example I

Your speed is 4.8 knots as indicated on your speed log. Assuming there is no current, how long will it take you to get from your present position to a buoy 6.25 nautical miles away?

$$\text{Time (hrs.)} = \frac{\text{distance (6.25 n. mi.)}}{\text{speed (4.8 n. mi./hr.)}}$$

$$= 1.30 \text{ hours}$$

To convert 0.30 hours to minutes, place 60 on the C-scale over an index (1) on the D-scale. Opposite 3 on the D-scale, read 18 on the C-scale.

Answer: 1 hr. 18 min.

I prefer an even simpler way of solving the same type of problem. Mathematically it is the same, but the slide settings are a little different, and much easier to remember.

Think of the problem as a proportion:

$$\frac{4.8 \text{ mi.}}{1.0 \text{ hr.}} = \frac{6.25 \text{ mi.}}{x \text{ hr.}} \quad \begin{matrix} \text{C-scale} \\ \text{D-scale} \end{matrix}$$

Place 4.8 on the C-scale over either index (1) on the D-scale. It is immediately apparent that if the 4.8 were over

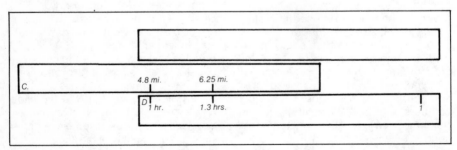

Figure 1

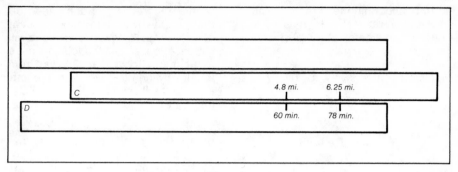

Figure 2

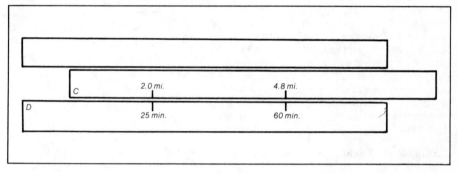

Figure 3

the *right* index, the 6.25 on the C-scale cannot be read opposite the D-scale. So, just put the 4.8 opposite the *left* index in this case. The slide rule will look like this: (Fig. 1)

Or, do the same problem in terms of minutes, rather than hours: (Fig. 2)

$$\frac{4.8 \text{ mi.}}{60 \text{ min.}} = \frac{6.25 \text{ mi.}}{x \text{ min.}} \quad \text{C-scale} \atop \text{D-scale}$$

Answer: 78 minutes (or 1 hr. 18 min.)

Example II

You run on a steady course between two objects known to be 2.0 miles apart in 25 minutes. What is your speed between those objects?

$$\frac{2.0 \text{ mi.}}{25 \text{ min.}} = \frac{x \text{ mi.}}{60 \text{ min.}} \quad \text{C-scale} \atop \text{D-scale}$$

Answer: 4.8 knots (or 4.8 mi./60 min.) (Fig. 3)

Practice for an hour or so with all the combinations of time, speed and distance you can think of, and you will become quite proficient. The same problems can be solved using other scales on the slide rule, too, but for the time being, the C and D scales alone will do nicely.

For those of you having a rule containing the sine functions (the S-scale), the following elementary examples may make you more familiar with their use. Wherever cosines are employed, just recall that Cos θ = sin (90° − θ), or cos 30° = sin 60°, for example.

Example III: Heeling to reduce draft

An old-timer on the Chesapeake Bay once asked a yachtsman if he had ever run aground. "Never!" the yachtsman declared indignantly. "Well, then," the old-timer replied, "you ain't sailed the Bay much." Soon, the yachtsman fetched up on a mud-bank with his deep fin keel (draft 6.0 feet), and found

99

with his sounding lead that he was in 5.0 feet of water. How far must he heel over his craft before the keel clears the mud?

Inclined draft = draft x cos θ (θ is heel angle)

$$5.0 \text{ ft.} = 6.0 \text{ ft.} \times \cos \theta$$

$$\frac{5.0}{6.0} = \cos \theta = 0.83$$

By matching up both indices we read 56° on the S-scale opposite 0.83 on the D-scale. This is the sine value. The corresponding cosine value is 90° − 56°, or 34° (answer). The yachtsman put one anchor out toward deep water and took a good stress on the cable. Nothing happened. He put another anchor out abeam from his main halyard at the masthead, and winched till the heel angle was about 30°. And off he came.

Example IV: Tacking downwind

A downwind run is rarely the fastest point of sailing. This is especially so for boats having no spinnaker, or only a small one, and employing high-aspect-ratio sails in a modern rig. The problem is this: if you don't head directly for the downwind mark, but bear off to fill the sails better, your speed will increase, but so will the total distance to the mark. So what angle away from the downwind mark will permit reaching it in the least time? Figure 4 illustrates the situation:

There is a formula easily computed on the slide rule to give the total distance sailed. Knowing the speed for each divergence angle (θ) you may readily determine the angle that will permit you to reach the leeward mark in minimum time. For this problem to be solved you should have a good speed log.

Total distance sailed =
$$\frac{2 \times \text{Base distance} \times \sin \theta}{\sin 2\theta}$$

Let us say that the leeward mark is directly downwind, distance 5.0 miles. When sailing directly for it the speed log indicates 5.0 knots. By hardening up 10° the speed increases to 5.3 knots; by 20° to 5.7 knots, and by 30° to 6.0 knots. What is the optimum divergence angle (θ)?

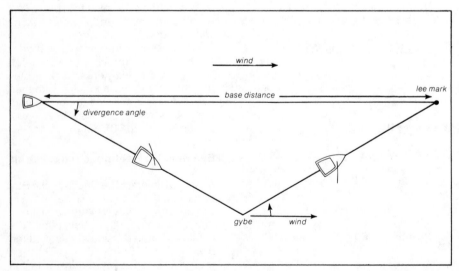

Figure 4

Make a table of the data:

θ	Speed	Total Distance	Time (in hours)
0°	5.0	5.00	1.00
10°	5.3	5.06	0.96
20°	5.7	5.34	0.94
30°	6.0	5.77	0.96

In order to conserve space, the calculations I'll make will be only for the θ = 30° case. You can calculate the others to confirm the results:

$$\text{Total Dist. (mi.)} = \frac{2 \times 5.0 \text{ mi.} \times \sin 30°}{\sin 60°}$$

$$= \frac{10 \times 0.50}{.867}$$

$$= 5.77 \text{ miles}$$

It is apparent from the table that a divergence angle of 20° is about optimum for minimum time. It makes little difference how many tacks you make toward the mark (if your crew is good at gybing) as long as the divergence angle to the wind is optimum.

I have presented just a smattering of examples showing the utility of the slide rule. If you are a serious navigator, you will find many more uses for it in celestial navigation, the sailings, conversion factors, and all kinds of things.

In retrospect, Napier was right and the schoolchildren were wrong. Logarithms, as depicted by the slide rule, *can* save us time, space, effort, and mental gymnastics. The slide rule *can* enhance our amateur or professional proficiency in sailing. This simple tool, stuck in a shirt pocket, or tacked to a convenient bulkhead with a bit of Velcro fabric, can make your cruising and racing more convenient, and pleasant, than ever before.

Clearing Bearings, Danger Angles

How to tell where you are not   John Mellor

At certain times in the life of a navigator it can be more useful for him to know, not where he is, but where he is not. Navigation of small boats tends, at best, to be a somewhat imprecise science, and probably one of the greatest sources of error lies in simply steering an inaccurate course. This can be due to a variety of things such as helmsman's error, an imperfect assessment of the tidal influence or leeway, a less then spot-on fix and so on. All very difficult things for even the best of small-boat navigators to get exactly right.

In the course of an offshore passage these small errors are not generally very important as there is plenty of space and there are plenty of opportunities to keep the position constantly checked and updated. Working in confined waters, however, such as entering harbor, negotiating a narrow

pass and so on, the situation is rather different. A very small error can lead to disaster.

Undoubtedly, the best way of avoiding such disasters is to adopt the technique of knowing where you are not. The advantage of this is that the navigator can define where he is not far more accurately than he can where he is. He does this by means of clearing bearings. Clearing bearings, by marking precisely the limits of where he must not go, enable him to know exactly how far he can safely stray from his ordered course. Thus, absolute precision accuracy in his course is not essential. Let us look at an example.

In Figure 1 you are entering harbor from the left, running in on the church on a previously calculated, safe bearing. The approach is fairly straightforward except for the outcrop of dangerous underwater rocks to port and

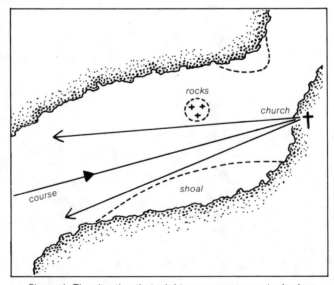

Figure 1: The situation that might appear as you enter harbor

the shoal water to starboard. There is plenty of room in between, but not so much that you can afford to stray far from your course. As long as you stick precisely to that course you will be all right. However, there are many factors that could cause you to wander a little: the vagaries of tide, wind and other boats. So it is essential for safety that you know exactly how far you can afford to stray.

In Figure 1 two clearing bearings are drawn from the church, one passing the safe side of the rocks, the other clearing the shoal water. These mark the limits of safe navigation, and as long as you remain between the two you will be clear of all the dangers. Thus, a navigator only has to keep a continuous check on the bearing of the church (he can appoint a crewman to hold a hand-bearing compass on it constantly, calling out the bearing whenever it changes), and he will know instantly the moment he begins to drift towards the dangers. He will also know (and this is the best part) precisely how far he can afford to go. In fluky winds or congested waters the benefit of this knowledge is, of course, enormous. It will enable him to make the best advantage of the wind, tide and space, and

prevent those heart-stopping moments as he wonders just how close he is to the rock!

Calculating and drawing these clearing bearings is simplicity itself. As you can see in Figure 1 they are drawn from a convenient mark to pass close on the same side of the danger as you will be passing. Obviously, the nearer they are to being parallel to your course, the more effective and less restricting they will be.

In Figure 2 we see a slightly different way in which they can be used. When sailing along the coast one often passes a series of headlands, frequently with off-lying dangers in between, as shown by the rocks in the diagram. In this instance clearing bearings are drawn both from the headland you have just left and the one you are approaching. Sailing from right to left in the diagram, one keeps outside the first clearing bearing (from the headland you have passed) until the other bearing has been crossed. The first can then be safely ignored and the second used as the safety limit.

This technique of safety limits extends far beyond just bearings. Transits, fathom lines, vertical danger angles—all can be utilized as clearing

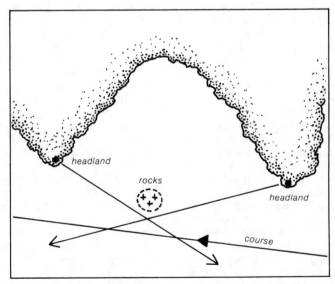

Figure 2: Playing the headlands can keep you clear of off-lying dangers

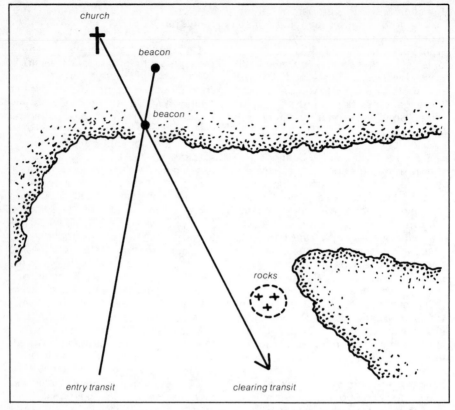

church

beacon

beacon

rocks

entry transit

clearing transit

Figure 3: You can use an entry transit and a clearing transit

safety markers. I would hesitate to use RDF bearings as I do not consider them sufficiently accurate, although they could be helpful in certain circumstances when nothing better is available.

Let us take a closer look at transits, fathom lines and vertical-danger angles. The first largely speaks for itself. In the entrance to many harbors one will find transits marking the line of best approach. Sometimes, however, there will be transits that do not appear to be on the best line at all. These will generally be marked "so and so in line with such and such clears what-do-you-call-it rocks" or something similar. Like the clearing bearings we have just looked at, they mark the limit of safe navigation and, if used properly, will lead the navigator clear of the danger. In Figure 3, we see an example. The two beacons in line mark the best

course for entry, while the leading beacon in line with the church is a clearing transit for the rocks to starboard. Thus the navigator knows that he can safely stray from the entry line as far as this transit. As long as he keeps the church open to the left of the leading beacon he will be safe.

Don't limit yourself to transits already plotted on the chart. When you plan your entry into any harbor look for any transits you can find for yourself that will form clearing lines for the dangers. If you can find them, you will realize that they are much easier and more reliable to use than even clearing bearings, for a compass is not necessary. You have only to keep the rear mark open to the requisite side of the front one.

Fathom lines can be used in a similar manner, and often are by larger ships when going along the coast. A check of the chart might show the ship's master that the 10-fathom line encloses all dangers relevant to his ship. He can then switch on his echo-sounder and, using the 10-fathom line as a clearing line, simply ensure that he does not stray over it. (He must, of course, allow for the height of the tide at the time.) On the average yacht, of course, it is not feasible to run the echo-sounder constantly while coasting, but the technique can sometimes be very useful for a short run in confined waters.

The vertical-danger angle is a slightly more complicated concept, but for the man who can wield a sextant it can be most useful. In the same way that the clearing bearing is simply a compass bearing used as a limiting danger line, so the vertical-danger angle is a distance off by sextant used to mark the limit of a danger. Its most useful application is when passing a headland with off-lying rocks or other dangers.

Measure off from the chart the distance from the headland to a point comfortably outside the danger. Then, taking the height of the headland, lighthouse or whatever from the chart, look up in the tables of distance off by sextant the angle subtended by that height at that distance. Set this angle on the sextant. This is the vertical-danger angle, and to remain safely outside the danger limit all you have to do is take regular sextant readings of the height of the object you have measured and ensure that the angle shown on the sextant is always lower than this danger angle. As you can see in Figure 4 this will keep you outside the danger zone.

The concept of limiting danger lines, bearings, etc., is a general one, and once you understand the idea of them this concept can be applied in many homemade ways. Take the business of finding distance off a cliff by timing the echo of a foghorn—a navigation technique of fairly limited application I will admit, but one that can be useful at times. If we happen to be sailing along past a coastline of high cliffs, especially in fog, we can utilize the method to set up a limiting danger line. Simply measure off from the chart the minimum safe distance we must be off the cliff, then calculate the time interval between blast and echo for this distance. (Remember the sound has to travel both there and back, so we need the time taken for sound to travel twice the distance we want to be off the cliffs.) Knowing this time, we have what we could call a Minimum Safety Time—the least time that must elapse between

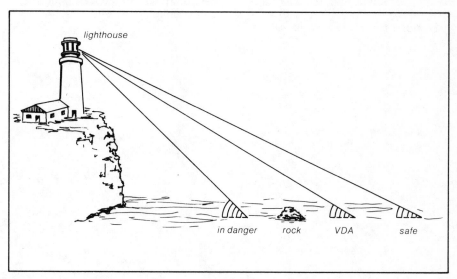

Figure 4: Different vertical angles show where you are relative to dangers

blast and echo for us to be a safe distance from the cliffs. A blast on the foghorn every now and then while consulting a stopwatch to ensure that the sound always takes longer than this to return to us will ensure that we are a safe distance from the cliffs.

Apply your own mind to the question and I am sure you will be able to come up with some limiting safety ideas of your own. If you are lucky enough to have a radar set aboard your boat, you can draw limiting distance lines on the face of the set with a grease pencil. First, ascertain which part of the coastline the radar set is showing—if it is a low coast with hills behind, the set may only show the hills, so if you are not experienced at interpreting a radar picture don't try this. If you are experienced, and are absolutely certain you can identify what the set is showing, then measure off from the chart the minimum safe distance you wish to be from the part of the coast the set shows, and draw a line on the face of the set that distance from yourself at the center and parallel to your course. Then simply make sure the coastline does not come within that line. As long as it stays beyond it, you are more than the minimum safe distance from the coast.

Another interesting point, not directly connected with this subject but very close, is the business of taking bearings of ships you think will pass too close for comfort. If the bearing of the ship from you remains steady then you are on a collision course. If the bearing draws ahead then the ship will pass ahead, and similarly if it draws astern. If you are approaching a headland, beacon, buoy or whatever with a strong cross tide, or making a lot of leeway, you are in a similar situation. Take a bearing of the object and keep checking it. If it remains steady you will collide with the object; if it draws ahead you will pass down wind or tide (whatever is setting you sideways), and if it draws aft you will pass clear.

A quicker way of doing this is simply to line the object up with something on board, like a shroud. Then, making sure you remain in the same position, so that the line between your eye and the shroud always makes the same angle with the centerline of the boat, simply keep checking the position of the object relative to the shroud. If it stays constant you will hit it.

The great value of clearing bearings, transits, fathom lines and vertical danger angles is that they tell the navigator *where he is not*. They provide limit lines that mark the edges of zones of danger. They are not substitutes for a well-plotted and accurately steered course, they merely back it up. Taken with this proviso, they can be very helpful indeed to the navigator and a great panacea for his nerves.

Finding Distance Off

Little-known methods for coastwise fixes   John Mellor

One of the most useful items to a navigator, and one of the most difficult to measure accurately, is calculating distance off. There are various methods for finding this rather elusive information and they range from the extremely accurate *vertical sextant angle* to the Boy Scout's thumb and 12-inch-ruler method. You can also determine your distance off from a DR position, or an EP (Estimated Position is a DR with allowance made for tide, leeway, etc.) run on from the last *decent* fix. You can also get a fix on the spot (if there are suitable marks to use) or an RDF fix. All these techniques are fairly well-known and if you pride yourself as a navigator you should be familiar with each method.

However, there are two other methods not so well known that can be useful to a small-boat navigator. These are the *four-point bearing* and *doubling the angle*. Both are based on the same simple trigonometrical facts, the former being in fact, a special case of the latter. Let us take a look at what we mean by *doubling the angle* and see

how it can find our distance off for us.

The two methods are particularly useful for finding distance off headlands while you are sailing along a coast, for they measure distances on the beam. They also require an absolute minimum of plotting, even with a complex tidal factor. In fact, with no tidal influence you need no plotting at all to get your distance off. You just use the distance and bearing to obtain an accurate fix. This, as you can imagine, is a tremendous advantage for a small-boat sailor in bad weather or when sailing short-handed, for it is under such conditions that any complex plotting becomes time-consuming, physically difficult and demanding, tiring, and very prone to errors. It is the one big advantage that doubling the angle on the bow has over a running fix, which it is closely related to.

Assuming there is no tidal influence, we begin, in Figure 1, with a boat proceeding on a course to pass the headland and lighthouse off the port bow. While still a fair way off, the navigator takes a bearing on the lighthouse

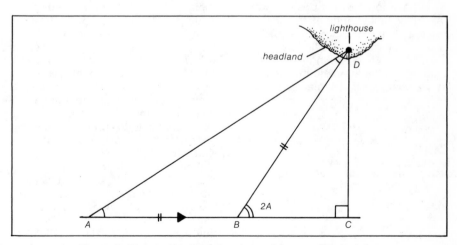

Figure 1: The standard solution for a distance-off calculation

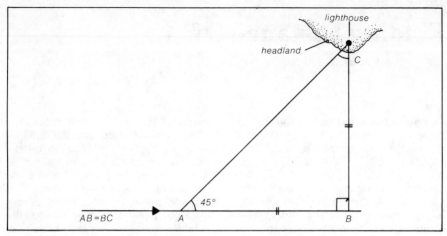

Figure 2: One solution for doubling the angle off the bow

(preferably when it is in the region of 30 degrees on the bow). If the angle on the bow is too small, any errors due to a slightly wobbly course will be greatly magnified.

Having read the log at the precise moment of taking the bearing he then continues on a steady course until the-angle the lighthouse makes off the bow has doubled. He then reads the log once again. The distance he has run between the two bearings will be his *distance off* the lighthouse measured along the second bearing. He then can plot his position from a simple range and bearing of the light. And that is the only plotting he has to do. He does not even have to know his position when taking the first bearing as the distance run equals the distance off regardless of where he is along the first bearing.

Those of you who understand trigonometry will appreciate the theory of similar triangles that explains this.*

---

*The theory explaining why the distance run equals the distance off is straightforward trig. and I think it will be instructive to run through it briefly.

(L denotes angle)   /LADB = LADC – LBDC

      LADB = LADC – LBDC
      LADC = 90 – LDAC
      LBDC = 90 – LDBC
but as LDBC = 2LDAC
      LBDC = 90 – 2LDAC
therefore LADB = (90 – LDAC) – (90 – 2LDAC)
           = 90 – LDAC – 90 + 2LDAC
      LADB = LDAC
therefore ∧ ADB is isosceles
   so AB = BD (opposite equal angles)

You will also realise that any line parallel to AB that joins AD to BD will produce a similar triangle and therefore the distance run along the course will *always* equal the distance off from the lighthouse along the second bearing. If you skipped the footnote don't worry. The theory is not essential, but, as with most things, understanding the whys and wherefores does help you remember the end product.

The four-point bearing has exactly the same theory and principle but is simply a special case in which the first bearing is 45 degrees off the bow. Doubling this, of course, brings the lighthouse abeam and once again, the distance run between bearings is equal to the distance off measured along the second bearing. The disadvantage of this one, as opposed to *doubling the angle* off the bow is that if the distance you must pass the headland to clear danger is critical then you are going to find it out a little late to be of much help! If the distance is not crucial it can provide you with a very simple, convenient and error-free figure (Fig. 2).

Well, that's the good news. Now for the bad. If we all sailed in tideless waters that would be all you would have to know. Unfortunately, we do not sail in motionless water and if you find tidal allowance calculations difficult for a running fix, you will really scratch

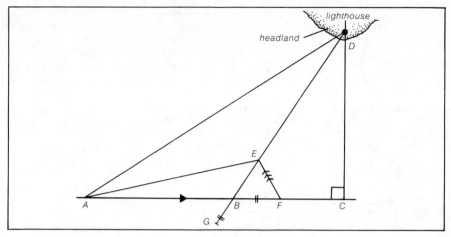

Figure 3: Distance-off solution made more complicated by the effects of tide's setting boat inshore and backward

your head over this bunch. They are, of course, basically the same. But if we allow for tide by applying the tidal vector to the transferred first bearing we destroy the great attraction of the methods, namely the absolute minimum amount of plotting. We would, therefore, have to treat them merely as special cases of a running fix which would be a pity.

To solve this problem for myself I have worked out a way to apply the tidal corrections by using just one extremely straightforward vector diagram. It's a very simple one (though the theory is quite complex) that can be plotted quickly and easily in any old corner of the chart. It requires no transferred position lines and no original position.

In Figure 3, we see that a tidal stream setting onto our starboard bow will have two effects on us. It will set us inshore and cause us to cross the line of the second bearing closer in than we otherwise would. It will also set us backward causing us to cross the line later, with a higher reading on the log.

It should be possible for us to resolve the tidal vector into two parts: one acting along the line of the course we steer; the other acting along the line of the second bearing. Now, because we are always sailing onto a fixed bearing, the actual effect of the tide on us will be purely in terms of our distance off. In other words, whatever point of the compass the tide comes from, the moment we reach the second bearing its total effect will have been simply to alter our distance off *along that bearing*. So if we can find this change in our distance off, the allowance for tide will consist simply of adding (or subtracting) this error to the log reading to get our correct distance off.

In Figure 3 the tide is setting on our starboard bow. We steer a course AC, but the tide sets us inshore and back so that we do not strike the second bearing at B but at E. Thus our true distance off along the second bearing is DE. The log reading, however, is AF, for that is the distance we have sailed through the water in order to reach our bearing at E. Therefore the log reading will give us a distance off of DG, where BG is equal to BF. Subtracting BF and BE from the log reading, therefore, gives us the correct distance off along the second bearing, without transferring either the first bearing or plotting a complex tidal vector digram on the chart.

How do we find BF and BE? We know the course we have steered and we know the rate and direction of the tide influencing us between our first and second bearings. So, anywhere on the chart, or on any old bit of paper

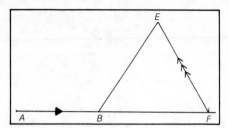

Figure 4: Simple vector diagram can be plotted on unused section of chart or on piece of paper

for that matter, you can plot (Fig. 4), AF (distance run by the log along the course steered), FE (distance and direction you have been set by the tide during that period), and EB (direction of the second bearing). This will give you the same triangle of forces as BFE in Figure 3. The reason for plotting this on its own is to avoid the necessity of plotting all the details of the triangle ACD. This way we can retain the one big advantage of the double angle on the bow, which is that no starting position and no plotting are required.

After plotting the simple tidal vector diagram in Figure 4, you only have to measure off the distances BF and BE and apply them to the log reading. This becomes your *true distance off* along

the second bearing and it works no matter what the direction and rate of the tide, and no matter where you begin along the first bearing. You have not been able to eliminate your plotting entirely, but you have been able to reduce it to an absolute simplified minimum.

The only thing left is to decide whether you should add or subtract the BF and BE corrections. Look at it logically and take the line of the second bearing as a datum. If the tide is running from ahead of this line, clearly it will push you back so your log reading will be too high. Therefore you *subtract* the component (BF) along the steered course. If the tide is from astern of the bearing your log will read low so you add BF.

If the tide is from the starboard side of the steered course, it will set you in causing you to sail a longer distance and cut the bearing at a shorter distance off. Thus, to obtain the true distance off you must subtract the component BE. If the tide is setting you out from your port side, it will cause you to strike the bearing sooner, at a greater distance off. So you must add the component BE to obtain your true distance.

The tidal vector diagrams in Figure 5 show this more clearly. If the tide is di-

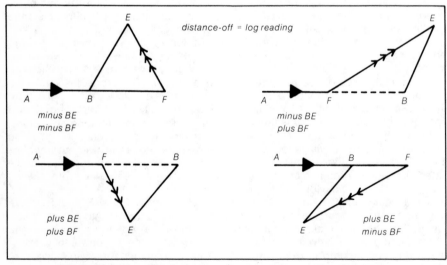

Figure 5: Many variations are possible using small vector diagram

rectly along the second bearing then, of course, there will be no component BF along the course. Similarly, if it is right ahead (or astern) there will be no component BE, which makes things considerably easier as there is then no need to draw a vector diagram at all. You have only to calculate the amount the tide has pushed you back or forward during the run and add or substract it to the log reading to give true distance off. With the tide along the bearing you do exactly the same, adding or subtracting the distance it has pushed you along the bearing to the log reading.

All this may seem rather complex, and it is. However, it does produce an end product that is a remarkably simple method for finding distance off without the need for a sextant (the best way by far), the complex plotting of a running fix, or even a starting position. In the majority of instances the tide, in all probability, will be either ahead or astern. All you have to do is to take the first bearing, note the log reading, run on until the angle on the bow doubles,

take the log reading again, calculate how far the tide has set you back or forward during the run and add (for tide astern) or subtract (for tide ahead) this figure to or from the log reading. The result is your true distance off along the second bearing.

I have given all the theory for those of you who want to follow and understand the process and assumptions. It also enables you to allow for any direction of tide.

To remember how to apply these correction vectors I always think of the *Miner said I'm out*. It reminds me that the vector is minus for tides ahead and from outside. The head or stern vector is the one plotted along the course while the sideways one is that plotted along the bearing. It may seem complex but with a little application, you will find it's logical in the extreme and the vector diagram could not be simpler for a tired, cold, wet mariner. It is certainly easier to plot and less prone to errors than all the paraphernalia of a running fix. Try it.

Longitude Minus Sextant or Clock

Handy methods for insuring position at sea   William V. Kielhorn

There are days at sea when the air is clear, the spume is blowing, the deck is lurching — and it is darn near impossible to handle both a sextant and yourself safely on deck.

This is a time when finding your longitude becomes a problem. Latitude is not quite so difficult because you can usually find the time over a five- (or even ten-) minute meridian passage period to obtain, and then average, some fair sextant shots of the sun between breaking seas. But how do you find the longitude without a sextant?

There are several ways, including some special cases which are more of classroom interest than of practical utility. In any case, each requires a knowledge of *time,* which is quite synonymous with longitude. Fortunately, radio time signals now are easy to come by. And the advent of the tuning-fork or crystal-controlled watch has all but eliminated the need for the old "standard chronometer." No longer is there an excuse for not knowing the time good to a second or so.

The first way to obtain longitude without a sextant is also the simplest way: just observe true sunrise (or sunset); then work out a regular sun sight using zero degrees as the true altitude of the sun. There are, however, a couple of difficulties with this method.

First, one of our best and most common sight-reduction methods, *Tables of Computed Altitude and Azimuth* (H.O. 214), doesn't tabulate below about 5° of altitude. Second, most of us really don't know the technique of observing the instant of true sunrise or sunset. And finally,

atmospheric refraction anomalies at very low sun altitudes can introduce significant errors.

Inasmuch as the remarkably useful H.O. 214 fails us in this one case, we have to select another sight reduction method. Among these (and there are many more) are:

Cosine-haversine
H.O. 208 (Dreisenstok)
H.O. 211 (Ageton)
AAA (Ageton modified 211)
H.O. 229 (Sight reduction Tables — Marine)
H.O. 249 (Sight reduction Tables — Air)

There are slight differences in the techniques used in determination of rising or setting. Bowditch (H.O. 9) gives 34' as the refraction correction for a body at the horizon; amplitudes of the sun (with sun's center at the horizon) are calculated with a 42' correction; a 36' correction for lower limb contact is mentioned both in Bowditch and in Dutton; 35' is used in the Nautical Almanac for stars and planets on the horizon.

But, with the apparent altitude of the sun's lower limb, a full semi-diameter above the horizon (16'), the correction to the center is almost exactly another 16'. This is the instant of true sunrise or sunset when viewed from near sea level (Fig. 1).

The proper technique follows: while you are seated comfortably in the cockpit and well-braced, use your marine binoculars to observe the sun. Have your stopwatch or hack watch set to GMT. At the instant the lower limb is one semi-diameter (its radius) *above* the horizon, note the time and write it down.

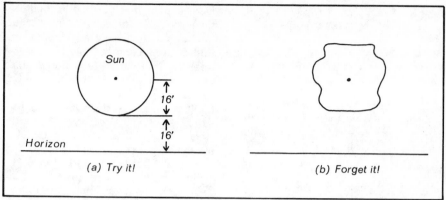

Figure 1: True sunset or sunrise. If the sun is badly distorted by uneven refraction as in (b), do not attempt to determine the instant of rising or setting

Try to do this when you are on the top of a high swell or sea.

You can also use a bright star or planet the same way, estimating when it is one full sun *diameter* above the horizon as the instant of rising or setting. But they are not quite so accurate as using the sun because of the difficulty in estimating the altitude. But a word of caution — *don't* use this method with the moon. The moon's parallax is so great that it is on the true celestial horizon almost as its *upper* limb disappears.

Some textbooks describe ways to obtain approximate longitude either by use of the sunset/sunrise tables in the Almanacs, or, for approximate latitude, by using "duration of daylight" tables. These methods are, in my view, so inaccurate that they are virtually useless unless you are *really* lost in the open sea. My reasoning is that sunset/sunrise tables are constructed on the premise of the rising and setting of the sun's *upper limb* at the horizon and this doesn't correspond at all to the zero degrees true altitude method of observation I described in the preceding paragraph. Furthermore, the interpolations for latitude are not precise and the calculations easily could result in time errors of about

two minutes — or a longitude error of up to half a degree from this cause alone! In addition, the setting or rising of the sun's upper limb is not so frequently seen as the "true" setting because of clouds or haze at the horizon.

If it is inconvenient to sit below and work out and plot a regular *zero altitude* sun sight, you still can determine the longitude quite accurately if you can observe the time of both the rising and setting. This is the method: Add the time of rising to the time of setting, and divide by two. Convert the time to GMT if GMT was not used. In other words, you find the GMT of the *average* time between sunrise and sunset, and this gives you the time the sun was on your meridian. By using either Almanac you can determine GHA sun at this moment as equal to your longitude.

Let us take an example: You are cruising in the North Atlantic on 30 July 1974 and observe a true sunrise at 09^{h}17^{m}24^s GMT. Later, at the end of the day, you obtain a true sunset at 22^{h}31^{m}14^s GMT. Assuming your rate of change of longitude is more or less constant during that time, what was your longitude at the moment the sun passed your meridian; and at what time did that occur?

$22^h - 31^m - 14^s$ GMT Sunset
$+ 09 - 17 - 24$ GMT Sunrise

$2|31^h \ 48^m \ 38^s$
$15^h \ 54^m \ 19^s$ GMT Time of
                 meridian

Look at the Nautical Almanac for that date and determine the GHA sun at that moment (which was your longitude), as follows:

1500 GMT 30 Jul 74

GHA sun =	43°24.1'
$54^m \ 19^s$ correction	+13°34.8'
Long. or GHA sun	56°58.9'W
	(answer)

If you are using the Air Almanac, the calculations are as follows:

GHA sun at 1550 GMT 30 Jul 74

Corr. for $4^m 19^s$

At 1554 GMT Long. or GHA sun

$$55° - 54.1'$$
$$+ \ 1° - 04.8'$$
$$56° - 58.9'W$$

There are other ways of determining longitude without a sextant, but they are not accurate. One way is the special case where the sun or moon passes almost exactly overhead at meridian passage; another takes place when a star or planet passes the meridian close enough to the horizon so that you can take a good compass azimuth and note the time it passes the true meridian. In either case, the GHA of the body at that time equals your longitude west of Greenwich. These methods are to be used, however, only when sunrise or sunset cannot be observed, and when you feel you have lost your reckoning by at least a degree or so.

As I mentioned earlier, knowing the exact time is not much of a problem any more. But if your chronometer has been damaged or has stopped can you find the time again without using a sextant? Yes, you can if you have kept a good dead reckoning position on the chart.

The problem is the same as be-

fore, except that you just substitute time for longitude. All the same methods given earlier are applicable, but for the sake of brevity (and practicality) I will illustrate a method using a single observation at sunrise (or sunset). In the following example I will use *Sight Reduction Tables for Air Navigation — Vol. II* (H.O. 249). Remember you *can't* use H.O. 214 for the *zero altitude* problem.

You are sailing in the North Atlantic on the night of September 1, 1974 and discover that your chronometer has stopped. The next morning it is too rough to obtain morning star sights, but you would like to restart the chronometer and determine its error as soon as possible. You estimate that your D.R. position at sunrise is 30°15'N 50°45'W. What do you do?

1. Re-start the chronometer, or set another good watch to your "best guess" of Greenwich Mean Time (GMT).

2. Observe true sunrise; when the sun's lower limb is a full semi-diameter above the horizon. Note the time on the restarted chronometer is $09^h 06^m 14^s$ GMT 1 September 1974.

3. You note in the Almanac that the sun's position at that time was as follows:

$09^h 00^m$	314°58'
$6^m 14^s$	1°34'
GHA sun	316°32' Dec. N 8°22'

4. Work out the sight, using an observed altitude of 0°00'

assumed Lat.	30°N
GHA	316°32'
assumed Long.	50°32'W
LHA	266°W
or LHA(t)	94°E

H_c	00°34'	d = +30
corr.	+ 11'	Dec. 8°22'N
H_c	00°45'	Z_n = 081°T
H_o	00°00'	
a	45 mi Away 081°T	

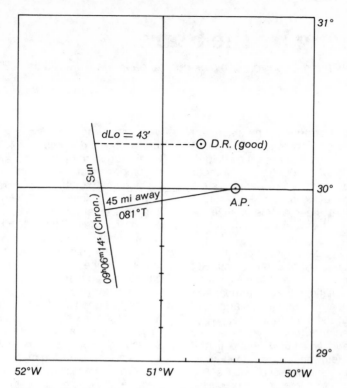

Figure 2: Sun line of position for determining error of the chronometer

5. Plot your line of position (Figure 2) and measure the difference of longitude, parallel to the latitude, from the "known" position (in this case it is your D.R.). It measures 43' of longitude. 43' corresponds to 2ᵐ52ˢ arc-to-time, so that is your chronometer error. The error is "fast" of GMT because the true position is eastward of the "observed" line. To double check on whether it is fast or slow, work the sight out again using the chronometer error. This time the sun line should fall right through the D.R.

So you can see that a good deal of accurate navigating can take place without using expensive instruments, or if there is heavy weather. When you cruise offshore remember these things. It will take away a lot of worry when you approach your landfall.

Steering by the Stars

If you know the groups you can pick out the bearings   James B. Kane

To **steer a course** by the stars, you first must know how to identify at least a few stars. And if you want to belong to the group of old-timers (without being old) who can identify stars merely by looking at the sky — and if you want to steer a true course by these stars — what follows is meant for you.

During a clear night thousands of twinkling stars might confuse you. But remember, only the brightest stars form constellations or star groups. And once you learn to identify a star group, picking out the stars in it is easy.

Let's begin as though you're at sea at night and you know you're in the Northern Hemisphere. You don't know where north, south, east or west is. Before orienting yourself more precisely, you must have a rough idea of where north is. To do this, watch which stars are rising and which are setting. Those due east rise the fastest and those due

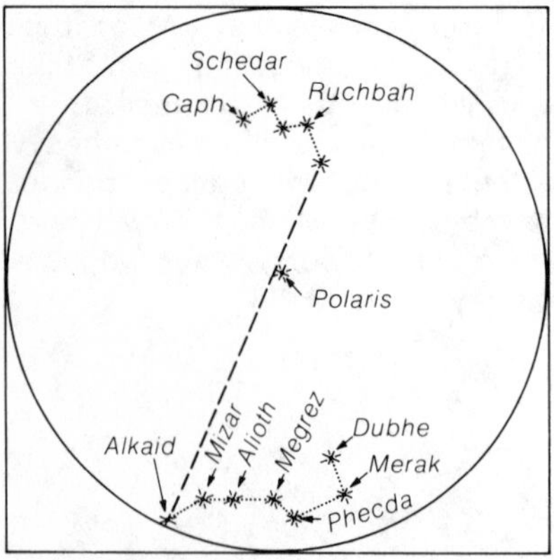

Figure 1: The Big Dipper
(Ursa Major) and Cassiopeia
rotate around Polaris the
same way as the hour hand
on a clock, but going
counterclockwise

west set the fastest. Those closest to the two poles don't set at all. They revolve around the poles and are called circumpolar stars.

Once you've found a general northerly bearing, look for the Big Dipper. The Big Dipper forms part of the group called Ursa Major. Naturally it's shaped like a dipper and the two stars at the far side of the dipper away from the handle, Dubhe and Merak (sometimes called the pointers), point to Polaris, the pole star (Fig. 1).

Now is a good time to stop looking at the sky for a few minutes and get back to earth. Here is a way to steer any true course you want using the pole star.

You do this by using a pelorus. Suppose you want to steer a true course of 135. Set the disc on the pelorus to 135 degrees on the lubber line. Next set the sight vane to north (000). Keep Polaris in the sight vane while steering to automatically steer 135 degrees true.

Ordinarily, the most you could be off on a bearing of Polaris is about one degree either side of north. But in latitudes above 65 degrees you could be as much as two degrees off. Consequently, it's best to use the Nautical Almanac to get the true bearing of Polaris when steering above 60 degrees latitude.

Using a pelorus to steer by is tricky at first because you have to look at the bearing of north instead of the heading of your boat.

More about just how to steer by the other stars later—after you see how to find the ones you'll need.

You can use the Big Dipper to find many other stars. If the line created by Dubhe, Merak and Polaris is extended past Polaris, it aims almost right for *Caph* in the *Cassiopea* group. Depending on how you look at it, *Cassiopea* is shaped either as an M or a W.

Follow the arc the handle of the Big

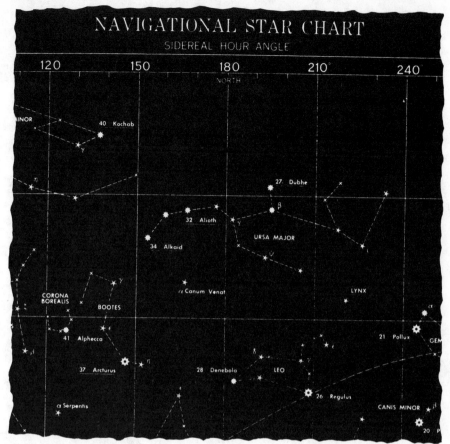

Figure 2: The Navigational Star Chart, a portion of which is shown here, is helpful in finding the stars you want to use

Dipper forms away from the bowl and you'll see *Arcturus*. You'll have no difficulty recognizing it for it's a bright star. Keep following this arc and you come to another bright navigational star called *Spica*. Go a bit farther on this same arc and you hit a group of four stars *(Corvus)* somewhat dimmer than Spica. Sailors from the clipper ship days called this Spica's Spanker. The four stars in this group form the shape of a spanker, the aftermost fore and aft sail on a ship.

Naturally, you should use the star chart (Fig. 2) in helping you find all these stars. The grid of vertical and horizontal lines on the chart show declination and sidereal hour angle. Of course, declination in the sky corresponds exactly to latitude on earth.

You can see stars on the right half of the chart generally from September to March and those on the left half from March to September. Star charts show north on top, south on bottom, east on the *left* and west on the *right*. When you hold the star chart overhead, with the north end toward north, the left edge is east, the right edge is west and you'll see the stars exactly as they appear in the sky, except for stars with high declinations (circumpolar stars).

During a period of slightly less than 24 hours, the Big Dipper and Cassiopeia revolve completely around Polaris, as the hour hand on a clock but in the opposite direction (Fig. 1). In autumn, Cassiopeia is near your meridian and to the north.

If you're in latitudes of the United

States or Canada, the square of *Pegasus* (the winged horse) shines slightly south of you. A line running through Polaris and Caph, extended about the same distance, ends near the four stars which form the Pegasus group (Fig. 3). *Markab* and *Scheat*, which shape the west side of Pegasus, create a good north-south line.

Use Pegasus to locate other bright stars. A line running from *Alpheratz* and *Algenib* (on the eastern side of the square) to the south almost hits the bright star *Diphda* in the *Cetus* (sea monster) group. Similarly, a line running from Scheat and Markab (on the western side of the square) to the south almost hits the star *Formalhaut*. Formalhaut shines slightly more brightly than Diphda. A line through Scheat and Alpheratz (on the north side of the square) to the east nearly points to *Hamal* in the *Aries* (ram) group.

There are three stars which shape a triangle, but actually belong to three separate groups. In the summer sky, *Vega* (brightest star in the Northern Hemisphere), Deneb and Altair create a right triangle at Vega. Their brightness makes them easy to find.

You can readily identify Altair by a dimmer star on each side of it. Altair, with its two dimmer stars, points directly to Vega and Vega, with three dimmer stars, shapes a parallelogram.

Orion is the most conspicuous group in the entire sky (Fig. 4). Because you find it near the celestial equator, sailors from both the Northern and Southern Hemispheres recognize it. In the Northern Hemisphere you see it in the winter sky (summer sky in the Southern Hemisphere).

It's a good thing to bear in mind that *Delta Orion*, the northmost of the three stars close together in the center of Orion, is practically over the equator and such a star always rises and sets exactly east and west. But don't look for it in the summer sky for it won't be there. In summer you should use *Gamma* in the *Virgo* group. It's almost as good. *Gamma Virgo* is in the same group as *Spica* and is nearly on a line running between *Arctarus* and *Spica*.

Using a bit of ingenuity you can use your pelorus with either Delta Orion or Gamma Virgo, as they rise and set, to steer a true course, just as you did with the pole star.

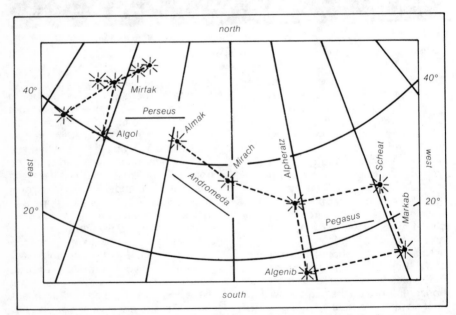

Figure 3: The groups Pegasus, Andromeda, *and* Perseus *with their own stars. Note how* Markab *and* Scheat *form a north-south line*

118

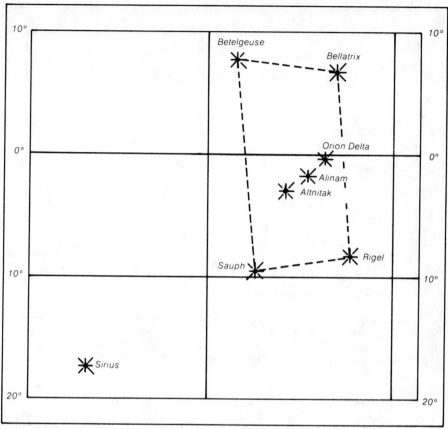

Figure 4: Orion, with its four stars, is the most conspicuous group
in the entire sky. Note how the three stars, Altnitak, Alinam and Orion Delta,
point to Sirius which is the brightest star in the sky

If you have no pelorus, here is something to help you. Everyone knows it's easier to steer by a star than to steer by a swinging compass. So, if you're lucky, you can find a star whose bearing is on the course you want to steer. But most times you're unlucky and the bearing of a star and your course line are so far apart that you're unable to use it. When this happens you can use your hand to measure angles horizontally from the star.

If you want to measure 15 degrees stretch your arm out straight. The span between your thumb and middle finger with your hand comfortably spread open is about 15 degrees. The distance between the tip of your thumb and the tip of the pinky is about 22 degrees. Now turn the palm of your hand down and clench your fist. Your fist will cover about 8 degrees. These angles are to the nearest degree and of course they apply to the average person.

Using a bit of ingenuity with stars that you know the true bearing of, such as Delta Orion, Gamma Virgo and Polaris, will enable you to use them as guiding stars as well.

Just to check your own "fist angle" hold it up to the Big Dipper. The two stars at the bottom of the bowl, Phecda and Merak, create an eight-degree angle. And in the Orion group Betelgeuse and Aldebaran create a 22-degree angle.

In the Southern Hemisphere aside from Orion the most important set of stars is the Southern Cross. The

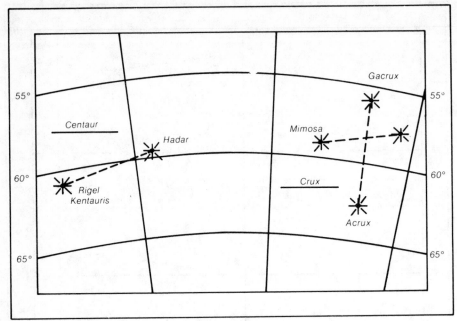

Figure 5: Stars to watch in the Southern Hemisphere. A line through
the two stars forming the long arm of the Southern Cross, extended nearly
five times the distance between the two stars, ends at the south pole

groups *Centaur* and the *Cross* lie to the south of *Virgo* and *Libra*. Although you have no star in the Southern Hemisphere to guide you like Polaris, a line through the two stars forming the long arm of the Southern Cross, extended nearly five times the distance between these stars does end at the south pole (Fig. 5).

Of course to steer by the stars all the time, you're going to need more stars to steer by than just Polaris, Delta Orion and Gamma Virgo. Table A lists 30 But most times you're unlucky and the bearing of a star and your course line are so far apart that you're unable to use it. When this happens you can use your hand to measure angles horizontally from the star.

If you want to measure 15 degrees stretch your arm out straight. The span between your thumb and middle finger with your hand comfortably spread open is about 15 degrees. The distance between the tip of your thumb stars with their declinations and Table B shows the true bearing of the stars when they are rising and setting. Grind

into Table B your latitude and the declination of the star you got from Table A and you can reel out the true bearing.

Before using Table B, however, keep in mind that you measure the bearing from north *clockwise* toward south when the star is rising, and north *counterclockwise* toward south when the star is setting. You, therefore, must subtract the bearing from 360 degrees when the star is setting to get your true bearing.

Example: While in latitude 10° N you want to find the bearing of Arcturus when it rises and sets. Table A gives you 19.3° N as the declination of Arcturus. Go into Table B with Latitude 10° N and Declination 20° N (the nearest declination to 19.3° N), and you come out with 70°. This means Arcturus bears 70° rising and 290° (360° — 70°) setting.

To use this system to its fullest capacity, use it with the Nautical Almanac. The Almanac gives the declination of 173 stars (pages 268 to 273) as well as the sun and four planets (daily pages).

Table A: 30 stars and their declinations

Star	Declination	Star	Declination
ACHERNAR	57.3 S	DENEB	45.2 N
ACRUX	63.0 N	DUBHE	61.9 N
ALDEBARAN	16.5 N	FOMALHAUT	29.7 S
ALIOTH	56.1 N	GACRUX	57.0 S
ALKAID	49.4 N	HADAR	60.3 S
ALNILAM	1.2 S	MIRFAK	49.8 N
ALPHERATZ	29.0 N	PEACOCK	56.8 S
ALTAIR	8.8 N	POLLUX	28.1 N
ANTARES	26.4 S	PROCYON	5.3 N
ARCTURUS	19.3 N	RIGEL	8.2 S
BELLATRIX	6.3 N	RIGEL KENTAURIS	60.7 S
BETELGEUSE	7.4 N	SCHEDAR	56.4 N
CANOPUS	52.7 S	SIRIUS	16.7 S
CAPELLA	46.0 N	SPICA	11.0 S
CAPH	59.0 N	VEGA	38.8 N

By knowing the sky, you'll know what stars to expect to rise next. This is important for you hardly ever see stars as they pop over the horizon. They rise about five or 10 degrees above the horizon before you're able to see them. In the Northern Hemisphere, they slide a bit toward the south when rising and toward the north when setting. In the Southern Hemisphere the reverse is true.

Now let's see how this works. It's shortly after sunset in January 1977. Your latitude is around 30° N and you want to sail a course of 100 degrees. First, go along the 30-degree latitude line (Table B) and look for bearings that are within 25 degrees to each side of your course. In this case, by measuring angles with your hand or with a pelorus, you can use any bearing between 75 degrees and 125 degrees. Note the highest and lowest declinations these bearings come within. A bearing of 125 degrees matches under 30° S declination. A bearing of 75 degrees matches 13° N declination (you have to interpolate 10 degrees and 20 degrees north). This indicates you can use any star whose declination is between 30 degrees south and 13 degrees north and which is on the right half of the star chart. Go to the star chart or Nautical Almanac and list the stars in the order they rise. From Table A you get the declinations of these stars so you can get the bearings from Table B. Naturally by looking over your

Table B: True bearing of stars when rising and setting

Decl.	S 50°	S 40°	S 30°	S 20°	S 10°	0°	N 10°	N 20°	N 30°	N 40°	N 50°
Lat.											
N 70°	—	—	—	180°	121°	90°	59°	0°	—	—	—
60	—	—	180°	133	110	90	70	47	0°	—	—
50	—	180°	141	122	106	90	74	58	39	0°	—
40	180°	147	131	117	103	90	77	63	49	33	0°
30	152	138	125	113	102	90	78	67	55	42	28
20	145	133	122	111	101	90	79	69	58	47	35
N 10	141	131	121	110	100	90	80	70	59	49	39
0	140	130	120	110	100	90	80	70	60	50	40
S 10	141	131	121	110	100	90	80	70	59	49	39
20	145	133	122	111	101	90	79	69	58	47	35
30	152	138	125	113	102	90	78	67	55	42	28
40	180	147	131	117	103	90	77	63	49	33	0
50	—	180	141	122	106	90	74	58	39	0	—

stern, you can use some of the same stars when they are setting.

Table B is good forever and at least 40 years will go by before Table A becomes obsolete. The declination of stars changes slowly through the years.

So, if you want to steer a true course during the night without a compass it's fun and informative to try hitching your boat to a star, and steering by it.

Pilot and Routeing Charts

New ways to interpret data

Mike Saunders

A **Frenchman I** met once in the tiny South Atlantic island of St. Helena, asked me what a pilot chart was. I showed him. For an hour we pored over the chart, planning the next leg of his voyage. But finally he shook his head skeptically.

"You say that to go to Cape Town, which is 1,700 miles direct, it is better to go west first, a distance of 2,700 miles? But, *mon ami,* my boat is more than 50 feet in length. It goes well to windward."

In the end he sailed directly to Cape Town. It took him over 50 days of merciless pounding to windward to do that 1,700 miles. My proposed longer route, using 100 miles a day made good as a rule of thumb, could be expected to take half that time, and would probably have been more comfortable to boot.

This admittedly somewhat extreme (but nonetheless true) example illustrates the value of pilot and routing charts in planning an ocean passage. They enable you to plan a route that either is quicker or more comfortable (or

both if you are lucky). And the charts can be a real contribution to safety where the more savage moods of the sea prevail.

The pilot charts were originated by Matthew Fontaine Maury, a lieutenant in the United States Navy, who began assembling weather data in the early part of the 19th century. In a nutshell they are a graphic representation of the ocean climate. Each chart is the condensation of thousands of meteorological observations made over the years, and shows some 10 different variables. Pilot charts are published in the United States and routing charts in Britain. Although the two are similar in essentials, there are small but significant differences. Each chart shows the average climate of one ocean for one month of the year or, in certain cases, for a whole quarter. Figure 1 gives the areas, numbers and references of charts currently available.

At first sight, the charts look as involved as a plate of spaghetti. But color coding helps to unravel the tangle

---

Pilot Charts published by the US Naval Oceanographic Office

	Chart No.
North Atlantic	16 (monthly)
North Pacific	55 (monthly)

	Pub. No.
Atlas of Pilot Charts—Central American waters and South Atlantic	106
Atlas of Pilot Charts—South Pacific and Indian Oceans	107
Atlas of Pilot Charts—Northern North Atlantic	108

Routeing Charts published by the Hydrographer of the Royal Navy

	Chart No. (numbers in bracket refer to months of the year)
North Atlantic Ocean	5124 (1) through (12)
South Atlantic Ocean	5125 (1) through (12)
Indian Ocean	5126 (1) through (12)
North Pacific Ocean	5127 (1) through (12)
South Pacific Ocean	5128 (1) through (12)

Figure 1: Numbers and references of charts currently available

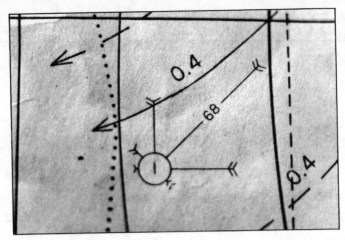

Figure 2: Typical trade wind rose

which in due course reveals itself to be composed of a great deal of data.

Each ocean is chopped up into five-degree squares (i.e., roughly 300 miles x 300 miles) and a *wind rose* in the center shows the average wind conditions in the area.

Wind roses are the most important item of information on the chart for the sailor; a typical rose is shown in Figure 2. The length of each arrow indicates the percentage of wind blowing from the direction, and the number of feathers shows the average wind strength. The number in the center is the total percentage of calms, variables and light winds. A rose like this one has the power to evoke in me memories of flying fish for breakfast—with 68 percent from the northeast: it can only be the northeast trades!

Roses on routeing charts give more information than those on pilot charts. As shown in Figure 3, the rose gives not only the overall percentage of wind from that direction but also the percentage at each individual strength. Many of these roses, moreover, cover 16 points of the compass as opposed to the usual eight.

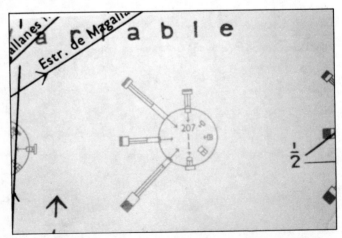

Figure 3: Routeing chart wind rose with the various strengths shown in differing thicknesses. Numbers in center are (top to bottom) number of observations, percent calms, percent variables

Currents are perhaps the most uncertain of the data given on these charts. Few measurements are available, and apart from constant streams like the Southeast Equatorial Current, currents are notoriously variable. Green arrows show the prevailing direction, while adjacent figures indicate the strength in knots. Some idea of their constancy is given by solid and dotted lines. Remember that the charts deal only with ocean currents. Tidal or inshore streams may be totally different.

Another principal interest to sailors are the main shipping routes given complete with distances from port to port. Most sailors, of course, will want to know where the routes are so that they can sail clear of them.

Both types of charts give the sailor the same essential information to plan a voyage, and so the choice of pilot or routeing charts will probably depend on what you can easily get. I have used both and admit to a slight preference for routeing charts, mainly because of more detailed wind data. They also separate the various bits of information with insets, and are therefore easier on the eye. Finally, the British charts are made of stronger paper—a point not to be dismissed when every boat I have ever sailed on seems to have a drip over the chart table!

Now, here is a common-sense approach that can be used by cruising yachtsmen, and a method that will give you a sound route to sail. First look at extremes, then examine the winds, and finally consider the "secondaries."

By first considering extreme conditions, times or routes that are very hazardous, or very difficult, you can eliminate them. Tropical revolving storms (hurricanes) are the first things that spring to mind.

And on the other side of the weather spectrum, I personally will go a long way round to avoid calms, for there is nothing so wearing on nerves and gear as a bad dose of the calms. But if the boat is a motorsailer with a handsome range, then calms may possibly be acceptable.

Two other extremes to check on are contrary ocean currents or a high incidence of fog. Extreme and constant currents are few, but where they exist they can make a passage either very fast or almost impossible. Examples of the former are the Southeast Equatorial Current, 1½-two knots, and the Agulhas Current down the East Coast of South Africa, 2½-five knots. Fog that is extreme enough to affect your route also is rare, but an area such as that to the east of Newfoundland, showing 30-percent incidence in June, is best avoided if possible.

After you have examined the extreme conditions, and decided what routes are impossible, possible or desirable, you now can carry on and look at the route itself.

Wind patterns will affect your choice of route more than any other climactic factor. Since pilot charts give the average wind for every 300 miles square, you can sail from square to square, always picking the most favorable ones. Bernard Moitessier called this "sailing the squares."

What is the most favorable wind? For a racing machine it is the fastest wind; but a cruising man wants a modicum of comfort as well. This is of course a snare and delusion—every wind cunningly contrives to specialize in producing at least one uncomfortable motion; the stronger the wind the more uncomfortable the motion, while no wind at all will drive you mad. Good progress, on the other hand, will raise morale.

On the whole, you must admit, it is an indistinct problem composed of vague and personal factors, out of which you must determine a rational route. In the end you have to draw the line somewhere between; and to help you decide where I suggest a rule of thumb for speed and a *Polar Discomfort Diagram* (Fig. 4).

The speed rule is simple—I have found that an average type of medium- to heavy-displacement cruiser, about 35 feet overall will sail 25 to 30 nautical miles per day per wind force, i.e., a Beaufort scale force of three will take you 75 to 90 miles, four, 100 to 120 miles and so on. Above Force five

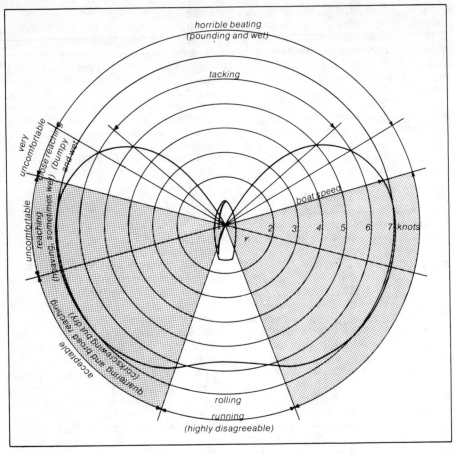

Figure 4: The Polar Discomfort Diagram

the day's run levels off as the boat reaches her maximum waterline length speed. Above Force seven or eight the speed tends to fall as you start to hoist storm canvas; below Force two much depends on your light-weather sails. Much also depends on the boat. Light-displacement boats are generally faster in moderate and light winds, and heavy or large boats can be superior in strong winds, if for no other reason than they toss their crew about less.

The boat's speed also depends, of course, on the wind direction, and this is what a polar diagram illustrates. But this one considers the crew as well as the boat. The effect of wind direction on the crew is considered in terms of degrees of discomfort—which is the only sensible way to look at things.

The combined result is a sort of wind

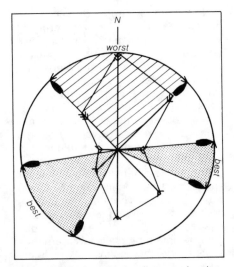

Figure 5: Wind rose polar diagram showing best and worst courses

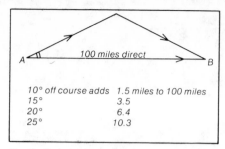

10° off course adds	1.5 miles to 100 miles
15°	3.5
20°	6.4
25°	10.3

Figure 6: Actual extra distance involved in sailing off course

rose polar diagram (Fig. 5). By imposing a simplified polar diagram showing only the desirable sectors, you can see at once which are the best and which are the worst sailing directions.

After several long sessions, the shape of the weather is soaked up, and routes do begin to emerge. It is always a good idea actually to plot alternative routes and measure distances. It is surprising how little difference there is between routes that swing far away from each other. Figure 6 shows how much extra distance is involved in sailing off course. A few hundred miles is only a few days and might be well worth it in terms of less discomfort.

Finally, there are the secondaries to consider. While shaping up a route from the wind patterns, it is worth looking at these secondaries, i.e., weaker currents, fog, sea temperatures and shipping lanes. All will obviously affect boats and crews differently. A vessel with six crew standing watch around the clock, for example, will be indifferent to shipping lanes, while a singlehander should avoid them like the

plague. Personally, I find my well-being closely relates to the sea-water temperature, and have seriously considered sailing round the world on the 76-degree F isotherm, in bland disregard of every other factor!

But after you have gone through the laborious (though fascinating) studies I have described you will eventually shape a route that curves beautifully across the ocean to the farthest shore. You steam out of the harbor, set the bows on the chosen route and find that a contrary wind springs up. The pilot chart says the chance of such a wind is less than one percent but the wretched breeze whistles about your ears for three whole days.

This has happened to me more than once. The point is that pilot charts show only average conditions, and you must be flexible in the face of actual conditions. If you are forced off your route then you should go back to the chart and start "sailing the squares" again. Your original route is, after all, merely a line on paper and it may no longer be the best course from the new position. But it is astounding how many people are determined to get *back on the original course* again, come what may.

Pilot charts and routeing charts are absorbing things, and very useful in the fascinating art of the mariner. They will help you to follow the first part of Joshua Slocum's advice to young sailors. But to follow the second you will need more than an armchair and pencil. He wrote, "You must then know the sea, and know that you know it, and not forget that it was made to be sailed over."

Great Circle Distance

It sounds complicated, but it isn't   Peter W. Rogers

The number of major distance ocean races and voyages going on has increased the interest about just how long a course distance actually is. Aficionados of prevailing winds, currents, and great circle routes all manage to get their opinions in. But given the fact that rarely do you find someone with a miniature pilot chart or great circle chart in his or her pocket or printed on a cocktail napkin, nothing conclusive about distances is likely to emerge. The result can be a heated argument.

Most people have heard the term "Great Circle Route," and they know that such a route is shorter. But shorter than what? A great circle is a line whose plane passes through the center of the earth. Every meridian of longitude is a great circle, but only one parallel of latitude is; that is the equator. In the Northern Hemisphere, a great circle (or Gnomonic) chart shows lines of longitude tending to converge at the north; the latitude lines sag in the middle to the south. A great circle would appear as a straight line, and if it were transferred to a Mercator chart it would bow to the north.

I used to sail in icebreakers, and since icebreakers really go only north and south, we didn't worry much about these strange bo⋅ ⋅haped courses, for north-south tracks are great circles anyway.

But on one of those icebreakers, the *Glacier,* a warrant bos'n named Ken Kramer showed me an interesting way to determine great circle distance with a maneuvering board (either NO 2665-10 [the smaller version] or NO 2665-20) that can be purchased from any chart distributor.

Let's assume we want to determine what the great circle distance is from New York to the Cape of Good Hope at the southern tip of Africa.

The first step is to assume that the horizontal line along the top of the maneuvering board represents the equator. Note that it intersects with the 0-degree mark on the circumference of the board (Fig. 1).

Everything to the right of 0 degrees we designate north latitude, and everything to the left as south. New York's latitude is 40°42′N, so we put a mark on the circumference at 40°42′ (Fig. 2). The latitude of the Cape of Good Hope is 34°22′S, so we mark off the amount *to the left* of 0 degrees. Then draw a perpendicular line up from each of these marks to the horizontal line (equator). The two resulting lines (a and b) are linear representations of angular measurement (latitude) taken from the base line (the equator), and the distance along this base line represents the difference in latitude (Fig. 1).

Next, assume the maneuvering board's circumference also represents the equator. New York's longitude is 74°01′W, so starting from the bottom of the board (180 degrees) mark off 74°01′W *to the left* of 180 degrees. The Cape of Good Hope is at 18°23′E so mark this off *to the right* of 180 degrees. If you draw a straight line between them this would represent the difference in longitude if both New York and the Cape of Good Hope were located at the equator.

But they are not, and so we take the distance at the top of the board (a) and plot it toward the center of the board. Do the same for the distance (b). The

128

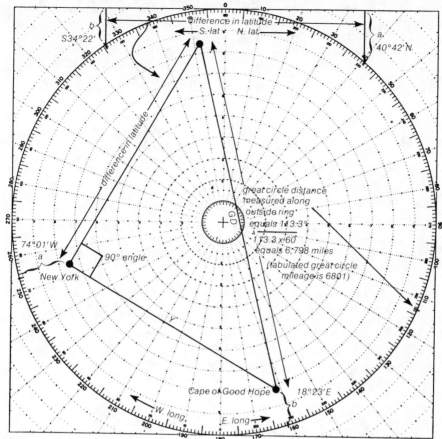

Figure 1: Solving the great distance route by maneuvering board looks complicated at first.

resulting distance (Y) between these two points (Fig. 1) now represents the difference in longitude at the *proper latitudes*. If it's hard to visualize, imagine the maneuvering board as a transparent globe, and line Y is a slice through it. Looking from the North Pole, New York is on the upper side of the globe and the Cape of Good Hope is on the under side.

But so far we have ignored the difference in latitude. To include this you have to plot a perpendicular to line Y that is equal in length to the difference in latitude you have already measured at the top.

The resultant vector, line GD (Fig. 1) *is the great circle distance*. In short, you now have a right triangle, one side of which is the difference in longitude

and the other side of which is the difference in latitude; the hypoteneuse is the Great Circle distance.

Now take a pair of dividers and plot the exact distance of the line (GD) from 0 degrees along the outer circumference. It comes out to 113.3 degrees. Because we have already used the circumference to measure latitude on a global projection and longitude at the equator, we can now multiply 113.3 times 60 because there are 60 miles in a degree. Therefore, 113.3 x 60 equals 6,798 miles for the Great Circle route.

According to HO Pub. 151, *Distances Between Ports*, the actual tabulated great circle distance is 6,801 miles, which is a three-mile error. Given the small size of a maneuvering board

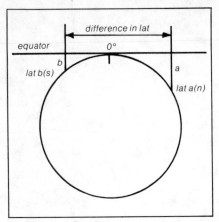

difference in lat

equator 0°

b
lat b(s)

a
lat a(n)

Figure 2: Plotting latitudes on maneuvering board and then moving them "up to equator" is first step

board my average was one mile of error for every 335 miles of track. My best result was the 7,350-mile run from San Francisco to Singapore. The maneuvering board gave me 7,348 miles, only two miles off!

The New York—Cape of Good Hope example is a case using north and south latitude, and east and west longitude. It is slightly simpler to use latitudes that agree and longitudes that agree. Always remember that you are looking for *differences* in latitude and in longitude. If both latitudes are north, for example, you would mark *both of* them off to the right of 0 degrees, and the *difference* in latitude would be the distance between the two and not back to 0 degrees.

It looks complicated at first but once it's understood, it is *very* fast. So, go back to the verbal arguments about how long a distance may be. But before you go, stuff a maneuvering board in your pocket!

(10-inch diameter), such a small error is remarkable. For practice, I worked out 10 of these, totaling over 52,000 miles of track. Using the maneuvering

A New Way to Plot Celestial LOPs

A graphic solution reduces plotting time

Joel H. Jacobs

Historically, there have been two traditional methods for celestial navigators to plot their lines of position. One, of course, was to plot directly on the chart you were working with, and the other was to use universal plotting sheets which were either constructed by the navigator or were preprinted forms available from the Defense Mapping Agency, British Admiralty, or companies who deal in navigation aids.

Plotting directly on a chart has some disadvantages which include the large size of the charts in relation to the navigator's working space on yachts, and the confusion that occurs when a number of LOPs of the same celestial body are plotted at near simultaneous times.

Commercial (i.e., non-governmental)

universal plotting sheets, then, have much to recommend them. Their 8½" x 11" size makes them handy to use on a small boat; charts are kept free from numerous erasures, and multiple series of observations can be plotted to average out variations in readings (Fig. 1).

The major disadvantage of the plotting sheets is mostly the time it takes to extend the various lines to the mid-latitude mark to establish the correct ratio of the difference in longitude to the difference in latitude.

Remember, one minute of arc on a great circle is equal to one nautical mile, but the difference in longitude technically, and more properly referred to as *departure*, varies with the cosine

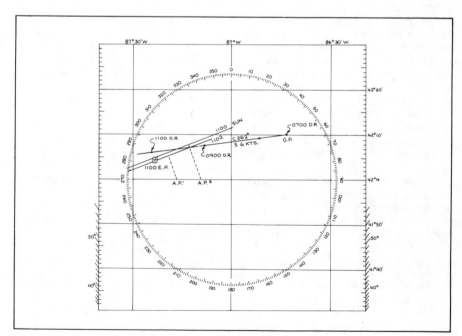

Figure 1: A typical plotting solution using conventional commercial plotting sheet

131

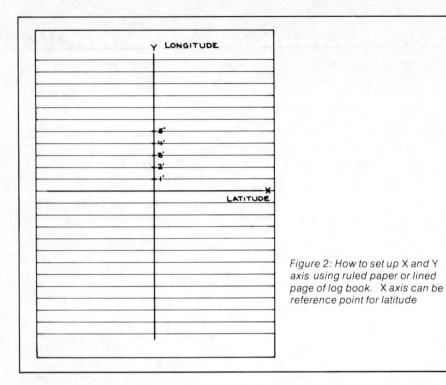

Figure 2: How to set up X and Y axis using ruled paper or lined page of log book. X axis can be reference point for latitude

of the latitude. What this really means is that the distance around the earth at the equator is the same for both latitudinal and longitudinal measurements. But, the distance between meridians *becomes less* as latitude increases so that the distance between meridians at latitude 60° north is only one half (cos 60° = ½) as much as it is at the equator. Universal plotting sheets mechanically solve this trigonometric function, and they expand the length of a meridian, i.e., they make each unit the same length.

You probably are asking yourself why all this fuss about something you are already familiar with when you thought you were going to read something new? Well, it's just a starting point to introduce certain new concepts that can be applied so that you can dispense with constructing and plotting on universal plotting sheets. With this system you can make all your entries directly in your log. There are no offline records to keep, and your plotting time is reduced by 50 percent to 60 percent.

Here is how it works. Take any horizontally ruled book or paper pad and draw a vertical line through the center of the page. This is your reference point for your dead reckoning (DR) or assumed longitude. Label this line Y. Next, draw a horizontal line through the center of the page and label this line X. It is your reference point for latitude (Fig. 2).

Now let each pre-ruled line, where it intersects the Y axis, represent one nautical mile, or one minute of arc in terms of longitude. And make the center of the graph represent your assumed position when plotting only one sight. If you are plotting two or more near simultaneous sights, the center of the axis (for simplicity) should represent your DR position or you will have to convert differences in longitude into minutes of arc as I will explain later.

Now let's proceed to plot a line of position (LOP) from the following sight reduction information we have obtained by working out two sextant sights from a DR position of 30° north latitude and 60° west longitude. Sight 1 has the following solution: Zn 315° intercept 5.5 miles towards; sight 2, Zn 230°, intercept 10.0 nautical miles towards.

First, draw the Zn of 315° as a broken line (Fig. 3, detail a). Now measure the solution intercept distance of 5.5 nautical miles, detail b, along the Y axis and then strike your LOP 90° to the azimuth line and 5.5 nautical miles from your DR position, detail c.

Now do the same thing with your second sight. Draw your Zn of 230°, detail d, and mark off 10.0 nautical miles and draw an LOP at 90° to it, detail e. Extend these two LOPs to a point of intersection which is your fix position.

All you have to do now is to construct lines parallel to the X and Y axis from your fix position to the X axis, detail f, and a horizontal line from the fix to the Y axis, detail g.

The Y axis scale gives us the difference in latitude ΔY, detail h, which is expressed in nautical miles and in minutes of arc of a great circle. Do the same thing to determine difference of longitude ΔX by using the Y scale.

The Y scale thus used is in nautical miles, however it *has to be converted* into minutes of arc when it is used to measure difference in longitude. You do this by using a simple formula: difference in longitude $= \Delta X/\cos L$.

Great, you say, but how do you solve this formula? You do it by using an engineering or scientific calculator with trigonometric functions, or you can use a navigator's slide rule; most serious navigators should already have one. Now all you do is to add or subtract your difference in longitude and your difference in latitude from the DR coordinates as follows: your DR position we know is 30° north latitude, 60° west longitude.

DR latitude	30°00.0′ north
minus	2.7′ (Y Scale)
Fix latitude	29°57.3′ north

To get your longitude you simply convert ΔX of 10.6 nautical miles by using the formula I have given above. The answer is 10.6/cos 30° which

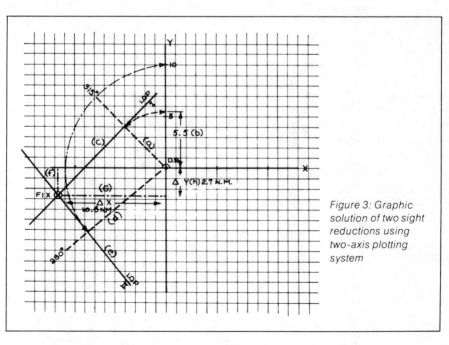

Figure 3: Graphic solution of two sight reductions using two-axis plotting system

equals 12.2 minutes of arc. So your solution for longitude is:

DR longitude	60° 00.0′ west
plus	12.2′ (*X* scale)
Fix longitude	60° 12.2′ west

You might ask whether you should always add or subtract the figures obtained from the *X* and *Y* axis and the answer is that the differences could both be additive or subtractive factors; it all depends upon the fix position relative to the DR. Where the fix position is to the left of the *Y* axis (longitude), the increments are added in west longitudes. When the fix position is to the right of the axis the increments are subtracted in west longitudes. The re-verse holds true for east longitudes.

When the fix position of the *X* axis (latitude) is above the axis, it is added; and when it lies below it is subtracted.

That is all there is to it. Your fix is latitude 29°57.3′ north and your longitude 60°12.2′ west. There is no further plotting. On your first reading, all this probably sounds long and complicated, but if you work through it a few times, you will see how quick it is to do.

Portions of this system were first brought to my attention by George R. Campbell, a former Navy navigator and hydrographic officer with both the Navy and Defense Mapping Agency. Campbell, who has an engineering background, prefers to use quadruled graph paper. My own preference is to do it right in my log.

4

Safety

Coasting Without Power

Precautions for engineless cruising   Larry Pardey

If **your engine** fails can you handle your boat under sail offshore in all conditions? Engines should be considered a convenience on an auxiliary sailboat, not a necessity. Sailing vessels have been handled without them for centuries. The British Navy blockaded Napoleon's French coast for 20 years. They never lost a ship except in battle, though they patrolled the English Channel and the Bay of Biscay in all weather, winter and summer, working close to shore in extremely clumsy and unweatherly vessels. Surely, we can safely sail our own outside-ballasted, close-winded yachts at ideal times of the year without depending on an engine to get us out of bad situations.

Time and time again we've watched people wasting cruising time in miserable harbors waiting for parts to arrive for their engines. With confidence in their sailing ability, they could have sailed on to a larger, more pleasant port where parts and service were available and had fine cruising along the way. So the suggestions that follow will help you be prepared to enjoy your cruising whether your engine works or not.

First: Have all your sailing gear in good order with plenty of spares on board. Have extra food and water in case you are delayed. A simple sailboat should not be hard to keep shipshape. Unlike engines, most potential problems with sails, masts, spreaders, hulls and rudders can be checked by eye or touch.

Second: and most important, after you clear port, get out to sea. The greatest danger to a sailboat is the land, not the sea. Very few large commercial sailing ships ever foundered at sea. Most were driven ashore because of poor windward ability, and not having enough sea room. Enough distance off varies with wind strength, di-

rection and sea conditions. If you are coasting and the wind is off the land, you can stay quite close to shore; 10 fathom-curve perhaps or a quarter mile, whichever is safer. If the wind increases, you can go in and anchor. Often, it is better to be anchored in the lee of the land, resting, than to be hove-to and blown offshore. But, if you are anchored, be careful that the wind doesn't swing and drive you ashore. When we are in this position with an unsteady barometer, I set the alarm clock for every two hours in case the wind veers or backs. It could be disastrous to be awakened by Force 8 onshore winds and a nasty sea.

Keep farther offshore if the wind is blowing onto the land, at least two or three miles even in the lightest breezes with a steady glass and good weather report. If the wind increases to 25 or 30 knots, head way offshore, especially if you aren't making port. Twenty-five or 35 miles is a fair margin, but I would keep working offshore because the wind could increase more. The farther off, the safer you are. We have hove-to quite comfortably in 50-knot winds in the North Atlantic for two days. We lost approximately 18 miles to leeward. Our 24-foot *Seraffyn* has a long, moderately deep keel and does not make much leeway. Hove-to with a fin- and skeg-type boat, with its smaller lateral resistance, you do need extra sea room. Remember, you can't turn and run with the storm if a rocky coast is to leeward. You must have sea room.

Third: Heaving-to is the classic safety valve of the sailing vessel. If you keep well to windward and become tired, you can stop and rest. You can heave-to and wait for morning or until the fog clears to run in on your landfall. During *Seraffyn's* sea trials we left at 1900 one day to sail to Fisherman's Cove, Catalina Island, California. Lin was practicing her navigation and when we approached the island two hours before dawn, she elected to heave-to and wait because she just didn't like the way things looked in comparison with the chart. It was a good decision too, as the bay was blocked with a temporary log boom that was being used in some marine biology experiment. That's not exactly a good thing to run into at night.

We cruise for fun, and beating to windward in steep seas and heavy head winds doesn't fit that category, so often we heave-to for the night and get some extra rest while we hope for a windshift. What's eight or 10 hours extra on a long passage?

Fourth: To sail without relying on your engine, you need a boat that will go to windward when necessary, even in gale conditions. You need easy reefing and good strong storm sails, plus real familiarity with your gear *before* the storm conditions are upon you.

Fifth: Keep to windward! What a temptation it is to ease off the wind and roar along on a beam reach, rather than staying close-hauled gaining to windward. No matter how tempting, don't start your sheets on a long haul if the wind is forward of the beam. Always keep about 10 or 15 degrees to windward of your rhumb line. If the wind falls aft the beam you can safely sail your rhumbline course. Many times I have been tempted into easing my sheets and close reaching only to be headed and have to make several tacks to clear a headland or to make port.

Sixth: Sailing without depending on your auxilary requires thinking ahead. The prudent single-engine-plane pilot always is looking for a patch of decent ground to land on in case his engine fails, especially when he is flying over unknown territory. An alert sailor should do the same, looking at his chart and checking ahead for the depths and bottom conditions near shore in case that nice offshore breeze dies. If you know you can anchor ahead (shoaling water and sand bottom), it is safe to stay near the land. But if the chart shows deep water, steep to

the shore and a rocky coast, keep a good distance off. Remember your ace in the hole when sailing with or without an engine is your ground tackle.

I have seen a sailor motoring in a light breeze within 25 yards of a steep rocky headland which was on a prevailing lee shore. There was a long, large, onshore swell. He had his sun cover over the boom, mainsail furled and covered, the jib and anchor stowed below. What faith he had in his engine. Just a bit of water or dirt in his fuel and the engine could have died, giving him no time to get sailing or even to anchor.

Seventh: Keep clear of high, large points of land because major headlands often have unusual effects. They can create strong currents, sudden down-drafts or a blanketing effect that eliminates your nice breeze. I once got in trouble this way. It was during the first week of our cruise, eight years ago. We sailed into the lee of Isla Guadalupe, less than a quarter mile off-shore, all sail set, after two days of reaching along in a lovely 15-knot Pacific northwesterly. The 3,000-foot-high cliffs of this narrow island caused a fierce williwaw that laid us down with cabin sides awash before we could react. Water poured through the open companionway and I prayed as I shoved the helm down. *Seraffyn* rounded surely into the wind and I was able to douse most of the sails, but not before we had 50 gallons of sea water below. I had learned my lesson. It pays to approach headlands with caution or to keep two or three miles off unless you have good local knowledge.

Eighth: Learn to use tides and currents to your advantage. The merchant sailing men had to plot their voyages to deliver cargo where it was wanted as quickly as possible, and usually they weren't able to use the classic round-the-world trade-wind route. So they learned to recognize and use every favorable current. They were able to sail in and out of ports and places today's cruising sailors rarely attempt.

For coastal sailing in places with a large rise and fall of tide, you have to schedule your movements with the help of a good tidal almanac. On long passages the ocean currents also can be used to great advantage. One passage we made in *Seraffyn* that I am particularly proud of went from the Panama Canal to Kingston, Jamaica, via Cartegena, Colombia. When we were in San Diego, California, on board *Wanderer IV*, I discussed our plans with Eric Hiscock. We planned to cruise to Panama, and from there to the east coast of the United States. Eric's comment was, "I wouldn't try that passage in a straight sailing boat, the wind is against you, the Gulf Stream is against you, and we have spent more time running under bare poles in the Caribbean than anywhere else!"

I took this advice under consideration and sewed a third reef into our mainsail. We left Panama and the usual northeast trade wind was blowing so we beat along the Panamanian shore using the Caribbean counter-current (1½ knots average) on our stern all the way to Cartegena, Colombia. We gained much needed easting this way. By studying the Pilot Charts for each month we learned that the prevailing trades swing more to the east in late spring.

We left in May with wind from the east, heading 25 degrees high of our rhumb line to counteract the Gulf Stream. We made our landfall four miles to windward of Kingston, five days and five hours later (480 miles). We used the British Admiralty publication *Ocean Passages for the World* and the US Pilot Charts to turn an extremely difficult beat to windward against the Gulf Stream into one close-reaching tack, and averaged 95 miles a day!

When you are near the coast, it is simple enough to figure out if the tide or current is setting you by taking compass bearings astern or on the beam. If you plot them hourly, you will know the exact effect for the distance and time run. Offshore you can use multiple sextant sights (LOP) to plot the effect of the currents. When we were leaving Cartegena, I took five separate sun sights, a half hour apart. The first four showed I had not headed high

enough and I was being set below my rhumb line. By the time I had taken the fifth sight I had hardened the sheets to steer 25 degrees above my rhumb line to counteract the effects of the Gulf Stream. These lines of position were almost parallel to my rhumb line as we were headed north and the sun was bearing east.

Ninth: Don't miss a fair wind. Once in Gibraltar we watched numerous cruising people who wanted to sail west to the Canaries, staying in port because an easterly was blowing at 30 knots with heavy gusts in the harbor. The weather forecasts stated that these gusts were only local and the barometer was steady. But these sailors were timid and were waiting for perfect conditions. By the time they left, the easterly winds had quit and the prevailing 12-15-knot southwesterly had set in. The result was that they had to beat against two or three knots of easterly current or resort to power.

When you are under sail you must be ready to leave the instant the winds are fair, day or night, and not when it's most comfortable.

Tenth: Your boat must be able to move in very light airs. Looking through our log books, we show only six-and-a-half days of complete calm during the past eight years, and this probably would equal the hours spent just maintaining a diesel engine. But we do have the maximum working rig the designer would recommend for *Seraffyn* plus a huge spinnaker and nylon drifter. We're glad to have these because we spend about 50 percent of our time cruising in winds of less than 12 knots.

Light-air sailing with little or no sea is definitely the most comfortable and enjoyable. You are making 70 or 80 miles a day and the windvane is steering happily. It's warm and dry and the boat is moving like a magic carpet as you lounge back and quietly read a good book. The majority of cruising people miss these idyllic conditions because, to them, winds of five to seven knots means being "becalmed." To move well without using your engine in light conditions you have to sail harder. You must have light-air sails and be rigged so you feel secure with lots of sail set. And you also must keep your bottom clean and reasonably smooth.

Almost all short-handed cruising sailors we meet with boats ranging from 25 to 50 feet, with or without engines, say that they average about 100 miles a day on long passages, year in year out. We find we do the same. I know that when I am sailing larger boats and am alone on watch, I am not so keen to change headsails or reef the main or generally sail the boat near its potential. It's a matter of size and handiness. A genoa on a 40-foot boat is a handful for one man to carry, let alone set. So I suppose the reason boats of 25 or 30 feet average about the same as boats 30 to 50 feet is that they are easier to sail efficiently.

Naturally, when a person is sailing without using his engine, he is continually learning to sail better in all conditions and keeps his sailing gear in better order. He simplifies sail-handling procedures and smooths out all the wrinkles to get a better sailing machine, so he too can keep up his 100 miles a day average.

Eleventh: You must sail defensively. Only two or three times have I thought I really needed an engine. I realize now that it was only because I was not sailing defensively. After we had transited the Kiel Canal by hitching a tow from a fishing boat, we left Cuxhaven with a strong fair tide flushing us out the river Elbe. The wind was from the northwest so we could just make our course. We had gone 20 miles when the wind lightened and the tide started to turn. We weren't gaining over the ground so we decided to work outside the deep channel and anchor in about two fathoms behind the marker buoys until the tide changed.

The ships were bumper to bumper. We attempted to squeeze through two or three times only to tack back into the channel as ships bore down on us. Finally, we made our bid, and just then we saw a large coaster's lights with red and green, and masthead lights in line; and we barely had steerage. As the ship steamed down on us, I was sure we were in for a collision. I flashed our large light on the mainsail and Lin ran down and got the Freon foghorn and started blasting away. The coaster cleared our stern by 50 feet. Eventually, we managed to anchor in two fathoms outside the channel. My mistake was not studying the charts before I left and staying out of the big-ship channel for there was lots of water and room outside the buoyed channel for yachts. If you study your charts beforehand you can elect to stay well out of the heavy traffic zones in areas such as New York Harbor or the Straits of Florida.

Twelfth: Don't make more than a daylight passage by yourself, with or without an engine. It is believed that the great singlehanded sailor, Joshua Slocum, who disappeared at sea, was run down by a ship just after the turn of the century. Our own experience has proven that merchant ships don't necessarily stick to shipping lanes and sea-going tugs rarely do. You must keep a 24-hour watch to be safe.

In Dartmouth, England, we watched an excellent singlehanded sailor without an engine wait for three weeks for perfect conditions to make his dash up the Channel to the Solent. As he told us, and rightly too, he was very concerned about being out in the heavy channel shipping without someone to keep watch all the time. He figured he could make it to the Solent in perfect conditions without having to sleep. Still I feel this is a very chancy way to go to sea.

Thirteenth: Carry a large flashlight, or spotlight and use it to alert ships to your presence. If necessary, flash the code for D on your mainsail. It means *I am maneuvering with difficulty, keep clear.* Also constantly check that your running lights are easily visible and burning all night.

Fourteenth: Carry a complete medical kit. Having someone on board who is sick could create a problem offshore without an engine unless you are prepared to cope with emergencies. But having a serious illness coincide with complete calms is highly unlikely.

Finally, be careful of being towed. If you sail without an engine or your engine breaks down, you might wish to accept a tow someday. But try to avoid this because you rarely will know the ability of the man or vessel offering assistance. Few people in power vessels realize how much way a sailboat carries and the effect of windage on a mast and rigging. If you do need a tow, give the other boat your line but be able to release your end quickly by securing it with a round turn and two half-hitches. If the towing boat goes too fast or puts you in a compromising position, you can release this knot while it is under strain. Also have your anchor ready. When you accept a tow in close quarters, the motorboat should tie alongside you with his propeller slightly aft of your rudder for better control.

If you lose your mast or rudder and need a tow, and you are not in United States waters, be sure you arrange the price at sea and get it on paper. When we were in Malaga, Spain, we met a sailor with a 30-foot cutter who'd been dismasted off Torremolinos. He was well offshore and in no immediate danger, but his engine would not start so he signaled a fishing boat and asked him for a tow into Malaga. When they arrived in port, the fisherman asked for $170 for four hours of towing, not really a lot. The yachtsman didn't have the ready cash so the fisherman was held in port for three full days getting a lien on the boat. The final outcome was that the port authorities awarded the fisherman $1,000 for the tow and time lost fishing! Whatever the situation, remember you are trusting your vessel to someone else's seamanship the minute you take a tow.

I have delivered a lot of auxilary yachts and I do find myself turning on the motor when the boat speed drops below three knots. I'm basically lazy and instead of getting out the light-weather sails, I take the easy way and mindlessly power along hoping the wind will freshen. When I get into port I don't have the feeling of accomplishment that we do after making a passage on our own engineless *Seraffyn*.

Leave your auxilary in neutral to charge your batteries and pump bilges, but don't turn the prop shaft. I guarantee your self-esteem and sailing ability will improve immensely as you learn to make ocean passages completely under sail.

When There's a Man Overboard

Preventive procedures for saving life   Robert C. Martin

Man overboard at sea is undoubtedly the most serious of all dangers in sailing. There are certainly some amusing stories of such things happening, but be assured, unless you have a total disregard for the value of human life, the situation of a man overboard at sea is deadly serious.

Unfortunately, people seldom fall overboard in swimming suits. It usually occurs during heavy weather when you are wearing warm clothes and foul-weather gear. In the water this clothing soaks through and resists any motion you try to make. Lifting a sopping-wet sleeve out of the water and over the head is enough to submerge your body. Trying to swim in soaked clothing is about the same as swimming in molasses.

With all your foul-weather gear on, try jumping into shallow water (make certain you can stand on the bottom). Not only is swimming impossible, but even treading water becomes exhausting after only a few minutes. That is why life jackets should always be worn when you put on heavy clothing at sea. If you do fall in the water, you will be powerless to move more than a few yards; and without flotation, your surface time will be limited.

A serious consequence of going overboard in most areas is the danger of exposure in the water. The colder the water, the less survival time you have. A normal man can remain immersed indefinitely if he is in water with temperature above 68 to 70 degrees Fahrenheit. At around 65 degrees, the maximum upper limit for survival is 10 hours. Hypothermia sets in and, if this is prolonged, it will kill you. Hypothermia is a big word that simply means the cold water sucks the heat out of your body until the vital organs can no longer function. After that, it hardly matters whether you get picked up or not.

Obviously, the colder the water, the more the cooling effect. So while you may have 10 hours in 65-degree water, your absolute outer limit at 32 degrees is less than one hour. This is all true if you are a normal adult, in warm clothing, and you have robust health. If you are already cold (shivering) or tired, survival time can be measured in minutes.

If you ever do fall in cold water, it is best to remain as motionless as possible, conserving body heat. Violent exercise will increase the surface blood flow and speed the cooling process. Your body only has so much heat to conserve. It is not true that you can generate enough heat through exercise to replace the cooling loss. So remain calm, try to float with your back to the waves and hope for the best. If you can see the boat, make noise and try to maximize your own visibility by waving an arm, but don't try to swim unless perhaps an overboard pole or life ring is very close at hand. Conserve your energy.

It is too bad people don't always fall overboard on bright, sunny days but they don't. Offshore, they fall off wildly pitching boats, in heavy winds and big seas. There are no other boats around, no land, no points of reference, only open sea in all directions. Once that tiny head drops behind the first wave behind the boat, it is only visible when both it and the boat are near crests at the same time — a statistical rarity. This is the principal reason why people can't be found at sea; you just can't see them.

So what do you do about it? The Offshore Racing Council's safety regulations require competitors to carry overboard poles, life buoys, high-intensity lights, whistles, and dye markers—all of which are to be ready for immediate use if needed. Sadly, some of this

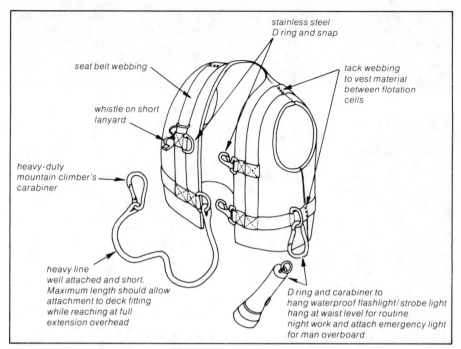

Figure 1: The author's own custom vest and harness for use outside foul-weather gear. Use of D rings and snap hooks allows vest to be donned quickly without his having to fumble with zippers or lacings; rings and hooks are very strong

In the figure, the following labels appear:

- stainless steel D ring and snap
- seat belt webbing
- tack webbing to vest material between flotation cells
- whistle on short lanyard
- heavy-duty mountain climber's carabiner
- heavy line well attached and short. Maximum length should allow attachment to deck fitting while reaching at full extension overhead
- D ring and carabiner to hang waterproof flashlight / strobe light hang at waist level for routine night work and attach emergency light for man overboard

equipment is not always as effective as it could be. The overboard pole is a weighted and buoyed staff with a flag that is intended to provide a highly visible target, easily seen from the boat. The rules read that the flag must be at least eight feet above the surface of the water. Most commercially sold poles do qualify but unfortunately, in anything but calm conditions, some of the poles blow over into the water because they are insufficiently ballasted.

Life buoys are a good idea but they are only slightly more visible than the man who is overboard. High-intensity lights are an excellent idea, if they work when needed and whistles also are good if the person in the water can get to them. In a heavy seaway, he would be lucky even to see the overboard pole, let alone swim to it to retrieve the whistle. Finally, dye markers are excellent for air-sea searches but I think they have limited usefulness when the searchers are at sea level.

The problem, simply stated, is to find the man in the water: it is a visibility problem.

What then, do you do when the horrible cry of *man overboard* is heard? The man in the water, if he is able, must do all he can to be seen and heard. Personally, in heavy weather, I always wear a life jacket (to stay afloat), a whistle around my neck (to be heard), and a flare pen in my pocket (to be seen. Fig. 1). Flare pens are the best insurance for a person in the water to be seen. The pens fire a small flare several hundred feet in the air which can be seen day or night, are easy to carry, and well worth the small investment they cost. I don't care what the racing rules require, the object is to find the person in the water. Carry plenty of flare pens. One isn't enough.

Aboard the boat, there is usually a problem with having enough people, but ideally you should do the following: Instantly, when a man falls off the boat, wake the dead by shouting "man overboard." Bang on the mast with a winch handle, scream, anything, but get the whole crew on deck. There is no other time more necessary for an "all hands" call.

Simultaneously, all safety gear should be thrown in the water. The more jetsam you can create the easier you can see the spot. Throw the poles and life buoys first, but anything that will float is good. It is also ideal if the overboard gear can be released by the helmsman, quickly and easily. Such times are no good for fumbling with complicated mechanisms or procedures.

Also simultaneously, one crew should watch the man in the water and do nothing else. If visual contact is lost with the man overboard or the general area, you lose most of your chance of recovery. As long as a crew can see the floating person, he should point and constantly advise the helmsman of the position.

The helmsman has a terrible responsibility at this point. It is not easy for me to give general rules because the boat may be going in any direction and on any point of sail; but always remember you must return to the exact spot the man went over the side. If you are going into the wind, note the course, turn around and sail a reciprocal course which should get you close to the spot you're seeking. Timing is important too. Especially if you can't see the man, all you have to work with is a search pattern. If you're going to sail a reciprocal course, note the time you take from when the man went overboard til when you turn around. It will take just as long to get back.

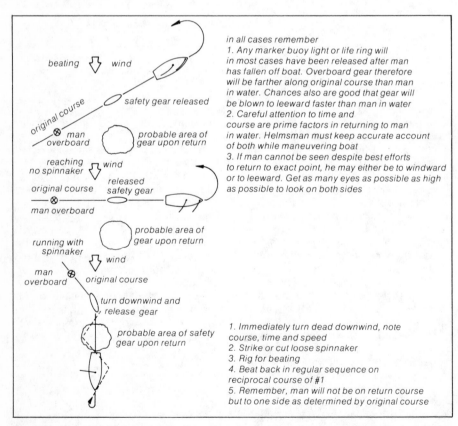

in all cases remember
1. Any marker buoy light or life ring will in most cases have been released after man has fallen off boat. Overboard gear therefore will be farther along original course than man in water. Chances also are good that gear will be blown to leeward faster than man in water
2. Careful attention to time and course are prime factors in returning to man in water. Helmsman must keep accurate account of both while maneuvering boat
3. If man cannot be seen despite best efforts to return to exact point, he may either be to windward or to leeward. Get as many eyes as possible as high as possible to look on both sides

1. Immediately turn dead downwind, note course, time and speed
2. Strike or cut loose spinnaker
3. Rig for beating
4. Beat back in regular sequence on reciprocal course of #1
5. Remember, man will not be on return course but to one side as determined by original course

Figure 2: Man-overboard courses. If beating or reaching without spinnaker, tacking to weather will gain some of leeway lost during return, can also be faster maneuver than by gybing around

Some sailors recommend immediately putting the boat on a beam reach, no matter what the point of sail. Then get the sails in order, turn on the reciprocal, and return to nearly the right spot, beam reaching all the way.

Off the wind is the worst possible situation. There usually are big, cumbersome sails set forward and it takes time to strike them, turn around, and then beat back. And you will likely have to *sail* back in any case. Most auxiliary sailboats racing these days don't have engines powerful enough to move well upwind in heavy airs and seas. Use the engine by all means, no matter what course you have to sail to return to the spot. But for the sake of the man in the water, get back there as fast as you can (Fig. 2).

Someone has to take command of the boat. You can't afford to have several people trying different things at the same time. Someone must decide quickly what you are going to do with the boat and then you do it—instantly —and pray you have made the proper decision.

Within reason, the hell with equipment. If it means destroying a spinnaker or cutting a sail loose, do it. There are stores that can replace sails:

not so for the person in the water. Also keep in mind that the object is to get back so you musn't endanger the boat in doing so. If you have to cut a sail loose, do it correctly so you won't end up broaching, breaking a mast, or driving over a sail in the water. If you have to spin the boat quickly and lose some gear doing it, have at it. Just think about what is the most important thing to do, then proceed with it.

Everybody left on the boat must always remember to work quickly but carefully. It is a high-stress situation and all hands are required. Don't get injured at a critical moment and become a burden to your already overtense mates. Worst of all, don't fall off the boat yourself. A second man overboard is certain death for the first. Stay calm, do the job at hand, and be careful.

The last item I would mention is how to stay on the boat. Use a safety harness—but use it properly. Most commercial harnesses are made of heavy nylon webbing which is strong and durable. They have safety lines of varying lengths. The critical construction of a good harness is in the hook, line, and attachments, and these *must be strong*. Most harness assemblies

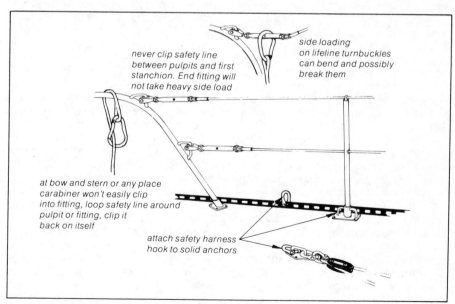

never clip safety line between pulpits and first stanchion. End fitting will not take heavy side load

side loading on lifeline turnbuckles can bend and possibly break them

at bow and stern or any place carabiner won't easily clip into fitting, loop safety line around pulpit or fitting, clip it back on itself

attach safety harness hook to solid anchors

Figure 3: Correct and incorrect locations to attach safety line

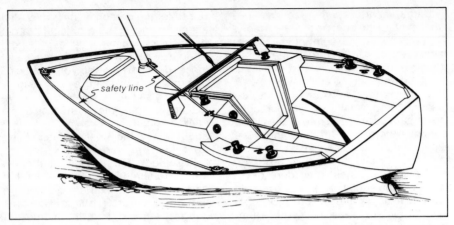

Figure 4: In heavy weather rig continuous safety lines between major work areas and over exposed or slippery part of deck. Anchor lines securely and lead them clear so crews' safety harness hooks can remain attached at all times while moving from place to place. Be sure to lead safety lines under all working lines so there will be no fouling or chafe

will easily hold your hanging weight but you won't be gently lowering yourself over the side to use it. You will likely be thrown violently off balance with only the safety line to catch you, absorb the shock, and hold. Choose strong materials for your harness, as hefty as you can find. They still won't be any too strong.

When you are using your harness remember two other things. Short lines are better than long ones. They will not let you fall as far and therefore can keep you under control better. There is a big difference in loading between falling three feet against your safety line and falling five feet. So opt for short lines if possible.

Finally, and this is more important than anything else, always snap your harness line onto a strong part of the boat. It will do no good whatsoever to have the best harness in the world and then snap it onto a weak fitting. Never snap onto the ends of lifelines running around the deck through the stanchions. The end fittings are not built for side loads. It is only marginally acceptable to snap onto these lifelines between stanchions; then your loading of the lines only bends the cable and puts the end fittings in tension for which they were designed. Whenever pos-

sible, choose anchor points that can't break: pad eyes, stanchion base eyes, shackles in the toerail, any really strong fitting will do (Fig. 3). Or you should rig safety lines of strong rope, well-belayed, so you can snap on and move about. You may fall farther, but the stretch in the lines will help absorb the shock (Fig. 4).

My standard offshore safety kit consists of a whistle about my neck, a flare pen in my pocket with plenty of flares, and a safety harness sewn to the outside of a life jacket. If it's rough enough to use a harness, it's rough enough to fall overboard; and I want to float. Besides, the life jacket adds warmth in cool weather and acts as a nice chest protector when you are being thrown about on a wild foredeck. I recommend the combination highly.

Man overboard when it happens, is something you cannot afford to think about. If you do have to do much thinking at that time, it may well be too late. Everyone must be forewarned and aware of the necessary procedures to follow if it occurs. So constantly be ready for that moment. If you are lucky, you will never have to practice what you have learned. If you are unlucky, you had better know just what to do.

Recovering an Overboard Person

How to retrieve the watersoaked victim   D. A. Bamford

I **first met the** problem of recovery one beautiful, sunny, and blustery day a few miles south of Toronto. We were ploughing along in a 15-knot breeze, enjoying ourselves, when a passenger, a 21-year-old woman, slipped off the foredeck.

I don't recall a conscious gybe action but I must have done it correctly, for in a few seconds we were alongside the victim. Only then did we realize how hard it is to lean over and lift 125 lbs out of the water over a two-foot freeboard. I'm sure I would have had a very difficult job of it myself.

Fortunately, my son was with me and, between the two of us, it wasn't *too* much of a problem. However, I frequently sail with only my wife, and I'm sure that if I were the person in the water, it would be the end.

A study of the literature yields many excellent articles on man-overboard drills, but very little has been written on how to get him or her on board again.

Peter Johnson, in his fine book, *Ocean Racing and Offshore Yachts,* says of retrieval: "Further difficult actions follow, including laying alongside and getting him aboard which is no easy matter. I am afraid that all this takes time and demands the highest seamanship and preparation." And that is all he offers on this difficult subject.

Even Eric Hiscock, one of the most experienced sailors and a man who takes safety and preparedness very seriously, devotes only one paragraph to the subject in all his books — *Cruising Under Sail*, page 390.

The person will, more than likely, be exhausted from swimming, even if just to keep afloat. He may be severely chilled; he may be weighted down 50 lbs or more than normal with waterlogged clothing; he may be unconscious, or panic-stricken.

Even under ideal conditions, calm seas, light winds, strong crew available, it is very difficult to lift 200 to 250 lbs the three-to-four feet from waterline over the gunwale. (If you don't think so, try it yourself. Get up on the kitchen table and try to lift your wife off the floor without help.)

I sail with Murphy as my unseen crew and believe that people are not so accommodating as to fall overboard under perfect conditions.

Heavy seas, strong winds, tired and reduced crews, darkness and cold, all add up to what is, at best, an extremely difficult proposition and make retrieval almost impossible.

It is all very well to say "don't fall overboard," "wear safety-harness," etc., but it can happen. And, as Terry has recounted, after finding a man, he may die in the water before you get him on board. This also hap-

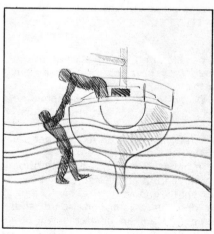

Water-soaked sailor is almost impossible to pull aboard.

pened in the Toronto area late in 1972.

Let's start out from where we have found the man and have him alongside (the lee side). Keep cool. Panic is the worst enemy of a successful recovery but speed is essential.

All those engaged in the rescue operations should be wearing safety harnesses secured to the boat to prevent them from falling overboard but giving as much freedom as possible. It may help if the boat is hove to. Generally, the boat will ride more steadily, and this position will lower the gunwale.

Get a line on the victim, looped

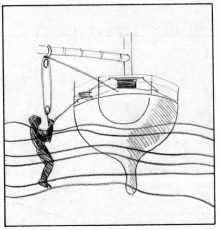

Handy-billy or mainsheet tackle also may work. Keep line attached under armpits.

Secure line under armpits; then with second line around legs, hoist aboard with halyard.

under his armpits and secured to the boat in case he lets go or slips out of the rescuer's grasp.

Do not have a crewman enter the water except in extreme circumstances. Even then, life jacket and a safety line secured *to the boat* are essential.

In general, a dinghy should not be employed but an inflatable can prove advantageous as it is relatively easy to drag the victim on board and, even if filled, an inflatable will still float. Again, secure it to the boat.

A ladder, rope, wood or whatever,

secured, will be of tremendous help if the victim is capable of helping himself. Hooking a safety ladder over the gunwale is not sufficient. It must be secured.

At the point where the retrieval will take place, foredeck or cockpit, it may be advantageous to let down the life lines as they may only add to the problem. This, however, is a matter to be decided, based on circumstances.

Modern designs, in order to get more headroom below, have increased freeboard and this adds a great deal to the problem of retrieval. My new 30 footer has 3½ feet from waterline to cockpit coaming, and the trend in modern center-cockpit cruisers is to much greater distances.

If your gunwale isn't high and if you have adequate strength of crew members, grasp the victim by the arms or better still, under the armpits (victim should be facing away from the boat), and heave him on board. This sounds simple, but in fact it is not, even if those two "ifs" are in your favor.

Assuming the victim is unable to help himself, what do you do after he is alongside? Here are some possible solutions, as described in *Yachting Monthly* (Apr. 1970).

The main or foresail halyard may be secured to the victim and he may be hoisted up by the winching of the halyard. He may get bruised but this is better than drowning.

The main boom or spinnaker pole may be swung out over the victim and a handy-billy from boom to victim will permit relatively easy retrieval. Note: The handy-billy should be inverted. A strong topping lift is necessary, or secure the halyard to the boom end.

If the victim is secured alongside aft, perhaps the mainsail can be used as a parbuckle. Take the sail off the mast, but leave it on the boom and keep the halyard attached. Drop the sling into the water and feed it under the victim, then hoist away. A broom, swab or a boat hook may be helpful in working the sail under the victim.

If the person is secured alongside forward, drop the jib but leave it hanked on the forestay and leave halyard and sheet attached. Again,

Get sail underneath and take up on halyard and jib sheet.

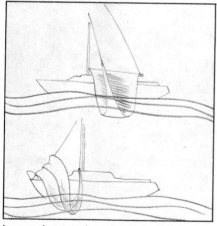

Lowered mainsail or jib can act as sling.

drop it overboard, work it under the victim and hoist away, tightening the sheet simultaneously.

Many of us sail with a minimal crew — wife and family — or at best friends with limited strength and seamanship. They would be completely incapable of getting a victim on board without using some of the ideas proposed here.

There is no substitute for practice. If you expect to have any hope of rescuing a person who falls overboard or of being rescued yourself, practice repeatedly, but be sure the victim has a life jacket or a safety line secured before he goes overboard.

I think it could be a good idea for clubs to provide a dummy (not a living one) of proper size and weight for members to practice with.

Speed is essential, and of course, panic must be avoided.

Passing Ships at Night

How to judge bearings from range light angles　　　　John Mellor

One night a few years ago I was giving a promising young member of the crew his first experience of keeping watch alone. I retired to my bunk after leaving him with strict instructions to call me on sighting *any* ship *any* where, my concern at that stage being simply to let him experience the responsibility of being alone in charge of the boat. Well, I was duly called in the early hours with the report of a ship on the starboard bow. "How far off?" I asked.

"Oh, quite a long way."

So I lay back in my cozy bunk and decided to have a quiet smoke before going on deck to see the ship. About halfway through my cigarette there was a call from the cockpit. "It seems to be getting rather close, Skipper." Logic suddenly fell by the wayside and my skipper's instinct shot me out of the bunk and into the cockpit in about half a second flat. Whipping my eyes rapidly round the horizon I could see no lights anywhere. "Where is it?" The watchkeeper pointed up somewhere around the crosstrees, from where a huge red light stared down at me. A crash gybe all-standing saved the situation just in time for us to live and learn some lessons. The most important is that a ship's distance off and speed of approach are *extremely* deceptive and difficult to assess at night.

So let us have a look at this whole question of sighting, identifying, and calculating the approach of ships at night, for in the increasingly crowded waters today it is certainly one of the most important factors contributing to a safe arrival at our destinations. And let us begin with a little espionage, a touch of the "know thine enemy," and consider things first from the viewpoint of the other fellow — the coaster, the tanker, the fishing boat.

The first thing we must realize, whatever the rules may say about sail and steam, is that much of the time those fellows literally cannot see us. A 25- or 30-foot yacht bobbing about in any kind of sea presents an incredibly small, and continually vanishing target to a lookout. At night with a couple of small lights, sometimes half-hidden by sails, it becomes virtually impossible to see a small boat beyond a dangerously, or at the very least worryingly, close range. And before you mention radar, you must realize that radar can no more see through waves than can the human eye. In any sort of chop, a radar screen will be covered, out to a distance of anything up to 10 miles, with a solid mass of echoes from the waves. These echoes, known as *sea return,* will help obliterate any small echo such as a yacht. And beyond the range of the sea return a yacht will probably be too small to be picked up, anyway.

So right away you must understand that it is, on the whole, unreasonable to expect a ship, whether it be coaster or super-tanker, to see our little sailing boat in the middle of the night in any but the calmest and best of conditions. In my opinion the wisest rule of the road for a small sailing yacht is to keep clear of other shipping. And if you can adopt this simple rule, and it is one I have adhered to for many years now, you will find that the whole problem of meeting other shipping is considerably simplified. Never mind sticking out for your rights; never mind the vitriolic correspondence sometimes seen in the yachting press; just remember the old tombstone — *Here lie the bones of Johnny Dale who insisted steam give way to sail.*

The simple fact of the matter is that it is invariably far easier for us to see a ship than it is for her to see us, and this gives us far more time to take avoiding action with the minimum alteration of

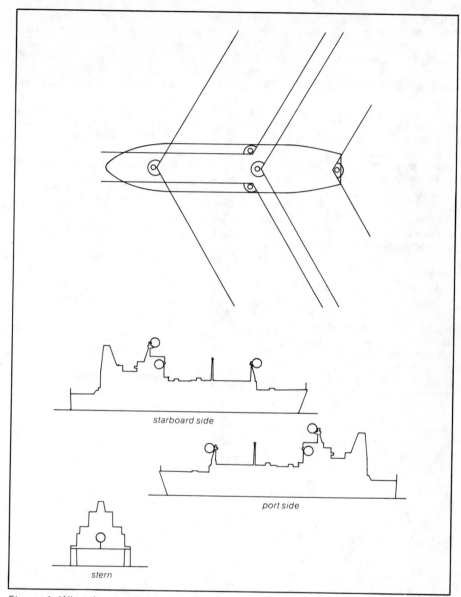

starboard side

port side

stern

Figure 1: What the standard set of running lights
on ocean-going vessel looks like at night

course. If we see a ship in good time
and take action in good time, we will
find that only a very small alteration is
required to take us well clear of her.
Which brings us to the meat of this article: seeing, identifying and assessing
the actions of the ships at night.

When we study textbook drawings of

ships' lights, it all seems very straightforward—a couple of big white lights
on the masts, a low one forward and a
high one aft, a red light on the port side
and a green one on the starboard side,
and a single white light aft, all dis-
played over various clearly defined
arcs (Fig. 1). It would appear to be a

simple matter to see and assess the attitude of a ship at night. Unfortunately, we don't see these nice clear diagrams in real life. What we see coming over the horizon is just a splodge of white light, a mass of deck and cabin lights that certainly swallows up the side lights and often the high white lights too, if they are dim. If you are close enough to see the side lights you are too close for comfort, so for practical purposes we can ignore the side lights completely. Whatever the books may say, very few ships drive around with only one white light. Every merchant ship I have seen in many years of sailing has carried two range lights, and if a ship has two range lights, of which the lower is forward, then you can always tell which way she is going.

So rule number one is to look for the two white lights. Although you occasionally find instances where these two lights are low and lost in the deck lights (fishing boats especially) or not clearly separated vertically, on the whole they do stand well clear of deck or cabin lights and are generally well separated both vertically and horizon-

tally. Thus, a glance at these white lights will tell us instantly which way the ship is pointing.

However, before we even see the range lights, just as soon as that first splodge of light appears over the horizon, we must take a bearing on it. By watching how the bearing changes, or if it remains constant, we can deduce while the ship is still many miles away whether she will pass ahead or astern of us, or whether she will hit us. And at this stage only a very small alteration of course generally will suffice to enable us to pass well clear. A look at her range lights will tell us which way she is headed, and therefore, which way we must alter course in order to pass astern of her; always the safest way to turn in a small sailing boat that could suddenly decide to slow down at a most inconvenient moment.

Now, though a ship's range lights will tell us in general whether she is moving to the left or right of us (the lower one is always at the forward end), they will not tell us whether she is moving away from us or towards us. If you look at Figure 2 you see that the lights

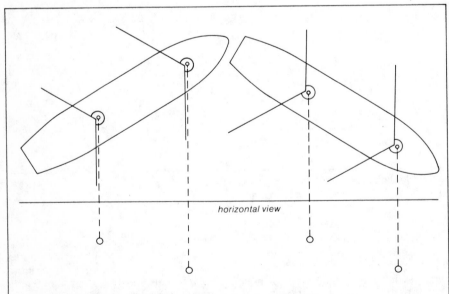

horizontal view

Figure 2: It is difficult to tell from certain angles whether vessel is moving toward or away from viewer's position

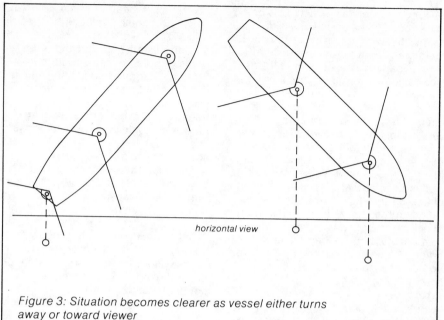

Figure 3: Situation becomes clearer as vessel either turns away or toward viewer

horizontal view

will appear exactly the same to you whether she is steaming slightly away or slightly towards us. If she is steaming well away from you then you will lose her two white light arcs and pick up the stern light, which will tell you beyond doubt that she is going away. Similarly, if she is steaming almost straight toward you, the lights will be nearly in line, and this will be equally obvious (Fig. 3).

It is the unclear situation shown in Figure 2 that you must be careful of. In many cases it will be obvious from the ship's behavior whether she is approaching or moving away. If she appears over the horizon and becomes bigger and brighter, then clearly she is coming toward you. If, however, she appears around the back of an island, you must be on your guard, even if the bearing is drawing well clear and the lights indicate she is steaming to the right. If she is going slightly away from you (and it will take a long time watching to deduce this from the fading lights) all is well. If she is coming toward you (again it will take a long time to deduce this from the increasing

brightness of the lights), you must be prepared for a possible alteration of her course that could bring her onto a steady bearing. Remember, you should assume that she doesn't see you.

The problem here is that if the ship is going away slightly as in Figure 2, and alters course to port away from us, her range lights will come closer together. If she is coming toward us slightly and alters course to port away from us, her lights will open out. Thus we find a situation in which a ship steaming away to the right, with her bearing drawing right, *appears* to be passing well clear of us. Then we see the range lights begin to draw together, indicating that she is altering course. But, unless circumstances prove conclusively that she is coming towards or going away, we do not know for sure whether she has altered toward us or away from us. We have to watch her bearing again for a further period to check; and all this time she may be getting nearer. It is this sort of situation that can change rapidly from a clear-cut, safe course into a close-quarters, possible collision case.

153

Our best defence against this is constant surveillance of any vessel that is not positively steaming away from us. It is tempting to simply check her bearing over a period, decide she will pass clear, then ignore her. By the time someone notices that she seems to be getting closer, she could be near enough to cause a panic. In calm or very rough weather, when a sailing boat's speed or maneuverability is limited, she could cause a lot more than just a panic. So we must be very aware of this problem, and keep a constant check on the distance apart of those range lights, as well as a constant check on the bearing. Remember my little anecdote at the beginning of this article. A ship that alters course toward you can be on top of you before *you know where you are.*

Now let us take a more detailed look at this business of taking bearings to see whether a ship will pass clear of us or whether she is on a collision course.

If we look at Figure 4, we can see just why a steady bearing will result in a collision. If we are on the yacht at A and take a bearing of the ship approaching on our port bow, we will find it bears 315 degrees in this instance. If we then take another bearing some time later (say, 10 minutes, although this will depend on the relative speeds of yacht and ship) and find that the ship still bears 315 degrees, it should be clear from the diagram that the ship will arrive at point C at the same time that we will. This, of course, will result in a collision. To avoid the collision, in this case, we should bear away to port and pass under her stern, invariably the safest place to go.

The actual size of our course alteration, and the rate of change of the bearing that will cause the other ship to pass well clear really can only come from experience. Practice this in daylight until you are thoroughly conversant with the effects of various course alterations and rates of change of bearings. Take a bearing, alter course 10 degrees, then take a bearing again a few minutes later to see how much it has changed. Then see how far she passes clear of you. A little experience with this in daylight and you will soon feel confident about the results of your avoiding action at night.

Now look at Figure 5. You will see what actually happens when the bearing of that other ship does change.

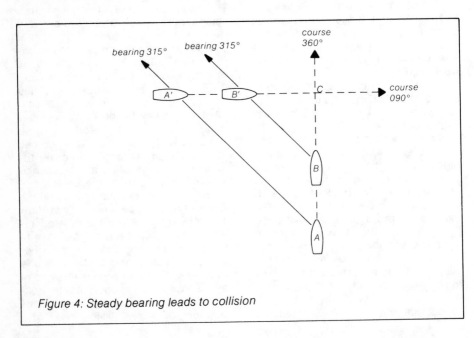

Figure 4: Steady bearing leads to collision

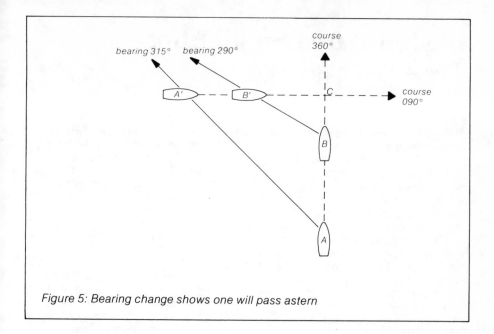

Figure 5: Bearing change shows one will pass astern

Once again we are in the yacht at A traveling north. We take a bearing of a ship on our port bow and again she bears 315 degrees. Ten minutes later we take a bearing again and this time she bears 290 degrees. We can see from the diagram that she has moved more astern of us, and we say that our bearing has *drawn aft*. It should be clear in this case that we will arrive at point C some time before the ship does. Thus she will pass astern of us. So when the bearing of another ship draws aft we can say that she will pass astern of us. Conversely if it draws forward, she will pass ahead of us. Imagine if we were in the ship traveling east. We can see that when the bearing of the yacht draws forward, it will pass ahead of us. Once again, precisely

how rapidly it needs to change in order for the ship to pass safely clear depends on the circumstances. So experiment in daylight to gain confidence in your own estimates.

These are very clear-cut examples, but if you can understand the principles involved, as shown in the diagrams, then those principles will apply to any situation. They will also enable you to visualize in plane view (as in the diagrams) what you see in a two-dimensional horizontal plan. You can then see far more clearly just what is happening. And it is this ability to *see* what is happening when a splodge of light appears on the dark horizon that enables you to make your way safely and confidently at night through the busiest of shipping lanes.

Big Ships and Small Blips

Efficient use of radar reflectors Don Grayson

While the small-boat sailor may not be able to afford radar, he can take steps to improve his chances of being seen by those boats that do have it. On large ships radar represents a major source of navigation information to the bridge. It is a sad commentary of modern times, but personnel are so expensive that the typical large ocean vessel is usually run in open waters with two men on the bridge: the helmsman and the watch officer. There are no dedicated lookouts, no radar watches, just these two men.

In your mind's eye imagine a large ship plowing north one fine night off Miami. The vessel is in the middle of the Gulf Stream's axis to get maximum boost from its current, which puts it well away from any landbound dangers. Ahead is the white stern light of a ship several miles away. All the helmsman has to do is play follow-the-leader and reminisce about his last port. The watch officer has little to do except nurse his coffee.

Under these conditions nobody outside the enclosed bridge is looking around for marine traffic, since there is no real need to. All the watch officer has to do is move the coffee cup over and look at the radar scope. There the whole situation is mapped out for him: several miles ahead is the vessel whose stern lights are visible; off to the left are a few bright splotches representing radar returns from the high-rise buildings along the coast of Florida; and all else is clear except for the normal speckled ring of sea clutter extending out for a couple of miles around the ship's position.

A small sailboat heading back from the Bahamas, cutting across the big ship lane has almost no chance of being spotted visually. And unfortunately, it is very likely that what little radar return it does present will be lost in the sea clutter and never spotted.

Under these conditions we have the making of another "Devil's Triangle" report. Visibility was good, the sea was slight, nobody saw, heard or felt anything. The actual contact between the sailboat and the ship was nearly a thousand feet in front of, 50 feet below, and several thousand tons in between the watch officer.

Consider the same situation, but with a slightly more persistent flickering dot on the radarscope drawing the watch officer's attention. It shows at a range of 3,000 feet. At 16 knots he has 74 seconds to evaluate the return, decide on a course of action and execute it before that bow nearly a thousand feet ahead of him inexorably passes through whatever was causing that flickering blip on the radarscope. With a ship that may take 30 seconds to answer her helm or five miles to stop, the watch officer has little safety margin.

Even under the best of conditions a wooden or fiberglass sailboat does not present a very large radar target. Since the aluminum mast and rigging present only rounded surfaces, they make very poor radar reflectors. Most of the radar return from a small sailboat comes from the engine, fuel tanks and galley equipment. To further compound the detection problem, all of these items are relatively low in the boat and thus will be hidden from the radar by waves.

Figure 1 gives the detection ranges of various targets for a typical commercial marine radar. Smaller radar-equipped fishing vessels would be expected to have ranges about one-half as great; larger military vessels (destroyer escorts and larger) would have ranges nearly twice as great under conditions of low sea state. In rough conditions sea clutter significantly obscures the weaker returns.

The first point of interest in Figure 1

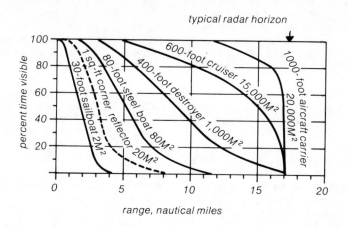

Figure 1: The maximum range a 30-foot sailboat could be expected to present a return on a radar screen continuously is around one-half mile

is that maximum range is a probabilistic thing. The probability of detection (which is a measure of the percentage of time the radar return is visible on the radar screen) varies with the target size and range. For example, the maximum range that a 30-foot sailboat could be expected to present a return on a radar screen continuously is something around one-half mile. At one mile the blob of light on the radarscope on which your life may depend would be visible only about 80 percent of the time. At three miles the probability that a 30-foot sailboat can be detected on a commercial shipboard radar drops to about 10 percent. That, I submit, is inadequate if you are crossing the shipping channel during the 12 to 4 watch and the watch officer is swapping sea stories with the helmsman.

The obvious solution to increase the range at which a radar-equipped ship can detect your boat is somehow to increase your boat's radar reflectivity. Short of getting a larger boat built out of metal, the best approach is a radar reflector. The second curve in Figure 1 shows the typical detection range of a one foot corner reflector. Now the 100 percent detection range has been increased to about one mile, the 80 per-

cent to two miles, with the 10 percent detection range out to five miles. Doubling the corner reflector to two feet will increase the detection range by a factor of about 1.5, making your 30-foot sailboat look like an 80-foot steel boat. Another doubling in size to four feet will make it look like a 400-foot destroyer and *another* doubling in size. . . . Of course the ultimate limit in detection range is established by the radar horizon.

Since it is the cross-sectional *area* of a corner reflector that establishes its radar reflectance, two reflectors will not be so effective as one which has twice the linear dimensions. Two reflectors may be used if desired and if they are far enough apart so that one does not physically hide the other, they will increase the total radar return.

There are a number of different kinds of radar reflectors that one can use to enhance a boat's radar return. Pots, pans, aluminum foil; in fact, anything metallic with a series of flat surfaces will work to a certain extent, especially if it is hoisted in the rigging where it can be seen well above the wave crests. The standard measurement of radar reflection is equated to a smooth, metallic sphere one square meter in projected cross section. Such a standard target will reflect any impinging radar energy equally well in all directions and thus represents a poor but stable radar target. The most efficient radar target is a flat, metallic plate which acts as a mirror. As an example of its effectiveness, a one-foot-square metal plate will give the same radar return as a metallic sphere 100 square meters in projected cross section. Like a mirror, however, the metal plate is extremely directional. Curve A of Figure 2 shows the searchlight-like beam from a one-square-foot flat plate. Imagine trying to hold it aimed at a distant radar-equipped ship from your pitching deck.

What is needed, obviously, is an educated mirror that automatically returns any radar beam back to its source. One such device is a Luneberg lens. Its return, shown as curve B in Figure 2, is almost as strong at 60 square meters as the flat mirror, but is omnidirectional. In other words, no matter from which bearing the radar-equipped ship is, the Luneberg lens will return the radar energy back toward it. Because it is omnidirectional, boat motion will have no effect on its performance. It is constructed, like an onion, of different layers of material, each with a different index of refraction so that the radar beam is precisely bent and sent back on the reciprocal of its original direction. While the Luneberg lens is undoubtedly an excellent tech-

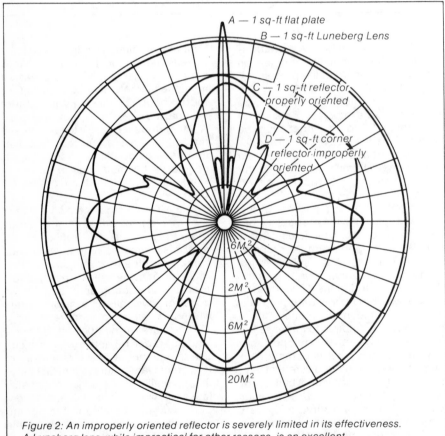

A — 1 sq-ft flat plate

B — 1 sq-ft Luneberg Lens

C — 1 sq-ft reflector properly oriented

D — 1 sq-ft corner reflector improperly oriented

6M²

2M²

6M²

20M²

Figure 2: An improperly oriented reflector is severely limited in its effectiveness. A Luneberg lens, while impractical for other reasons, is an excellent technical solution to the problem of being seen by radar

nical solution, it is impractical for several reasons. Compared to a corner reflector cluster, the Luneberg lens is heavier, more difficult to stow and much more expensive.

A more practical solution is the corner reflector cluster: a series of three metal surfaces arranged as an inside corner which act as mirrors to reflect back to the source any radar beam that hits it. To explain this action by analogy, throw a ball or shoot a champagne cork at the intersection of two walls and the ceiling—then duck before you get hit in the head. Another illustration of this principle is the myriad of little corner reflectors embossed within automobile taillight lenses to reflect headlights.

Curve C of Figure 2 shows the results of a one-foot corner reflector cluster. This curve shows that the corner reflector cluster gives reasonably good results in all directions since it has a nearly circular response. As a result, boat motion will have very little effect on its performance. With an effective radar cross section of 20 square meters, it is not so efficient as a flat plate nor Luneberg lens, but is still quite acceptable.

There are a number of things that can deteriorate the performance of a corner reflector. Just as a mirror must be accurately aimed to reflect a beam of light back to its source, the angles between the three "mirrors" in a corner reflector must be accurately placed at 90 degrees. A one-degree error in just one of the three angles will cause a reflected radar beam to miss returning to the radar antenna by 100 feet if the radar-equipped ship is 6,000 feet away. From this it can be inferred that the average commercial fold-up corner reflector would be a relatively poor performer. The non-square angles, the non-flat surfaces and the claims of up to X miles of radar detection should not engender confidence. Those neat little fold-up affairs made out of nice mesh are another example of technology gone awry. They may have a place on a life raft where nothing else is practical to stow, but as the main resource on your boat they

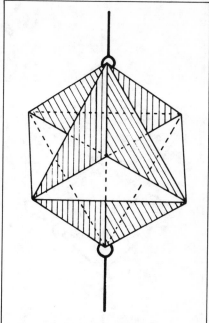

Figure 3: Radar reflectors are often oriented incorrectly apparently because they are easier to suspend from one corner and besides, they just "look better" that way

are woefully inadequate.

Another common mistake in corner reflectors is the orientation. The simplest (and unfortunately by far the most common) way to suspend a corner reflector cluster is shown in Figure 3, whereas the preferred way is shown in Figure 4. A little reflection (mental this time) will show that the incorrect orientation presents only four corners around the horizon while the preferred orientation presents six corners. The results of these two orientations are shown in Figure 2 as curves C and D. Note that the incorrect orientation only presents four main lobes around the horizon with four deep nulls representing bearings at which you will very nearly be invisible to radar.

You have a chance that a corner reflector cluster incorrectly oriented will cover these null areas if you allow it to rotate or twist in the wind at least 45 degrees to fill in the gaps of the cover-

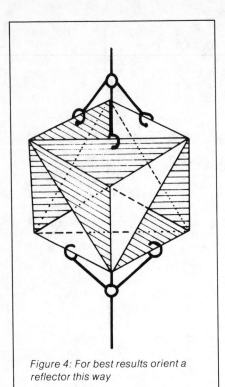

Figure 4: For best results orient a reflector this way

is easier to suspend from one corner and besides, it just "looks better".

The degree of precision required in both the construction and orientation of a good corner reflector design should provide a clue to the expected effectiveness of these "metallized" or "reflectorized" life-raft covers or even jacket hoods. One recent test of a "reflectorized" life-raft cover showed that it was completely ineffective in increasing the radar detection range over a life raft with a conventional cover. Being generally round, it is the least effective shape that could be chosen for an efficient radar reflector. Random wrinkles and triangular indentations in the cover's surface would be the only opportunity to provide an efficient retro-reflective surface.

At this point you should be convinced that you need a corner reflector if you are going to wander across shipping lanes at night and you know how to hang it. The next questions are: "How do I get one, and how big should it be?"

I recommend making your own, following the criteria outlined in this article. It should be made of light metal. Sheet aluminum, stainless steel or monel are probably best, but any metal will do, as long as it is not badly pitted. Painting the metal will not interfere with its effectiveness. There does not need to be any electrical conductivity between the metal plates. The sheets should be flat just as any high quality mirror is flat. The metal can be of any convenient thickness that is strong enough.

The exact size is not too important, but bigger is better. The usual limit is the size of your flat stowage space for a collapsed assembly and the amount of windage you are willing to put up with. Just from the performance standpoint, I would not recommend anything larger than two feet on a side—unless you want to masquerade in the fog as an aircraft carrier.

age. You are, in other words, hoping that the wind and the boat's motion will randomly aim a corner in the proper direction while someone is looking. A much better solution is to hang the cluster from a small tripod bridle where it can be snugged down in a seamanlike manner and not worry about it.

Unfortunately almost all of the corner reflectors that you see suspended in the rigging, even in brochures about them, are oriented incorrectly. The radar reflectors on the US buoyage system is a mixed bag, some correct, some incorrect. Almost all of Europe's buoyage systems (with the notable exception of Great Britain) are oriented incorrectly. The apparent reason is that a corner reflector cluster

Sea Anchors

What to use and when

William V. Kielhorn

Controversy has raged for years among deep-water sailors about what one should do aboard a small yacht if caught offshore in a gale. Some say the best bet is to lie ahull; others favor heaving-to using a storm trysail and backed storm jib. Others prefer to run before the sea, dragging long looped lines astern; and one fraternity insists that riding to a sea anchor, bow to the sea, is the best method. But which method is really best? There is no real answer. Each method has advantages and disadvantages depending upon the size and type of craft, the size and character of the sea, and the boat's location with respect to other hazards. This month let's look at the sea anchor and how to use one.

Most sea anchors sold in yacht chandleries are not very good. In the first place, they are generally far too small to keep the bow of a yacht into the sea; although possibly they could be of some use if trailed astern while running before the wind. Second, the "standard" sea anchor employs a heavy fixed hoop which makes stowage and handling difficult. Third, the designs are far from optimum, and each manufacturer seems to have his own ideas about strength, weight, inlet-outlet ratios, etc. I suspect that few have been tested in a towing tank, and fewer yet used properly and on a regular basis.

Parachute technology, on the other hand, has reached a high degree of sophistication, and there are designs carefully worked out for a variety of purposes: sky-diving, aircraft and automobile drag chutes, missile and cargo chutes. I carry aboard my 23-footer a small, nine-foot diameter parachute originally used to slow the entry of air-dropped naval mines. None of these chutes are specifically designed as a yacht's sea anchor, but if properly rigged, they can do an admirable job.

Some of the various types of drogues are shown in Figure 1. The drag coefficient (C_D) is a measure of water reistance per unit area of the device. Thus, a "window shade" drogue is somewhat more efficient than a parachute. However, the window shade is heavy and awkward. It is used primarily as a drogue for drifting oceanographic buoys, where it performs well both in calm and in storm, for it never collapses.

A yacht's sea anchor must have more than just a reasonable drag coefficient in order to be useful. Among the requirements are: light weight, compact stowage, and easy deployment and retrieval. The parachute sea anchor meets these criteria quite well.

The parachute does have some disadvantages. The shrouds can tangle if improperly handled, the drogue may tend to oscillate in the water if the relieving vent is too small or if the parachute material is insufficiently porous. Most important, the forces involved can be so great that they can become dangerous if the apparatus is improperly rigged. I have heard, but have not confirmed, that in the 1950s a commercial fishing vessel was capsized in the Pacific by a large parachute drogue that was allowed to sink too deep while the craft was subjected to a heavy swell.

The size of any sea anchor depends upon its intended use, and upon the size and type of craft. Obviously, a drogue intended to enhance directional stability while run-

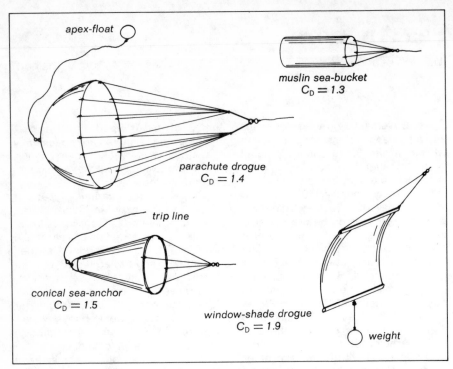

Figure 1: Types of drogues

ning before the wind should be very small, while one intended to hold a craft bow-on should be very large.

Once, I had the task of holding a small (40-ton) oceanographic research vessel precisely steady at an offshore location, while a delicate acoustic array was lowered to within 100 feet of the bottom in 10,000 feet of water. And I had to maintain that configuration for a full day with essentially "zero wire angle" as a necessary part of the experiment. In the absence of wind this would not have been difficult. But as it happened, the wind was blowing a little shy of 30 knots, and the significant wave height (the average height of the highest one-third of the waves) was 18 feet.

A surplus emergency personnel parachute 24 feet in diameter was deployed on 600 feet of ⅝″ nylon warp streamed from the bow chock, the average wave length of the sea at that time. Immediately after the drogue took hold, the little ship became docile and comfortable, and shipped not a drop of water again. Earlier her high bulwarks had been crested port and starboard and the oversized freeing ports had been unable to handle the sweeping seas. But from that moment on, the cook didn't even have to mount the storm racks on the mess table. Best of all, the 10,000-foot cable to the 40-feet-long hydrophone array stood obediently "up-and-down" for all the time required. Similar use of parachutes has been made many times, with equally salubrious results.

The key to any successful use of a parachute sea anchor lies in how it is rigged. If you have purchased a surplus parachute of some sort, the chances are it contains fittings and features not needed when used as a sea drogue. All should be carefully removed to keep the parachute as light and as simple as possible.

Ideally, it should be neutrally

buoyant in sea water, but this is quite impossible because the nylon, shackles, etc., are heavier than sea water. Therefore, it is of the *utmost* importance that a small float capable of supporting the *entire* rig be attached on a light polyethylene (floating) lanyard. This in turn should be attached to the apex of the parachute. From experience, it appears that this floating lanyard should be equal in length to the diameter of the parachute.

If a tripping line is used, it too should be of polyethylene or other floating material; it will be less likely to tangle with the heavier nylon warp. This line should be tied to the float of the apex-lanyard and led back to the boat. When the parachute is deployed the tripping line should be kept slack. To retrieve the sea anchor, just slack the nylon warp until the tripping line takes the strain and dumps the parachute. It can then be retrieved very easily and rapidly by hand-hauling the tripping line.

My experience, however, is that a tripping line ordinarily is unnecessary, and is somewhat of a nuisance. Often it is just as easy to motor or winch up to the apex-float, snag it with a boathook, and then haul the dumped parachute directly aboard. A standard rigging of a sea anchor is shown in Figure 2.

A sea-anchor warp should be regular-lay three-strand nylon with the smallest diameter compatible with the expected forces. This, incidentally, is also true of regular anchor warp. Many yachtsmen use line that is too heavy thus losing the advantage of nylon stretch and placing unnecessarily heavy forces on their bitts and anchors. As a rule of thumb, anchor warp and sea-anchor warp should be the same. For a 25-foot boat, 3/8-inch best quality nylon (breaking strength 4000 pounds) is about right. A 40-footer of heavy construction could use 1/2-inch or even 5/8-inch. Cousteau's *Calypso* (137 feet) has successfully anchored in 3000 fathoms of water using 5/8-inch line.

Regular-lay three-strand nylon is preferred as warp material for several reasons. First, nylon itself is light for its strength, even though it is a little heavier than sea water. Second, nylon stretches greatly under tension, usually about 1/3 to its breaking point, and thus absorbs sudden shocks to maintain relatively constant tension. Third, regular-lay construction exposes fewer nylon fibers to internal and external chafing than does line of different construction. Nylon does have the disadvantage of tending to unlay under tension, and therefore a swivel should be used in the system.

Two other caveats in using a nylon warp are worthy of mention. The first is in the use of chafing-gear, and the second is in the absolute necessity

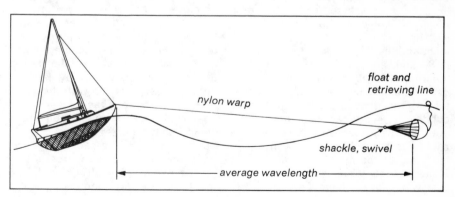

Figure 2: Rigging the parachute sea-anchor

of protecting the rudder from rearward surge forces. It is most important to protect the nylon warp from friction and abrasion where it passes through a chock and around a cleat or bitt if you expect to ride to a sea anchor for more than an hour or so. Usually a wrapping of rags or a rubber sleeve covering will do the trick. Even better, a short length of chain leading from the cleat or windlass, passing through the chock or hawse and bent to the warp will protect the nylon adequately.

A long warp, of the length one would use in a long, heavy sea, will permit the craft to surge backwards a considerable distance if it is struck by a breaking sea. This is a very desirable thing to have happen with respect to the forces working against the boat and the sea-anchor system. On the other hand, if the rudder is not firmly lashed and secured in an "amidships" position, the backsliding could well carry away the rudder entirely. The effect is quite analogous to the dangerous "tail-slide" maneuver sometimes attempted in aerobatics. Moderate power from the engine may ease both the stress on the warp and reduce any backward forces on the rudder. But be careful not to overrun the warp.

How much can one drift using a sea anchor? This, of course, depends on the size and type of anchor, the mass and windage of the boat, the strength of the wind. A good general estimate for a boat using a large parachute (say 24 feet in diameter) would be about 10 cm./sec (0.2 kn.). But, on top of this, one must add the Ekman drift, the Stokes drift, and the tidal current vector. Ignoring tidal drift, which must be determined from the tidal current tables (very inaccurate in high-wind conditions), you can estimate that your drift will be downwind, and very slightly to the right facing downwind in the Northern Hemisphere, of about two to three percent of the true wind speed. If you are threatened by a lee shore, you will need a good seaman's eye and sound judgment.

You could easily use a parachute sea anchor to good advantage to go into the wind as you ride a strong, favorable current. Riding the Florida Current northward against a northerly wind is one such case. But, because of possible opposing traffic, this might not be wise to do. You are *not under control* while riding to a sea anchor, and have no maneuverability in this situation. You should be alert to the fact that some large ships can be slow in their lookout duties, and they may misinterpret your dayshapes or lights which, by the way, should indicate, *under way but not under control.*

Few modern yachts are designed to withstand the immense forces of breaking sea waves coming from aft or abeam. Every cubic meter of sea water contains slightly more than one ton of mass. A breaking sea wave may easily contain 500 tons or more, curling and racing downslope at speeds up to 20 or 30 knots. This can be disastrous to a flat transom, an exposed cockpit, or inadequate companionway battens. Strong, streamlined bows, the intervening cabin-top, and the forward fittings, are far better able to withstand and deflect such an onslaught.

A Ukranian-born Polish immigrant to England, a sailor familiar with small ships and big waves, a man named Teodor Korzeniowski, gave to modern yachtsmen in his fiction a bit of advice, albeit inadvertently:

"Don't you be put out by anything," the Captain continued, mumbling rather fast. "Keep her facing it. They may say what they like, but the heaviest seas run with the wind. Facing it — always facing it — that's the way to get through. You are a young sailor. Face it. That's enough for any man. Keep a cool head." The man who wrote those words is better known as Joseph Conrad; the quote is from *Typhoon.*

Battening Down

Weathering a hurricane in port   George Nichols

Virtually every year at least one hurricane strikes somewhere on the Atlantic seaboard or Gulf coast of the United States, claiming among its more vulnerable victims hundreds of small craft trapped on exposed moorings or pinned into docks and marinas. Although hurricane tracking and warning services are constantly improving, there is usually relatively little time to take precautionary measures before the tearing winds take their toll. Long-range planning, including thoughtfully chosen ground tackle and a pre-selected hurricane hole in which to shelter one's boat will prove worthwhile when it comes to hurricanes or any really severe storm.

I was living in a small waterfront house near the head of Marblehead harbor on August 31, 1954, when hurricane Carol came, my first hurricane as a boat owner. At 6:30 AM, a fair sea was already running out in the harbor. Small boats moored in the open were starting to be flung about and the 45-foot yawl *Betise* I then owned was throwing a fair wave each time she pitched. The sky was remarkably dark, rain came in heavy squalls, and the radio was predicting a 45-to-60-mile-an-hour nor'easter for the day, the "backlash" — we were told — of a hurricane rumored to have passed offshore two days before.

At breakfast I decided to go aboard *Betise* for the day rather than to work. A few minutes later I was rowing out crab-wise across the wind in my son's six-foot skiff. Out from under the lee it was blowing harder than I had realized, and the rain squalls blotted out the shore when they swept down. It was a hard job to keep moving at all but after a

while I reached the boat in safety to find Pete Jeffries, who was working aboard for the summer, about to come ashore for orders. He had just heard a radio report that we were in for a hurricane.

First we had to face the decision confronting all boat owners before a hurricane: to seek safety ashore or to ride it out with the boat. We were confident of *Betise*'s ability to survive anything in the confines of Marblehead harbor and by staying aboard we hoped to take avoiding action if threatened by other craft wrenched from their moorings by the storm. Obviously in other cases prudence would dictate taking all the necessary precautions and leaving the boat to fend for itself.

The mooring, put down in 1913, was a rock of five to six tons. By 1954 it was probably four to five feet down in the mud. Thirty feet of wrought-iron chain of 1½-inch-diameter stock had been passed through holes in the rock and shackled to itself. To this chain we had shackled a new two-inch manila pennant about 30 feet long.

We carefully wrapped extra chafing gear around the mooring pennant in the chock — the port chock, since the wind was predicted to haul to the east and south — allowing us to place an anchor over the starboard side, if necessary, without risk of fouling the main mooring. Next we assembled a 75-pound Herreshoff pattern anchor, 10 feet of ½-inch chain and 200 feet of ⅞-inch diameter nylon rope. With this set up and lashed on deck we were ready; Peter went below to make coffee, and I surveyed the situation.

Things were far from peaceful when Pete and I came back on deck well secured in oilers, boots, and new orange life jackets. By now the wind was coming in great gusts which tore the top off the water and sent blinding spray over the boat. It was impossible to face the wind, rain and spray in the gusts which cut visibility to a few yards. These gusts were quite local, however, and between them one could look about. One could hear them coming with a strange high-pitched howl and see the top of the water come off under them. Sometimes they would pass quite close by without touching *Betise*. As they swept by to leeward the small boats in their track would disappear in the spume. After such a gust had passed the only thing showing would be a few bottoms of swamped dories or, if the boat remained upright, a mast snapped short at the deck.

Gradually, the wind blew harder and harder. The intervals between gusts became shorter and each gust seemed more powerful. With the wind by now east we were well sheltered by Marblehead Neck but even so the sea was running two to three feet high where we lay less than 400 yards to leeward of the shore.

About 11:45 with the wind east, despite several large boats maneuvering to weather, it seemed advisable to put down a second anchor. It would be impossible to dodge anyone in such a gale anyway. We secured a spinnaker sheet around Peter and, while I belayed one end in the cockpit, he dragged himself forward against the wind and spray on hands and knees to lash himself to the bitts on the foredeck. Gradually he managed to get the anchor unlashed and poised over the rail. When he was ready, I waited until a gust swung us to starboard before I put the helm up to port and drove her ahead with the engine as hard as she would go in order to lay the anchor out off the starboard bow as far as possible.

The placing of this anchor proved to be just right. In the next two hours the wind swung 45 degrees clockwise so that at the height of the storm when the wind was southeast we had 80 to 100 feet of scope out with the anchor well in. The strain was evenly divided between the mooring and the anchor, one on each bow, so that the gusts no longer were able to swing her bow off.

Meanwhile, things were really happening in the harbor. Between the bursts of rain we watched a big schooner slowly drag stern foremost onto the rocks. Her engine had failed to start. Several powerboats were under way in our vicinity and for a while one looked as if she would drift down across our bow. Luckily, she crossed us and managed to get up under the weather shore where she was beached and anchored. To leeward the various smaller craft unlucky enough to go adrift were piling in heaps onto the rocky shore.

At about 1:45 the weather started to improve. The rain stopped and for a few moments there was even a little patch of blue sky overhead. The wind even seemed to decrease slightly and swing quite rapidly from east-southeast to southeast and then southeast by south. We were lying securely between our two anchors so Peter went below to make lunch and check the radio. At 2:00 he handed me a large mug full of hot beef stew and the news that the storm center was just over Salem, four miles away!

Nevertheless, the worst was over. The wind picked up again about 2:15 but we were better protected by the shore as it worked around to the south. In the clearing weather we could see far fewer masts than had been visible before.

Damage to shipping in that storm was extensive. Over 150 yachts and boats were destroyed in Marblehead alone. How come some survived with so little damage? Doubtless, luck and the fact that Marblehead being on the open sea did not have as excessive a high tide as can occur during hurricanes in estuaries and shallow land-locked bays contributed importantly. But, certain things owners did before and during the blow were important, too; things one could group together under the general term, "good seamanship" — yet, all too easy for even good seamen to forget when one usually sails in protected waters under gentle summer skies.

First of all we had a really *big* mooring, far bigger in terms of weight of anchor, size and length of chain than most would have considered necessary. Moreover, it was so placed that there was plenty of room for the boat to swing without hitting anything even when the mooring was stretched out to its farthest extent. The amount of scope was more than three times the maximum depth of water and the chain so heavy that even at the height of the gale it never quite straightened out. The importance of these points cannot be over-emphasized. In these days of crowded anchorages, scope is cut to a minimum to save mooring space. If scope is too short, the mooring anchor will be pulled *up* off the bottom rather than *along* it so that it can dig into the mud.

Next to a good mooring, having adequate anchors and anchor lines probably contributed most to survival in Marblehead harbor that day. Our 75-pound Herreshoff, or modified "fisherman," anchor was backed up with 10 feet of heavy chain (to provide spring and keep its shank down) and plenty of heavy yet elastic nylon line.

Like chain, nylon line is essential for good ground tackle. Light, proof against rot, very strong and above all elastic, it does all the things chain does *except:* (1) hold the anchor down where it can bite, and (2) resist chafe. A short length of chain between the anchor and its anchor line will solve the first problem so the greatest danger to nylon rope is chafe and the ease with which it can be cut by a sharp rock, barnacles or old metal fouling the bottom of the harbor.

The amount of chafe which occurred that day astounded me and emphasized the importance of proper chafing gear. Five or six layers of heavy canvas were worn nearly through by the nylon anchor line and the mooring pennant moving in their chocks during the eight hours of gale winds. Tag ends of frayed rope hanging from the bows of boat after boat washed up on the shore that day were mute evidence of how often chafe had been the cause of their going adrift.

Once the blow has begun, there is little more one can do to prepare. Our only plan in Carol was to keep absolutely head-to-wind at all times and anticipate problems before they occurred. The excellent section on hurricanes in Bowditch's *American Practical Navigator* told us that we were in the hurricane's NE or dangerous quadrant when the radio finally informed us that the "eye" was coming from the south and likely to pass either over or just west of us. It went on to tell us which way the wind would veer — in our case, clockwise — and that once the shift had started we could depend on its continuing, barring major changes in storm path.

So much for "what to do" if your boat is on a mooring in the lee of the land; but, what if she is in a marina? What if she is quite small? Marinas, as many can ruefully testify, are dangerous places in a gale except in the rare instances where they are totally surrounded by high protecting land or buildings. Piles and floats are rarely as reliable moorings as anchors and chains; seas splinter hulls against sea walls and docks; tides several feet higher than normal carry boats over and onto docks which punch holes in them below the water line; and the force of the wind catching a hull broadside is far, far more powerful than when it strikes bow on. If you usually keep your boat in an exposed marina, look for a safe harbor nearby and arrange in advance to lie there to moorings or tied off four ways between trees or big anchors well clear of all docks when trouble threatens. This means, of course, that you must have long enough, heavy enough, lines to make the moor, if you need to. Think ahead. Supply stores and ship chandleries tend to be closed or sold out just when you need their wares most. If you must stay in your marina slip, look into what holds the docks in place and see what extra you will need to keep your boat safe. Try to move her as far from piles and floats as possible. Lay out anchors and heavy mooring lines in "all four corners" as needed well ahead of time. Laying them out from a small boat after the wind has begun to rise will probably be impossible and will certainly be risky for both you and your boat.

Planning for Emergencies

A checklist for a survival situation　　　　　Fred Martini and Russell Nilson

Some time ago, we examined the contents of a commercial survival kit. The case indicated that it was quite complete, and rather attractive. Inside, however, it was virtually useless. "Waterproof matches" were kitchen matches in a snap-cap vial; the malted milk tablets were a pasty mush; and the dye marker was too small to serve its purpose. The "fishing kit" consisted of a few feet of line with a feathered jig attached. The flashlight batteries were leaking badly. The flares included were hand-held (less than ideal in an inflatable raft), and the compass would not tolerate any movement. Most astonishing of all, the "medical kit" contained two rolls of gauze, nine Band-Aids, three feet of adhesive tape, some first-aid cream, and three ammonia inhalants. (No doubt the latter were intended to revive you after you had abandoned ship and looked inside your survival kit!) We were fortunate that our exposure took place ashore, where it was merely laughable; the Robertsons were not so lucky (*Survive the Savage Sea,* Bantam Books).

Time for acquisition is as important a consideration as the thoroughness of the preparations. In the process of stowing the provisions and equipment for an extended voyage, survival gear may end up in the corner of a locker next to the sea anchor, and the two are usually remembered at about the same time. Although there is time to prepare if and when you receive word or signs of approaching storms, the experiences of the Robertsons, Baileys, and others have emphasized that plans and preparations can be called upon in relatively calm seas, and far from reef or shoal.

On our 37-foot ketch *Serenity* we have repeatedly refined and condensed our preparations to the point where we are satisfied that our system is both complete and practical. Table I describes our survival gear in detail.

The dinghy was originally a stock 65-pound fiberglass model. Four inches of polyurethane foam, a raised sole, and a stern drain plug converted it to an unsinkable, self-bailing dinghy that weighs 135 pounds. Having it available in an instant is quite convenient; the nylon tie-down straps have bronze turnbuckles at each end, but at the center of each strap we added the buckles from auto racing-style safety belts.

The life raft is readily accessible in the main saloon. Although it is satisfactory in most respects, we do recommend rafts with a radar reflective canopy, and a modified color scheme. Our particular model is brilliant yellow throughout, and unfortunately this color (as well as international orange) is highly attractive to large pelagic sharks. This could prove to be disconcerting, if not actually dangerous, particularly if you are fishing or carrying an injured crewman. Our two-man inflatable is more suitably decorated, with international orange above and deep blue below the waterline.

A collapsible radar-reflector and an emergency radio beacon are comforting, but we felt it advisable to include sufficient navigational gear to give us the option of heading *somewhere,* if only for the morale boost of having a destination.

Our food supply may be larger than necessary, provided that fish or other prey are available; but freeze-dried food is so light and compact that stowage does not present a problem. With eight gallons of fresh water, plus the output of six solar stills, freshwater needs should be met even in the absence of rain.

The time required in an emergency is minimized by the fact that, with the

Table I — Survival gear aboard Serenity

Location	Item
On deck:	
Over skylight	9″ sailing dinghy with mast, boom, sail, rudder, and oars lashed within. Held to deck by quick-releasing straps
Starboard deck box	Life preservers
	Inflatable 2-man raft
Beside SB deck box	2 5-gallon jugs, ⅔ full of fresh water. Lashed with a quick-release knot
Below deck:	
Main Saloon	4-man inflatable raft with canopy. Flare-gun attached to case
Companionway	Nylon seabag, containing:
	4-month supply of freeze-dried food
	1-month supply of canned emergency rations
	4 quarts canned fresh water
	medical emergency kit
	4 solar stills
Companionway	Metal case, containing:
	H O 249 and worksheets Plastic sextant
	Pencils, paper Compass
	Smoking flares Radar reflector
	Extra flares Nautical Almanac
	10 Kendall Mint Cakes
	2 solar stills
	Canned pemmican
	Knife and can opener
	Assorted lures, lines, and leaders
	Signalling mirror
	Charts
	Inflatable splints
	Insect repellents, mosquito netting
Companionway (bracket)	EPIRB
Companionway (Mounted sheath)	Survival knife, double edged

exception of the uninflated life raft, all the packages float unassisted. The seabag, metal case, and EPIRB must be placed on deck, the dinghy and water jugs freed via the quick-release straps, and the deck box opened. With a few practice sessions, this can be completed in short order, and the raft inflated as well, by a crew of two.

Preparing for medical emergencies. Assembling and organizing a satisfactory medical kit can be quite a complicated operation. As with the preparations for abandoning ship, accessibility and thoroughness are the key criteria for evaluating your medical preparations.

Sampling local physicians will demonstrate to you the variety of professional opinions concerning the proper prescriptions and procedures for treatment at sea; we will not attempt to consider the pros and cons of these. Our primary concern here is with the organization and stowage arrangements. (For advice on proper treatments, check the reading list below and discuss them with your physician prior to departure.) The preparations we are describing were made with the assumption that we would be cruising for extended periods far removed from medical facilities. The listing of drugs and equipment provided in Table II represents the supplies aboard *Serenity* when we left the United States last August. The specific drugs listed are

Table II — Medical supplies aboard *Serenity*

Analgesics (Pain Relievers)
*Aspirin (-) tab.
Tylenol (-) tab.
*Tylenol w/codeine, tab.
Darvon, caps.
*Demerol, tab., inj.
*Morphine, inj.

Anesthetics
*Xylocaine, Inj.

Antacids
Gelusil, (-) tab.
*Mylanta (-) tab., fl.

Antiseptics
*Betadine (-) swabs, fl.
Hydrogen Peroxide (-) fl.
Povidine (-) fl.

Antifungal
Grifulvin V. tab.
*Haltex, cr.
Tinactin, fl. (-)

Antibiotics, topical
*Bacitracin-Neomycin-Polymyxin, cr. cr.
Chloromycetin, cr.
Garamycin, cr.
Polysporin, cr. (-)

Antibiotics, systemic
*Ampicilin, caps., inj.
Erythromycin, tab.
*Gantrisin, tab.

Stethoscope
Blood-pressure gauge

Anti-diarrhea
*Lomotil, tab.
Kaocon, tab.

Antihistamines
Benadryl, tab., inj.
Chlor-trimeton, tab. (-)
Dimetapp, tab.
Vistrail, inj.

Anti-inflammatory preps.
Aristocort, cr. (0.1%)
*Hydrocortisone, cr. (1%)
Prednisone, tab.
Valisone, cr. (0.1%)

Anti-malaria drugs
*Aralen, tab.

Anti-nausea drugs
Bendectin, tab.
*Bucladin, tab.
*Compazine, tab., inj.
Dramamine, tab., Inj. (-)
*Phenergan, tab., inj.
Tigan, caps., inj.

Antiparasitic preps.
Kwell shampoo

Anti-spasmodic drugs
Donnatal, tab.
Probanthine, inj.

Penicillin, tab., inj.
Prostaphyllin, caps.
*Tetracycline, caps.

Anticonvulsants
*Dilantin, inj.
*Valium, tab.

First-Aid Equipment (-)
*Band-aids, assorted
*Butterfly bandages
*Gauze, assorted
Disposable sterile gloves
*Sterile disposable syringes
*Sterile disposable scalpels
Tongue depressors
*Thermometers
*Adhesive tape
*Gelfoam hemostatics
*Triangular bandages
*Ace bandages
*Airway
*Ammonia inhalents
*Ammonia inhalents
*Suture material
*Tourniquet
Cast frames, wire
Cast padding
*Inflatable splints
*Absorbent powder
Sterile towels
*Trauma dressings
Cold packs
*Sterile sponges
*Surgical detergent

Astringents
Bluboro wet dressings (-)

Decongestants
*Dimetapp extentabs, tab.
Sudafed, tab. (-)

Diuretics
Lasix, tab., inj.

Stimulants
*Adrenaline, inj.
&Dexedrine, tab.

Sun Screens
*Eclipse, lotion (-)
&Pre-Sun, lotion (-)
RVP, lotion (-)
*Uval, lotion (-)

Misc. (-)
Calamine lotion   *Vitamins
Cepacol cough drops   *Vitamins
Nasal sprays   *Eardrops
Laxatives   *Alcohol
&Eyedrops   *Gatoraid

*Included in Emergency Medical Kit . see text)
(-) No prescription required
    Caps = capsule
    Tab. = tablets
    Inj. = injectable
    fl. = fluid
    cr. = cream

less noteworthy than the functional groupings (antacids, analgesics, etc.) —if Dramamine works satisfactorily for your entire crew, there is no need to carry other anti-nausea preparations. Pills, topicals, and injectables are each stowed separately, in alphabetical order, within labeled zip-lock bags. *An up-to-date record must be kept of the quantity and expiration date of each drug.*

Small amounts of the materials noted by an asterisk in Table II are stowed separately, in a small watertight case. This is normally packed with our survival gear, but it accompanies us on diving trips and when we are exploring ashore. Accidents at these times could be quite serious, and having a medical storehouse back on the boat would be little consolation.

A few general principles are worth remembering:

• Always be conservative in the use of antibiotics and other prescription drugs.

• Treatment should be as thorough as necessary to permit the arrival of the patient at a proper medical facility.

• Be aware of the risks and options available, and act only when inaction would be dangerous; remember that your diagnosis may not be correct.

• Leave surgery to the surgeons; even appendicitis may be survived with antibiotic therapy, while your chances of surviving a layman's attempts at major surgery are almost insignificant.

With reasonably good fortune, your medical supplies, like your survival gear, will cruise with you undisturbed. But should the situation arise, proper preparation may make the difference between an unfortunate incident and a major disaster.

Annotated reading list

Eastman, Peter F. (1974), *First Aid Afloat*, 2nd Ed., Cornell Maritime Press, Cambridge, Md., 132 pp.

The Merck Manual of Diagnosis and Therapy, Merck, Sharp, and Dohme, Research Laboratories Division of Merck and Co., Inc., Rahway, NJ. *The Merck Manual* is updated regularly, and contains chapters which give detailed accounts of the signs, symptoms, diagnosis, prognosis, and treatment of medical problems. It also contains useful sections on the rationale behind drug usage. It does not orient itself towards emergency and first-aid treatment—little on the technical procedures of suturing, setting fractures, etc., which Eastman deals with. Moreover, its size (ca. 2,000 pp) makes it rather unwieldy for use as a quick reference. However, it covers a wider variety of conditions, and complements the above volume quite handily.

The Physicians Desk Reference, published by Medical Economics Co., Oradell, NJ. This volume is published yearly, and considers the characteristics, uses, and precautions affecting the prescription of drugs. Usual procedure is to consult Merck, your list of available drugs, and then the *PDR* to check dosages and potential side effects.

Other useful volumes

Grant, Harvey and Murray, Robert (1974), *Emergency Care*, R. J. Brady Co., Bowie, Maryland, 334 pp.
A basic consideration of the mechanics of emergency treatment.

Wingate, Peter (1972), *Medical Encyclopedia*, Penguin Books Ltd., Middlesex, England.
Essentially, this serves as a medical dictionary—quite helpful in wading through the miasma of medical terminology.

You're the Doctor

Facing medical emergencies at sea   Bebe K. Wunderlich, M.D.

You have just been elected ship's doctor for an ocean passage without benefit of American Medical Association approval. In addition to first-aid supplies, what should your medical kit contain? How should you use it?

Since I have constructed medical kits for several ocean-cruising non-MDs, I think I can help you collect and suggest ways that you can wisely use medical supplies for your crew's care. This article extends beyond the principles of resuscitation and emergency techniques that you can learn in a first-aid course. I am concerned about the situation when, by necessity, you must function as the doctor until you can get help.

Be sure to stow any medical equipment in a readily accessible place. And remember, if professional medical help is available, take it. My advice here is intended as an emergency guide only in cases when you cannot find such help.

While cruising aboard our 42' ketch *Kismet* in the Great Astrolabe Reef of the Fijian Islands, a young native in a fishing village invited us to go spear-fishing with him. His equipment was one pair of goggles and a six-foot pole with a single barbed iron spike. He explained the routine. We were to row our eight-foot dingy over a coral head and tow a heavy monofilament nylon line with bait wiggling on a big hook. He disappeared into the crevices of the coral and we rowed.

Suddenly, he surfaced close to the dinghy. With a broad grin he said that he had found the evening meal for everyone: a six-foot shark. The idea of us, plus hooked shark, in the Dyer Dhow would surely resemble being in a Waring blender with a razor blade. There couldn't be enough suture material in all of Fiji to fix up this fracas. We passed on the shark dinner, but let's suppose we hadn't.

Lesson one: *Lacerations.*

The first concern in treating lacerations is adequate stoppage of bleeding. Apply FIRM pressure directly onto the wound with a clean cloth or gauze dressing. Hold it for five minutes (count that time because it will seem like launching a new era); and then gently remove the dressing. This will stop most bleeding.

If, however, blood has continued to pour into your firmly-held dressing after three minutes, or if heavy bleeding recurs as soon as you let up the pressure, apply a tight tourniquet above the bleeding site. The limb will turn pale and be tingly and then numb. This reflects the lack of oxygen of the extremity when you stop arterial blood from going to the limb beyond the tourniquet. The tourniquet, therefore, must be released for a few minutes every hour. When the limb becomes pink again, you can reapply the tourniquet if the bleeding has started again.

If massive bleeding has occurred (more than a pint in an average-sized adult), and has finally stopped, cover the wound with a clean dressing and leave it alone. Your pale crewman with a resting pulse rate of 120 beats per minute will need more than a Bloody Mary to tolerate another hemorrhage.

If minor bleeding has occurred, the wound should be cleansed properly and closed. If you have a hairy crewman, shave off the dense growth around the wound. Pour fresh water over it to remove loose dirt. After you have washed your own hands, spread the wound open and cover it with Phisohex. Using sterile gauze pads and cool, boiled water, wash the wound with as much gusto as the unfortunate patient will allow. Rinse the Phisohex and dirt and blood off very well.

Should you need to give an intramuscular injection for pain relief, you can use a 22-gauge, 1½"-long needle. Fill the syringe with the appropriate drug dose. Wash an area of the upper aspect of the arm where there is no infection or trauma. Insert the needle at right angles to the skin and stick it approximately an inch into the arm to get through the fat tissue. Draw back (aspirate) on the syringe to make sure that the tip of the needle is not in a blood vessel. If you don't get blood back, inject the drug. If you do get blood, remove the needle completely and move it a couple of inches away from your original insertion.

Small superficial lacerations with no muscle, tendon or bone sticking out can be closed by using Steri-strips. After cleansing the wound, dry it well. Spray each side with tincture of Benzoin. Approximate the wound edges neatly and hold them that way with multiple strips of Steri-strip aligned next to each other. Cover the Steristrips with a dressing.

Deep wounds need to be closed with sutures. After thoroughly cleaning the wound, dry it carefully. Draw five milliliters of local anesthetic (Novocaine 1%) into a syringe and attach a 25-gauge needle. Hold the syringe almost parallel to the skin surface (see figure). At every inch, inject half a milliliter of anesthetic just below the skin surface. Do this on both sides of the wound. A white wheal will form on the skin. Wait five minutes for the anesthetic to work. Insert the suturing needle about half an inch from the wound edge. Sew from top of the skin through the underlying tissues and come out the skin on the opposite side about half an inch from the wound edge.

Closer sutures are needed in cosmetically-important areas but usually the skin can be approximated with sutures every half inch. Tie the suture with two square knots but leave enough slack for tissue swelling. A dressing should be applied. It may vary from a Bandaid to a gauze dressing, depending on the size of the wound. The sutures can be removed in 10 days by which time you probably will be able to get a consultant with initials after his name.

A common injury occurring aboard an ocean-cruising boat is caused by a fish hook's becoming embedded into flesh — yours, not the fish's. Local anesthetic should be injected at the wound site. It is sometimes easier to push the barb out through the surface and cut it off with wire cutters. If it is buried, it will have to be cut out. A scalpel blade or razor blade that has been boiled can be used to incise through the area where you have injected the anesthetic. Cut cleanly and evenly down to the barb and either cut it off or back it out.

Bone and Joint Injuries: Ocean cruising attracts dreamers everywhere. In port on a glorious tropical evening we had on board such a landfast dreamer. His thoughts were of gentle Trade-wind passages and as he climbed on deck from below his eyes were on the myriad of stars that a small ship could follow to find Paradise. His earthbound feet tripped over the main traveler and he arose from the cockpit with an index finger shaped to point simultaneously to the North Star and the Southern Cross.

Dislocations such as these can be readily treated by you. Grasp the dislocated member and pull firmly and steadily. Do not jerk on it. You will feel it pop into place with even traction. Then immobilize it with a splint. For a finger, a small piece of smooth wood, a sail batten or even a small thole pin would do. Wrap the finger and splint together tightly. Be sure that the joint cannot move.

Emergency care of fractures involves three primary areas: pain relief; cleaning any open wound through which a bone end might be protruding; and immobilization.

Before attempting to care for a fracture, pain relief should be given. Demerol 100 milligrams by intramuscular injection will give this relief and it may be repeated every four hours as long as the pain is severe. Demerol takes about 15 minutes to start acting. Once properly immobilized, a fracture is usually not very painful.

If bone is protruding through the skin at the fracture site, a compound fracture has occurred. This should be cleaned in the same way that you clean a laceration, being meticulous to get out all dirt. Once cleaned, the wound should be sutured neatly and a dry dressing applied. Then the limb should be wrapped with casting flannel and the splint applied. This patient has some chance of developing a bone infection so he should be given an antibiotic (Ampicillin — 500 milligrams every six hours) until you get medical help.

Proper immobilization means that the joint above and the joint below a fractured bone are stabilized and cannot move. Included in your medical kit should be two-inch and six-inch-size casting flannel. Wrap the extremity with the appropriate width casting flannel. Also in your kit should be included plaster splints that are fast setting. Several sizes are available but I would recommend a pack of 3″ x 15″ and a pack of 5″ x 30″.

After wetting the plaster, it will set hard in five to eight minutes. Take off the outer wrapping and put the splint in water until it is wet throughout. Lay the wet splint along the bottom side of the extremity and it will serve as a moulded form into which the extremity rests. Once the splint is hardened, wrap the extremity with Ace bandage including both limb and splint. A lot of swelling can occur after a fracture so do not wrap it too tightly. This immobilization by splinting will remove a lot of the pain.

If the fractured limb is at an abnormal angle, you need medical help as quickly as possible. Some simple fractures that look grim can be reduced easily by appropriate direction of traction, though. This requires a professional evaluation but if you're 1200 miles from your Barbados landfall you will have to do it by yourself. To reduce a fracture in which a bone is obviously bent, pull firmly and evenly along the line that would be the weight-bearing line and along which the bone would normally follow. Once the bone appears straightened, it should be wrapped with casting flannel and a splint made to immobilize one joint above and one joint below the fractured bone.

Burns: My parents were terrified of the idea of fire at sea, and, since we were planning a circumnavigation on *Kismet,* we invited my mother and father to dinner aboard. Steak with appropriate trimmings and lots of reassurances were about to be served, when an orange ball of flame engulfed the stove area. Excess kerosene that had dribbled into the drip pan burned vigorously and the streak of exiting guests was exceeded only by the streak of exiting parental confidence.

We quickly put out the fire because our fire extinguishers all worked and then slunk off to HoJo's, nursing charbroiled egos. No one was burned.

But suppose someone had fallen into the stove, or we hadn't had the proper equipment handy. Minor burns are painful and can be disfiguring but not lethal. However, infection can be a serious complication. To avoid this, the area should be washed with cold water. Any remaining dirt should be removed with Phisohex and water. Then the burn should be wrapped with a Vaseline gauze dressing. To hold this Vaseline gauze in place, an outer dressing of loosely applied roll gauze may be wrapped over the Vaseline.

Dental Pain. Our kindly family dentist provided me with an apprentice dental kit and superficial information on handling dental problems. You will want a good dental check-up just before leaving for an ocean cruise, so ask your own dentist for help. I think that the idea of me on the other end of dental pliers so terrorized our crew that for four years all dental agonies remained private until we got ashore.

In the Galápagos Islands one person almost gave in, though. The only dentist in the islands was a prepubertal Ecuadorian military dentist. He indicated that he specialized in pain-relief by hypnosis.

As the drill screamed, our crew looked pleadingly for a dangling mustard seed or a crystal ball: nothing. Each day she returned to the dentist as instructed. Then yesterday's fillings were removed and new ones applied until the pain finally gave up. The dentist said that he was "curing" the teeth. I could have done it with Cuprinol.

If your crewman complains of a toothache, take a look at the tooth. If you see a hole, clean it out with a spoon excavator. Mix Eugenol and zinc oxide powder together until you have a thick paste. After the cavity is clean, fill it with the thick paste.

If your examination of the tooth shows a pimple on the gum over the tooth or if the patient has facial swelling, his tooth has probably progressed beyond cure by your filling. Then he should be placed on antibiotics. Give him 500 milligrams of Ampicillin by mouth every six hours for a week. Pain relief can be obtained with 15 milligrams of Codeine taken by mouth every three hours. Even if your ministrations do remove the pain, the patient should see a dentist at your next landfall anyway.

Gastrointestinal Maladies: While living aboard *Kismet* and anchored in Singapore Harbor, we often noticed pajama-clad old ladies rooting in the river mire at low tide. Therein lay wrigglies, large and small. At night we would go ashore for a tasty treat at one of the many outdoor stalls, at which steaming kettles of unnamed delicacies were served on beds of rice.

Thirty US cents bought a mound of your choosing and it could also buy organisms from the muck of Singapore Harbor. Although one of the great pleasures of ocean cruising is trying local foods of the world, considerable caution is necessary in taking aboard the ship's water and you should avoid filthy eating places. We remained quite healthy despite indulging in local specialties but we were stricken in a couple of countries.

Drugs may be necessary in treating diarrhea and vomiting due to eating new foods or water. Severe diarrhea can result in dangerous dehydration if not treated. The drug, Lomotil, serves to diminish movement of the gastrointestinal tract. It can be bought in plastic bottles and the adult dosage is two teaspoonfuls every six hours until the diarrhea stops. I found that in four years of cruising, Lomotil and Bandaids were the medical supplies most often needed.

Once you have acquired diarrhea in a new port, it is better to stay aboard and use ship's canned goods and water until you are well. Adequate fluid intake is important and soups, juices, carbonated beverages and water are needed. Stay away from coffee, tea and alcohol until you are cured.

Seasickness is a common plague of some sailors. If you are so afflicted, you will be glad to know that N.A.S.A. has applied some of your tax dollars into studying this problem. They have invented a rotating chamber guaranteed to dump the dinner of even the most iron-clad stomach. As men are rotated in this chamber, various drugs have been given to them to find the best remedy for seasickness. Many of the drugs that you may have tried for seasickness cause sleepiness. The alternative to Jason with his basin was Jason in his bunk.

But the newly found combination of 50 milligrams of Ephedrine and 25 milligrams of Promethazine given orally every three or four hours is relatively free of producing drowsiness and supposedly "fantastic." Unfortunately, this mixture of drugs is not available in a single pill but your doctor can write a prescription for each of these that you can get filled at your local pharmacy.

Many people ask if they should have their appendix removed before crossing oceans in a small boat. If you have not had pain attributed to it, I do not recommend a prophylactic appendectomy. Appendicitis is most often a disease of young adults, so as you get older and wiser you are also less likely to develop this emergency at sea. If your crewman does complain of belly pain, is nauseated and vomiting and has extreme tenderness in the lower right side of his belly, he probably has acute appendicitis. Get on your radio for any help that might be available. If help is available, do not give him anything to drink or eat.

On the other hand, what is the appropriate management when you are away from professional help? The patient should be taken off deck work and confined to his bunk. This is no time for heroism on his part, either. Give him nothing to eat but clear liquids—water, carbonated beverages, juices, etc. Keep a record of how much he does drink. He needs approximately six eight-ounce measuring cups more fluid every 24 hours than he puts out in urine and vomit.

If he has a lot of pain give him Demerol by intramuscular injection every four hours. An advanced first-aid course will teach you how to give such an injection or your own doctor or his nurse can instruct you in intramuscular injections. An adult weighing over 150 pounds should get 100 milligrams of Demerol and someone who weighs less should get 75 milligrams. This dose can be given every three hours if the pain is bad and if your patient is alert and awake at the time of injection. An imperative part of your conservative management of severe belly pain is antibiotic coverage. Give Ampicillin 500 milligrams by mouth every six hours. If the patient is

vomiting and the pills do not stay down, change to intramuscular injection. It is *most* important that the patient receive and retain the antibiotic. If you do not have Ampicillin another broad-spectrum antibiotic could be used. After the pain and fever subside continue the antibiotic for two days. When the patient feels hungry start him on bland food for half a day. If he retains this he may have anything that appeals to him.

Think how marvelous it will be when you and your crew hold the entire yacht club bar entranced as the two of you discuss *your* medical management of *his* appendicitis on your passage to Tahiti.

Antibiotics. The use of antibiotics is an area that can easily be abused. I feel that the overuse of antibiotics is all too common in this pill-prone era. A crewman may ask for "a little penicillin" to treat a runny nose and leg aches that herald a common cold. Antibiotics have no value in the treatment of *virus* infection and often can do harm. Viruses live inside cells and antibiotics cannot get them there. If you do take antibiotics you may destroy certain bacteria that are necessary to maintain the delicate balance of organisms. These bacteria often keep each other in check and protect us from overwhelming infection by any one of them. After one type of bacteria is killed by an antibiotic it is common to have luxuriant growth of another resistant group or a parasite indigenous to the area where you are cruising. Traveling from port to port we encounter new organisms and we need all our natural defenses at work. Indiscriminate use of antibiotics can be harmful.

Antibiotics should be used only for *bacterial* invaders that are causing serious problems. On a cruising boat with a previously healthy crew the most likely occasions when antibiotics would be needed are for a bad chest or head infection or an infection of the urinary tract. Boils may occasionally need antibiotic treatment. Antibiotics should be given in the dosage recommended and at the proper time as I will describe in each situation. Sporadic timing of the drug may promote an antibiotic-resistant strain so keep a record of when the drugs are to be given. They should also be continued for two days after the symptoms disappear. Never give any drug to which the patient believes he may have an allergy.

Antibiotics should not be used for an ordinary common cold as it is of viral origin. But if a cold does progress to a productive cough with thick, pus-like secretions and fever there is a bacterial invasion and antibiotics are appropriate. Also, if an earache or a very severe sore throat (probably a "strep throat") accompany the cold then give penicillin 500 milligrams by mouth every four hours.

Urinary tract infections should also be treated with antibiotics. These include cystitis (bladder infection), pyelonephritis (kidney infection) and veneral diseases. If the patient has burning on urination, has a strong urge to void and voids frequently, he probably has cystitis. This may progress to back pain and tenderness and pyelonephritis.

At the first sign of burning and frequency start the patient on Azo-Gantrisin, two tablets (they each contain 500 milligrams) every four hours. To flush the kidneys and bladder properly he must take *at least* three quarts of fluids every 24 hours. Two big glasses of water should go down with every pair of pills. Azo-Gantrisin will combat the bacteria and also will make your crew more comfortable. His urine will be orange from the medication contained in Azo-Gantrisin that eases the burning and frequency. He has much to suffer because abstinence from alcohol and sex are also important until symptoms disappear.

Pyelonephritis causes pain in the side of the back beneath the ribs and outboard of the spine. Often it is preceded by signs of cystitis—burning, urgency and frequency. To treat pyelonephritis add Ampicillin 500 milligrams every six hours to the management. This should be continued for two days after symptoms disappear.

Again it is very important that the patient drink a lot of fluids. Any penile discharge should be treated with penicillin—500 milligrams every six hours for a week. Professional help also should be obtained as soon as landfall is made.

Boils and other skin problems may need antibiotic treatment occasionally. The majority of such conditions come from poor hygiene and tropical conditions. They will usually respond to cleanliness, dryness and avoidance of prolonged salt and sun exposure. Rinse with a little fresh water after you swim and take care to dry your armpits, groin, and between your toes to help avoid bacterial and fungal invaders. If an open sore or injury develops keep it dry and salt free. If it does not heal and spreads or if bad boils occur antibiotics should be used. After cleansing the area with Phisohex and fresh water and drying it well bacitracin ointment should be applied twice daily. Ampicillin 500 milligrams every six hours may help clear the infection. If no improvement is noted in two days add tetracycline 250 milligrams every six hours. Careless, unwarranted use of antibiotics can spread or initiate parasitic and fungal infections that thrive in the humid, salt-ridden atmosphere of an ocean cruiser. Good nutrition, cleanliness and dryness are usually the answer to "jungle rot" and antibiotics should only be used for problems that do not respond to this conservative management.

I spent four years sailing around the world with three other healthy adults and a cat. After years of previous training and months of deciding which drugs to take and which instruments would really be necessary, the only creature that I needed to treat for a serious illness was the cat. He developed cystitis and he responded successfully to Azo-Gantrisin. The sandbox brigade sighed with relief, the cat sighed with relief and so did I, that 35,000 miles of drugs had not sailed in vain.

This is a suggested list of medical supplies needed in addition to first-aid equipment:

Lacerations:
Phisohex 5-ounce plastic bottle—2
Gauze sponges 4" x 4"—12 packs
Steri-Strip Skin Closures—1/2" x 4"
—2 packs of 6 strips each
Tincture of benzoin spray—12-ounce
can—1
Surgipad—5" x 9"—12
Novocaine—1%—30-milliliter bottle
Syringe—5 milliliter with 25-gauge
needle—5, 22-gauge needle, 1½"
long
Straight cutting needle swaged to
3-0 Ethilon, black monofilament

Bone and joint injuries:
Plaster splints—Johnson and Johnson fast setting 3" x 15" and 5" x 30"
—box of each
Casting flannel—2" and 6" width
—2 rolls of each
Demerol 50 milligrams per milliliter
—1 bottle of 30 milliliters
Ampicillin—500 milligram pills—30

Burns:
Vaseline Petroleum gauze 3" x 18"
—12
Thermotabs—bottle of 100
Codeine 15 milligrams—50 pills

Dental pain:
Spoon excavator
Eugenol
Zinc oxide powder

Gastrointestinal:
Lomotil Liquid—2 ounce
bottles—12
Ephedrine 50 milligrams — 50 tablets Promethazine 25 milligrams —
50 tablets

Skin care:
Desenex Powder—3 ounces—2 cans
Bacitracin ointment—½-ounce
tube—1

Suggested amounts are selected for a crew of two for extended ocean cruising.

Guarding Against Fire

Make sure the chances are as low as possible   Christopher Knight

It was hard to sleep soundly because the forward berth was acting like a roller coaster, and the slight smell of kerosene from our cabin heater didn't make the ride any more pleasant. When Gabe yelled, I knew something was wrong even before I was fully awake.

I looked into the main cabin and saw a blossom of yellow flame on the bunk where he was lying. Kerosene from the heater had spilled onto his sleeping bag and it was burning like a giant lampwick with Gabe still inside.

I grabbed my own bag and used it to smother the flames. Nothing else had ignited, but the sight of a fire below while we were 50 miles offshore in the Gulf of Maine had given me a memorable scare. Since then, I have tried to analyze the pattern behind this and other potentially dangerous problems we have encountered while sailing.

This particular incident was caused by a small leak in the filler cap of the Aladdin heater which only showed up when the tank was full and the angle of heel was extreme. The dripping kerosene was ignited because the chimney had vibrated loose leaving the flame exposed. It was one small problem complicated by another.

Most trouble encountered aboard my boat has followed this pattern, which was first discovered by the famous Irish seaman Mr. Murphy. "What can go wrong, will go wrong, usually at the worst possible time." I've found a mathematical corollary which says: "When more than one thing goes wrong, the total trouble is larger than the sum of the parts." Big trouble can be caused by two or more little troubles which interact.

Fire aboard a boat is big trouble. Each year fires and explosions cause the largest property loss and second largest number of injuries in all boating accidents. Small fires can be stopped if they are attacked early enough with the equipment normally aboard, but if an explosion comes first or the fire gets into a more advanced stage involving large amounts of fuel and inaccessible areas of the hull, the chances of putting it out are slim. Start thinking about saving the people. The best time to stop a fire is before little troubles have a chance to start it.

It takes three elements to make a fire or explosion: air, fuel, and a source of heat for ignition. Removing any one of the three will stop a fire which is burning, and keeping any one isolated from the other two will prevent a fire from starting. For prevention purposes, air is the least controllable of the three elements because it is present almost everywhere in the boat, so let's forget about air and concentrate on fuel and ignition sources. There is no shortage of either aboard boats.

Almost everything aboard except for the metal parts and water is potential fuel for a fire. This includes materials like fiberglass resin in the hull, plastics, wood, paint, nylon, Dacron and other fabrics, along with the liquid and gas fuels we think of first. However, gasoline, propane/butane, alcohol, diesel, or kerosene is almost always the prime ingredient in boating fires. Gasoline and its explosive vapors are the worst offenders.

By carefully examining your boat in terms of fuel location you can make a good estimate of where fires could break out. Start at the bow and work your way aft. Is there a cabin heater? Where is its fuel stored? How about the galley stove? Is there a gas or liquid fuel piping system? Paint thinners? Extra gasoline for the dinghy outboard and the outboard itself? How about the main fuel supply tanks and the line to the engine? Do you have an auxiliary generator? Modern boats with complex living accommodations multiply the places where trouble can start in the form of fuel leaks.

An essential characteristic of liquid fuel, gasoline vapors, and propane/butane gas is that they all flow downward like water and collect at the lowest point. Imagine even vapors flowing down along bulkheads or through cracks in the floor. A boat, unlike a car, is watertight and gas-tight at the bottom, so fuel and fumes can collect as if in a bowl waiting for a spark. The electrical system can supply plenty of sparks.

Every electric motor or generator aboard using commutator and brushes sparks unless is it shielded. This includes the starter motor, blower, bilge pumps, generator, freshwater pumps, and other electric motors. High voltage leads for the engine ignition system may produce sparks if they are near metal objects. Even a gasoline filler hose nozzle can make a static spark if it hasn't been grounded to the metal of your tank fitting. So you don't have to drop a cigarette in the bilge or have the stove on to get a healthy explosion if flammable vapors are present.

The first thing to prevent is any leakage of fuel into areas where it doesn't belong. In the main fuel system the filler and vent should be positioned so that any overflow will run over the ship's side, not into the bilges. Often a hole or damaged fitting in the filler pipe or vent doesn't reveal itself except when the tank is topped off.

The tank should be isolated from heavy objects which might puncture it through shifting or chafing. A tank

placed so low that fuel must actually be pumped out of it is safer than a gravity feed because it won't leak continuously through a break in the line. If you do have a gravity feed, there should be an easily accessible valve right at the tank and it's a good idea to keep it shut off when the engine isn't in use. Could you reach the valve to shut off fuel if there were a fire in the engine compartment? There are electric valves available which automatically shut off fuel when the ignition is off.

By following the fuel line along its run to the engine you can locate possible trouble points such as entry and exit from filters, unprotected passage through bulkheads where chafe can occur, or where it is vulnerable to being hit by heavy objects like anchors or shifting ballast, in rough weather. The fuel line should be well clear of the exhaust and electrical system. One trick for insuring against leakage from wear or cracks in the line is to slip a slightly larger PVC tube over the whole thing and seal it at both ends with pipe clamps. Use a transparent tube so that you can see if any fuel has collected in it. Remember that vibration is constantly at work on an engine, and leaks can develop where none were before.

A perfectly good installation can drip a lot of gasoline from the carburetor if the float valve sticks, not cutting off the flow when the float chamber is full. This has happened to me several times as a result of rust contamination in the fuel. Once, more than a gallon of gasoline collected in the engine pan after the carburetor dripped all night. If the engine stops for no apparent reason, check to see if something like this has happened before spending time with your finger on the starter button. Gasoline could be dripping steadily over the warm engine just waiting for a spark from the starter motor.

Engine room blowers and ventilation are there for a good reason. Because fuel fumes are heavier than air, it's necessary to suck them up and pump them overboard just like bilge water. The blower intake pipe should be positioned as low as possible in the likeliest area for fuel spills, usually under the carburetor. Blowing for five minutes really to clear the compartment is a must, even if the engine has been running earlier. This is particularly true after refueling. Have you ever noticed how many of the news stories of boat explosions mention that the victims had just pulled away from the fuel dock? Before starting, I always sniff the blower exhaust at the deck fitting after a minute or two with the blower running. Your nose is a very sensitive fume detector, besides being cheap and reliable. If a definite odor is present, take a look around the engine compartment before hitting the starter. A small spill can cause an immediate explosion.

Unsuspecting skippers can pull away from the fuel dock with a large amount of gasoline present in the engine compartment, because the vapor mixture is too rich to explode. The engine will run rough or stall in this situation, but when more air gets in and the engine begins to run smoothly, then the boat explodes.

Cooking stoves and some cabin heaters use liquid or bottled gas fuels. As most boating cooks know, alcohol-primed stoves are prone to flare up when there is too much priming or the burner is turned on too soon, but the low flame temperature makes alcohol less dangerous than other fuels. Putting a pot full of liquid on the burner even during priming saves fuel, decreases the height of the priming flame, and can be used as a handy extinguisher for *alcohol* flareups only. Make sure than nothing flammable like curtains or dishtowels is placed above the stove.

Kerosene in stoves is harder to ignite, but once burning it has a higher flame temperature than alcohol. All piping joints should be well sealed by threading or brazing, not solder which can melt. The fuel is under pressure in the tank, and a lit burner provides plenty of heat to ignite kerosene which gets loose through a failed joint. Burning kerosene, like gasoline or grease, cannot be put out with water because these fuels float and continue to burn. Keep an appropriate extinguisher within easy reach of the cook.

Bottled gas installations have caused many explosions. This fuel is different from the gas used in city homes because it is heavier than air and collects in the lowest part of a contained space in dangerous concentrations. Leaks from joints in piping or burners which have gone out while turned on are often the culprits.

If all the fuel on board is properly contained, the electrical systems in boats still offer some potential fire sources, particularly when 110 volt is in use. Unattended electric heaters and battery trickle chargers have burned boats at the dock while the owner was home asleep. Switching off the shore power and the onboard system when you leave will prevent this.

Even 12-volt systems can do nasty things, particularly at battery terminals or leads before they reach the fuse box. A metal object falling across uncovered battery terminals or shorting out the main leads can ignite other materials nearby. A proper fuse box can do a lot to protect against short circuits or overloads in the rest of the system, but watch out for electrical gear where high voltages are used like radio transmitters and radar. Chafe in the wiring or other damage to insulation can cause problems, too.

Last spring I was up in the bosun's chair screwing a fitting onto the mast when I smelled a nasty acrid odor. I looked down at the cockpit and saw smoke rising from under a deck locker where the light switches were located. By the time I got down and hit the main switch, the insulation had burned completely off two switch wires. A little detective work showed that my screw had neatly short-circuited the wiring to the mast-head light.

There seem to be nearly endless variations of the small problems which can sneak up on an unsuspecting sailor, but if you try to cure in advance as many of them as you can recognize, and keep a lookout for the others as they arise, the odds against big trouble go way down.

The underlying principles behind all this prevention detail are fairly simple:

1. Uncontained fuels are the prime dangers. Try to outguess the events which would let fuels get loose. Use your nose before the starter button to locate possible problems and correct them immediately.

2. The electrical system is the secondary source of danger. Monitor it, maintain it, and don't use it if you suspect that fuel is loose.

By keeping fuel and ignition sources under control, you'll be able to breathe the air happily, knowing it's not going to help destroy you, your friends, or your boat. But keep the extinguishers handy, because Mr. Murphy is always aboard.

Tips & Ideas

What It's All About

Why cruises succeed — or fail

Larry and Lin Pardey

Cruising is for pleasure. Therefore the people we have met while cruising who are not enjoying themselves present a sad contradiction. More than half the yachts we have met were inhabited by people who couldn't wait to finish their voyage or sell their boat.

In La Paz, Baja California, we saw deserted yachts rotting. In Costa Rica we saw deserted yachts rotting. The Panama Canal was a treasure chest of yachts for sale by disillusioned sailors. It's been the same everywhere we've cruised.

Why? According to recent surveys, cruising is a dream cherished by almost 80% of the people who build or buy a yacht. What changes the dream to a nightmare?

Our private survey and observations exposed three main reasons for a non-successful cruise: (1) too large a vessel; (2) financial difficulties; (3) over-planning.

The difficulties of too large a vessel are obvious: crew, maintenance, expense. Financial problems cannot be foreseen when one finds living costs to be greater than at home. Also, jobs are not always easy to get if you are a transient worker living on a boat.

Over-planning is the hidden danger in cruising. Where are you going? Are you headed round the world? How long will it take? A person leaving on a cruise is asked these questions a thousand times. The new sailor tries to answer; the experienced man says, "I'm headed south — I've got six months free."

In preparing for a cruise, we — and many of our successful cruising friends — plan only to the extent of carrying all charts of the area to be visited with detail charts of all intermediate ports. We carry food and supplies for the length of the cruise plus one third for emergencies. Finally, we invite people to join us only when we get somewhere and then by telephone or wire.

Breakdowns, bad weather, illness and clearance problems are all schedule ruiners. With no dates, the humor of the mañana spirit can turn a delay into a fiesta as you explore around that interesting bend on the way to the next anchorage.

The most pleasant aspect of an unplanned cruise is the element of surprise that enters when you can say, "That island looks interesting. Let's stop." Our three years of cruising were made into a wonderful adventure by our unforeseen stops.

One especially comes to mind.

As we left the Panama Canal and visited Porto Bello, Isla Grande, and Nombre de Dios on our way toward Cartagena, Columbia, we sailed past the Archipelago de las Muletas.

Larry: "Shall we anchor for the night or press on?"

Lin: "If we get our hook down by nightfall, let's stay."

We anchored at 1930 just as it became dark.

We stayed almost two months in the remarkable San Blas Islands. We visited 11 of the 360 islands and made friends we will have for life.

There are some people who just don't enjoy cruising once they start. After they give detailed plans to all of the folks at home, plus instructions for visits from dozens of friends along the way, it's impossible for them to turn back.

The owner of one large yacht with guests scheduled for a week each for a four-month voyage told us his sad story. He hated cruising. Couldn't sleep well, got seasick, didn't like fishing, but as he said, "I can't disappoint all the people I've invited to join me. I'll just have to stick it out!"

Even on a limited cruise of two to four weeks, a schedule ruins the purpose of the exercise. Cruising is an antidote to the pressures of modern life. Why bring your pressures with you? Cast off your mooring lines and sail with an eye to interesting stops.

Set your ultimate goal one half of the distance you think you can cover, and if you move quickly you'll have twice the time to enjoy the people and places along the way. If you are delayed, no bother, because you have lots of time.

And what about the guests who'd like to join you? The excitement of not knowing exactly where you will be going makes an adventure of a normal visitors' cruise.

Establish an approximate port for your meeting and call guests the day you arrive in your meeting port. Make final arrangements and then wait for your guests. The expense of a phone call is minimal. The fun of a jeep ride from somewhere to wherever you are will really add excitement to your visitors' arrival. Your calm greeting will prove that you are one of those who do enjoy dream cruising.

It's a shame that everyone doesn't enjoy cruising as much as we do. Then, everyone isn't prepared to slow down. There are other reasons for success (and failure) too, so the following information — gleaned from those who have cruised successfully — should give the would-be cruiser something to go on.

Improper choice and outfitting of a vessel has ruined many long distance cruises. Yet, how can a person know which boat is ideal for cruising? No one can name the ideal design for everyone; but a survey of the yachts we met while cruising presents some interesting conclusions.

Our survey limited interviews to those who had been outside home waters for at least three months without paid crew. Information requested included not only size and type of yacht, but also costs, crew, rig and equipment.

We gave 57 yachts the once-over and they ranged from 17' to 58' overall, with a minimum cruising time of three months to a maximum of more than 20 years.

Our conclusions are based on the answers of people who are actually doing the cruising, not on theory or speculation.

We divided the vessels into two groups: those owned by the average sailor who must earn his funds before or during his cruise, and those with an independent income. Of the 57 cruisers interviewed, 16 were what we call independents.

What size yacht do you need to cruise enjoyably?

The average length of all yachts was 37'. Those which had been cruising six months or longer averaged 36.6', but subtracting independents, the average dropped to only 32.9'.

Yachts cruising for more than a year (we met 14 non-independents in this category) averaged 31.6'.

The six vessels we met which had cruised for more than two years had an average length of only 29' LOA.

Original purchase price is only a partial reason for the use of a smaller vessel for cruising. Figures stated by the owners interviewed confirmed the adage that maintenance costs increase at close to the cube of the waterline length.

Ten of the vessels we met were built of fiberglass and their maintenance costs averaged close to non-glass boats of the same size which had been cruising for the same length of time. But, fiberglass boat owners all stated higher costs for repairs to both masts and hull because of lack of materials and knowledge in less developed countries.

Slip fees and all other expenses increased with size.

One must either hire extra help or stay out of the water extra days to clean and paint a larger vessel. Parts and fittings increase in size rapidly as length increases, therefore, replacement parts which never seem available in foreign countries cost more and have to be flown in.

Aside from cost, smaller cruisers are easier to handle. Most small yachts we met had been fitted with self-steering vane gear or had tried to substitute an auto-pilot with little or no success. Motorsailers or powerful auxiliaries, using their engines frequently, found their auto-pilots satisfactory but expensive to buy and maintain compared with a vane. *Under sail*, all auto-pilots also drained batteries quickly.

Smaller vessels also proved more satisfactory by eliminating the largest single source of trouble our interviews exposed: *crew*. Apart from vessels carrying singlehanders or husband and wife teams, every vessel except one reported difficulties with crew members, or crew members reported difficulties with skippers. The differences reported ranged from poor sharing of expenses to sailing inability, from difficulties in finding a crew to the problems of getting rid of an unpleasant crew member. The more crew a vessel required, the more problems it had. We met owners who were actually cancelling their cruises because of crew problems.

Windvanes helped solve some crew problems.

Of the 57 boats in our survey, 8 were single-handers, 11 were families, 16 were couples and 22 were vessels that required crew. Only four couples, one family and one single-hander — all in small yachts — had been cruising for more than two years.

Light displacement yachts were in the majority for the three to six month cruises, but were in a definite minority in the six months or more range. Low cargo capacity and quick motion led to tiring, uncomfortable passages.

Light displacement yachts reported a higher rate of gear failures. Almost all of them were below their load waterline. Too much gear on board contributed to poor speed under sail.

What rig is most successful?

We met twenty-two ketches, four yawls, three schooners and twenty-eight sloops or cutters. Only two boats were able to cruise completely without an engine — a sloop and a cutter.

Long distance cruisers tended toward the sloop or cutter rig because the efficiency of only one mast allowed yachts to depend more on sailing and less on their engines. Downwind efficiency on a sloop or cutter was highly praised.

Very few cruiser crews continued using twin staysails for steering as they could not spread enough canvas for light airs and found the rough correcting motion of the staysails uncomfortable.

At least 50% of all cruising was in winds of under 15 knots.

Engines came in for a large amount of discussion. No vessel reported using an outboard as a main engine successfully. Unreliability because of corrosion of aluminum parts was the most prevalent complaint.

Small diesel engines, such as the handstart Volvo-Penta MD-1 8 HP and MD-2 15 HP or the Saab were very successful except for spare parts, which were hard to get. (Note: since the survey there have been complaints that the newer Volvo MD-1B 15 HP and the MD-2B 25 HP are not as reliable, probably due to their trying to squeeze double the horsepower out of the old MD-1 and MD-2.) Those boats which carried the most complete spare parts inventory were the most content with their engines.

The problem of locating replacement parts and ordering spares from the United States or Europe, plus the boredom of lost cruising time, ruined many pleasant cruises.

Electronics caused many headaches. The most frequent complaint was the unreliability of alternators combined with the scarcity of alternator repair men. One remedy found was the replacement of the alternator with a simple and more rugged generator and regulator.

Other electronic problem-makers

ranged from so-called waterproof flashlights to marine radios and from depth sounders to spreader lights.

One brand of electronic gear, however, was praised by everyone who owned it. This was the Brookes and Gatehouse waterproof battery operated equipment. Special praise went to the Brookes and Gatehouse depth sounder.

A second highly praised piece of electronic gear was the Zenith Transoceanic portable radio receiver.

A poll of favorite anchors for extended cruising found the CQR patented anchor a hands-down favorite, especially when used with a good length of heavy BBB chain.

Hand-operated anchor winches were first on the list of "thank heavens I've got one," or "sure wish I had one," gear.

The Plath Albina hand-operated bronze winch with chain cathead and line gypsy filled the bill on several small cruisers.

Galley arrangements were shown to be all important. We found that more than 60% of the interviewed yachts used gas stoves with ovens. All gas users were very pleased with the arrangement and contrary to reports, found no difficulty in getting tanks refilled. All emphasized that gas tanks should be on deck with a shut-off valve where the fuel line comes through the deck.

Only one boat we met reported a gas explosion and he stressed the fact that he had his tanks below deck in the so-called airtight compartment with an overboard drain. As he was running downwind, the drain was covered by his boat's quarter wave and the gas overflowed the watertight cockpit and went down the companionway, filling the bilges.

With a gas tank above deck, it is almost impossible to get fumes into your hull.

On the other hand, the difficulty encountered in obtaining alcohol and its high cost made alcohol stove owners very unhappy. Frequent minor fires caused by overfilling the primer cups and by dried-out packing

glands, plus odor, made several wives eager to change to gas.

Kerosene stoves worked well for those who had them, but the trouble of priming plus absence of an oven was mentioned as a nuisance by some.

Coal or diesel fuel stoves, although a delight in colder climates, proved too hot for the tropics.

Refrigeration systems were mostly unsuccessful on cruising boats we met. Those using well insulated ice chests were most contented and all commented on the availability of ice except in the Bahama Islands. Gas refrigerators worked okay, but required a large supply of fuel and produced much cabin heat.

Fresh water pressure systems and hand pumps in the galley came high on the list of problems. High consumption of water and electricity caused complaints when pressure systems were used.

Gravity feed systems with a day tank and separate main tank were a handy inexpensive solution.

All production fiberglass boats and several non-production boats stated that poor through-ventilation made life in the tropics uncomfortable. A galley sail helped, but strong opening portlights instead of solid picture windows were desired.

Sixteen of the boats we met had windvanes for self-steering. These sailors all considered their vanes their best friend. All said that cruising would be a lot less enjoyable without a vane, but admitted that adapting the vane to their individual boat had taken time and patience.

And the cost of cruising?

Besides the size of vessel and the number of crew carried, we found costs depend on many factors including food preferences and entertainment preferences. We found that the more light-air sails a vessel had on board, the less the engine was used which lowered fuel costs and repairs.

A simple vessel with little electronics or mechanical gear was less expensive to operate.

All interviewed stated that cruising cost more than originally anticipated. Contrary to popular belief, cruising costs more out of home waters, although this is not true of the whole world. Many items considered necessities at home are luxuries abroad. Canned goods and marine supplies often triple their costs in undeveloped countries.

The number of unhappy crews we encountered proved that the most important factors necessary for enjoyable cruising are a modest and simple yacht, plenty of time, some money in the bank, and a good sense of humor.

If you qualify, why don't you join us?

The "Business" Side of Cruising

Money, mail, and other matters   Lin Pardey

Handling your financial and business matters when you are cruising can be a real headache, and should be carefully considered before you leave home.

You can't cruise enjoyably for long periods and still run a business back home. We've met people who have tried to and they either are nervous wrecks or have quit cruising prematurely. A year ago Larry and I were in Bayona, Spain. There we met a Swiss yachtsman named Rudi and we helped load his luggage off his 35-foot cruising yacht. Rudi had left Germany four weeks earlier to make a year's cruise to the West Indies. He only called home from Spain because he was curious about how a contract his firm had was getting on. What he heard made him cancel his voyage and leave his boat for the winter. "If I hadn't called, I would be blissfully sailing for Madeira right now," Rudi told us.

We have met many people who either close their business for a year, find a full-time manager to run it on a profit-sharing basis, or lease the business with an option to buy. These people often enjoy cruising so much that they sell their business and keep going. But if they find cruising isn't the fun they expected, they still can go home and build it up again. One very successful sailing businessman we know put it this way, "Building a business is a full-time job but so is cruising. When I'm ready to cruise indefinitely, I'll quit and put my money in the bank. If I want to go back into business, I'll just start again. I've learned a lot that I didn't know when I first started, so it will be easier the next time."

About half the people we know who have been cruising for over a year also own a home somewhere. Almost all have leased their homes through agents who take a 10- or 15-percent fee for maintaining and managing the house. Other assets seem to be best put into bonds or high interest bearing accounts that can be handled by your bank. Speculative stocks and shares are impossible to combine with cruising. You can't have both worlds. You just have to accept the fact that long-term cruising is getting out of the rat race *completely*, or you won't enjoy it at all.

Annabele, who cruises with her husband Gordon on a 28-foot sailboat, takes one month each year and flies back to check her house and banking matters. She says the expense is more than justified because it gives her a complete change of scenery. She takes care of the tax returns, checks the garden and house, cashes any retirement checks and takes time to visit some of their five children. She and Gordon have cruised for over six years and keep only bonds and deposit accounts. They gave up stocks that might fluctuate before they could reach a phone and call their stockbroker to save a loss that could have put a damper on their whole cruise.

The rest of us who go cruising aren't fortunate enough to have this kind of problem. We do own our boats and have some money in the bank, but we earn our cruising funds as we go along. Still, even for us, handling business matters, mail and money transfers can be a problem.

We've found that the best formula for us is to outfit our boat completely, and then take out six months cruising funds and buy small denomination traveler's checks with them. I stress small denomination because we've been in places where no one in town had the money or inclination to cash even a $20 traveler's check. We carry only $10 checks and don't find it much trouble to sign five at a time if necessary.

We purchase half our checks in Larry's name and the other half in mine. That way if one or the other of us is sick or too lazy to go to town, the other person can get money. Checks in US dollars have always served us well, and so far we've never been any place where the rate for dollars wasn't known. On the other hand, a year and a half ago when the dollar was devalued, we had to wait three days before any bank would cash our checks because of the scare. We do buy two currencies now to protect ourselves.

After we have our six month's supply of traveler's checks, we put another six months of funds in our checking account for which we have a check-cashing card. When we get low on funds we stop at some city that has a yacht club and we ask someone to recommend a good bank. We present our check and card and wait eight or 10 days while the check clears. If we're terribly clever we combine this with a haulout so the wait goes quickly.

We have tried other ways: We wrote our bank asking for a cashier's check to be forwarded to us in Acapulco. When we arrived two weeks later there was no check at the Port Captain's office. We wrote again to the bank. We waited. Finally, two weeks later, in desperation we called the bank and asked for a new check. The second check arrived and we proudly walked into a Mexican bank. "Sorry, we don't accept cashier's checks without a guarantor." Luckily, we met a Mexican gentleman who was a large shareholder in the same bank and he guaranteed the check for us. Two months later, the real Port Captain of Acapulco returned to work from his holiday and forwarded our first check which he had locked in his desk for safe keeping.

Much to our surprise and inconvenience, we have found that Danish banks won't cash cashier's or banker's trust checks either. There seems to be no easy way and to transfer large amounts of money you must be prepared to wait.

If you want your bank to mail you a check for any reason, ask them to issue a bank check guaranteed by a New York foreign exchange bank if you are American, a London bank if you are British or a Sydney bank for Australians. Ask the bank to send your check to you in a plain hand-addressed envelope, i.e., no bank letterhead. Have the check wrapped in a piece of paper. Envelopes that obviously contain checks seem to disappear in the mail quite often.

One final note. Warn the local bank you are dealing with about how much cash or traveler's checks you will be processing. Once in northern Mexico, we arranged for a transfer with the small local bank. But when the funds came through, the manager told us that the largest denomination bills he had were 10-peso notes (80 cents). We walked out with two paper bags full of money, and we had to clear a place on board in the linen locker to store it all!

A police chief in Colombia gave us a good suggestion. His town had a bad reputation for pickpockets, but what he said could apply to any big city. "Don't carry any more money in your wallet or pocket than you are willing to lose. Keep the rest stored carefully away in your boat. If you want to buy something very expensive, go back to your boat and get the extra money."

Handling foreign currencies is an interesting part of cruising. There are pretty, new bills, and there is also the fun of working with different exchange rates. Many banks in the United States, England and Australia offer a service that takes some of the pain out of your first days in a new country. They sell $20 packets in foreign currency with a guide to the value of each coin and bill you will use. It's nice to arrive in Mexico with enough pesos to take a taxi to the Port Captain's office or buy an ice-cream cone without a mad rush to find a bank.

Credit cards have some use while cruising, but are not always convenient. My mother tried to cash a check against her BankAmericard when she was visiting in Falmouth, England. She was told that Barclay's Bank in London (250 miles away) or in Bristol (100 miles) would be glad to accept her check.

Paying bills by credit card means involving a third person to do your accounting at your mailing address. You should give someone power of attorney and hope that he or she will recognize your legitimate signature if your card is stolen or lost.

A final thought on finances. Don't be surprised if foreign shipyards, marinas and yacht clubs won't accept checks and demand advance cash payment for services. Transient yachtsmen do have a poor reputation in many places. We worked with a Costa Rican shipyard owner who had over 3000 dollars in bad checks from yachtsmen who had work done and then disappeared. A Falmouth (England) boat company said they had about the same in bad checks and unpaid debts. Foreign yachtsmen had work done, then sailed off at night.

What about your mail? There is only one way we have found that works. Arrange for a permanent mailing address, your parents, a bank manager, an accounting firm. Have all mail sent there no matter where you are. Ask your mail agent to forward your mail on a specified date to a specified address — preferably to a yacht club. Ask that all of it be sent in one envelope or package, stay there until the one package arrives. The mail slots of yacht clubs world wide are full of old letters that missed the yacht they were intended for. How do you know how many letters are coming unless all your mail is in one package from one address?

We suggest yacht clubs as mailing posts only because yacht clubs are aware of the fact that yachts often arrive late. General delivery is good if you are sitting and waiting for your mail packet, but after 30 days your mail is returned to the sender. The address of yacht clubs world wide can be found by consulting a copy of *The Lloyd's Registry of Yachts*, the list at the back of the book has served us very well so far. *The Lloyd's Register of American Yachts* has a list of Yacht Clubs in the United States and Canada.

Very few people quit cruising because of storms, bad weather or calms. It's the little hassles like making a phone call, cashing a check, locating your mail or finding a hot shower that annoy you most. But then again, if cruising were that easy, everyone would be doing it.

A Proper Awning

How to construct your own sunshield   Tisha Whitney

It doesn't take many hours sitting under a hot sun in a cockpit or closed up below on a rainy day to make a boat owner realize his need for protection over his cockpit. Once he has decided on the need, some sort of awning gets put on a list of priorities; how near the top usually depends upon cost. Is an awning something that must be ordered from a firm that makes items such as sail covers and dodgers, or can it be made at home to last as long but at a fraction of the cost?

Let's look at the factors involved in designing an awning for a particular boat and then at what might be involved in making your own awning.

Before purchasing or making a cockpit awning for your boat, take into consideration the cruising areas you plan to visit, for an awning should be designed with these locales in mind. If your goal is the tropics, awnings that cover as much of the deck as possible, from the forestay to the mast and from the mast to the backstay, should be considered.

Such awnings will reflect the heat which would otherwise be absorbed by the deck, keeping the cabin cooler and helping to make it tolerable to walk about barefoot above decks, thus giving access to more space. On one occasion we were cruising without an awning and entertained the surrounding yachts by playing hopscotch as we leapt from one section of white to the other, avoiding the oiled teak because of its intense heat.

Not only should the awning extend fore and aft as much as possible, but also spreaders can be used to widen its beam so that four to six inches extend beyond the edge of the deck. This will give you a few more inches of shade, which is at a premium in the tropics, and it will shed tropical downpours over the side instead of inboard.

This feature should also be considered if the awning is planned for the cooler and wetter climates of New England or British Columbia.

Cruising plans will also dictate the color of the awning. In the tropics a white fabric reflects much of the sun's heat. It also creates more glare than a dark fabric, but all of cruising is a series of compromises. If most of your cruising is planned for colder climates, you need not use white material for an awning.

Side curtains are an additional consideration. Several boats we have seen have roll-up curtains on the aft-most portion of their awnings. These can be unfurled and lowered when the morning or afternoon sun comes sneaking under the awning.

A disadvantage to having the side-curtains permanently attached is that there is always the extra weight to worry about when the wind comes up on a wild night. To circumvent this problem we use one curtain which is laced into place through grommets when needed. We are counting on the sun attacking us only from one direction at a time, and presume that the rain will likewise be as obliging. When the side curtain is not needed, it is stowed below decks, out of the wind and weather.

A boat that heads for the tropics will have the sun to contend with not only in port but also while sailing. An awning can be constructed to provide shade for both occasions. If your boat has a dodger, the forward edge of the awning is snapped or laced to the aft side of the dodger. The aft portion of the awning can be secured to your gallows frame or backstay. This portion of the awning is rigged below the boom so that it can be used when you are sailing. When you are at anchor, the awning is secured above the boom, using a metal tube or wooden spreader to provide the support at the aft section, since the gallows is now occupied. The edge previously attached to the dodger can now be snapped to a forward section of awning, thus connecting the portions and providing an awning that reaches from the mast to the backstay.

As an alternative, the after section could be left rigged below the boom, while the second piece is run forward to the mast and aft to the dodger. One disadvantage to this arrangement is that headroom beneath the aft part of the awning is reduced. Moreover, the dodger must be left in place, restricting the flow of air into the cockpit and through the companionway.

As a boat cruises north to the higher latitudes, other considerations will influence awning design. The awning will primarily act as a shield rather than a sunshade, fending off the rain and making access to the hatch easier.

Cruising boats, both in the colder climates and the tropics, are faced with the problem of gathering water if they are in undeveloped areas. An awning can be equipped with side flaps which can be drawn up tight to form pockets for rain. The rain runs off the awning into the side flaps, then drains into a plastic through-hull fitting at the base of the flap. A hose is attached to the underside of the throughhull, allowing the water to pass down to tanks or jerry cans. It is possible to provide much of your drinking water in this fashion when you are at anchor.

Be sure that you allow the rain to cleanse the awning for several minutes before you begin to collect drinking water; the first water can be saved for laundry or baths. If birds happen to frequent your anchorage, beware of their droppings for they may contaminate your water. It is wise to check your awning regularly and keep it clean, using a mild chlorine bleach solution on trouble spots.

If you would like to see your awning last several seasons, indeed, many years, you had better construct it soundly or the first few rain squalls will begin to work it apart. All seams should be triple sewn; by using several rows of stitching the material is securely

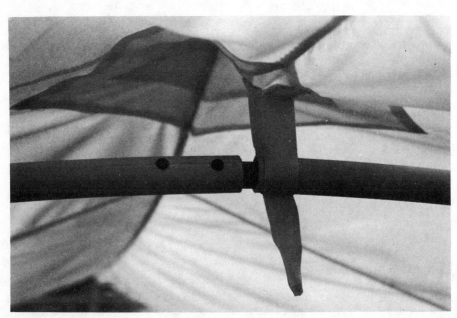

PVC pipe spreader consists of two lengths fitted together in the center with a sleeve. Loop of tape stitched to awning supports spreader

Outer ends of spreaders are secured in pockets applied at reinforced corners. Note how loop in boltrope incorporates lanyard. Grommet is used to lace side curtain to awning when needed

mine the life of your awning. Awnings made of light nylon are inexpensive but are not appropriate for cruising needs. They allow harmful rays to penetrate, providing the crew beneath with an unexpected sunburn. While nylon is easy to stow because of its light weight and flexibility, it pays for this later when it is subjected to the buffeting winds. Cotton canvas is an alternative but canvas is difficult to sew and, especially when wet, it is heavy and stiff. If is also highly subject to mildew and salt impregnation. By far the best fabrics for awnings are Vivatex (British trade name) and Acrilon (American trade name). They resist the sun and mildew, and are semi-waterproof, a helpful asset in a downpour.

To minimize stretching, a boltrope should be sewn to the entire edge of the awning as well as down the center. This aspect of awning construction is very important and does not receive enough emphasis by those who produce awnings commercially. In any kind of blow, the boltrope takes the strain off the fabric, thus keeping the shape of the awning intact.

When roping the material, bend the rope towards you so that the fabric is bowed out and remains on the outside as you work (Fig. 1). This allows you to draw the material into the strands of the rope as you sew, using up more fabric

locked, whereas with only one row the seam will work back and forth and soon the two pieces of fabric will saw through the threads.

The fabric you select will also deter-

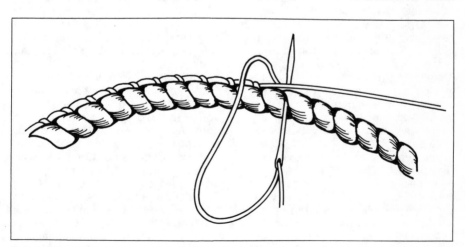

Figure 1: In roping edge of awning, keep fabric on the side of the rope opposite to you and with each stitch draw fabric into the strands of the rope

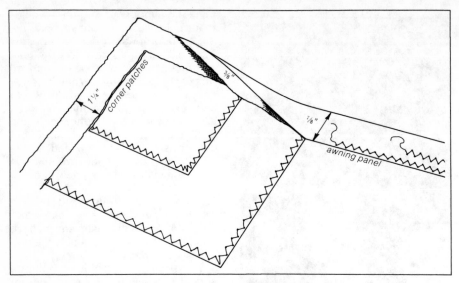

Figure 2: Detail of corner reinforcement shows how corner patches are first stitched to the panel of the awning. The edge is folded under ⅜ inches and then ⅞ inches are folded over before being hemmed with at least two rows of zigzag stitching

than rope. The stress will always be taken up by the rope, not the fabric.

When readying the rope for installation, first lay it out along the dock to get out the kinks, then draw a line along its length. As you sew the rope to the cloth, keep the marked line next to the seam. This will insure that you do not twist the rope as you work.

It would be quite expensive to pay a sailmaker to sew on your boltrope *by hand*, and the machines used commonly in sail lofts for boltroping are not recommended, for they frequently sew irregularly, thus producing unequal tension. I spent 18 hours sewing our boltrope and wouldn't like to think of paying someone else for the labor, especially when many shops charge 10 to 15 dollars an hour.

Another area that you should not "cut corners" on is the corner or any other section of your awning that receives stress, for it is constantly working when any wind is up. These areas should be reinforced with double patches. If you are constructing the awning yourself, you may wish to inset the reinforcement patches for your corners 1¼ inches, then fold over the

outer edge to form the hem (Fig. 2). Using this technique, you avoid building up too many thicknesses to sew through, ending up with five layers instead of nine when the hem is complete. The reinforcement patches reduce stretching and distortion of the corners as well as prolonging the life of the awning.

As you compile your checklist of requirements for a worthy awning, add "spreaders," for when cruising you will want your deck area to be usable, and complete headroom under the awning will help to make this possible. Because the headroom should extend forward and not be found only when you are standing in the cockpit, a spreader is needed to elevate and support the awning all the way to the edge. Our spreaders are constructed of PVC pipe, cut into two six-foot-long sections for ease of stowing below decks. These two pipes are fitted together with a sleeve to form a 12-foot spreader, a few inches more than the beam of our boat. The PVC has the advantage of being lightweight and inexpensive, but tends to flex noticeably when a strong wind wrestles with the awning. A laminated wood spreader or one of aluminum tubing is recommended for its strength and stability.

Having concluded that it is necessary to have headroom under an awning for extended cruising, we are committed not only to the spreader but also to a topping-lift arrangement to elevate the spreader. Keep plans simple; just a line secured over the center of your spreader that can be snapped to the main halyard and raised aloft should suffice. If the system of rigging an awning becomes too complicated, you will be reluctant to put up your awning when you need it, or, worse, reluctant to take it down when a gale threatens.

Once your awning is set up, with the spreader in place and the halyard hoisted, the corners and spreader ends should be secured with lanyards. Take advantage of your upper shrouds by running the forward corner lanyards out to them. The spreader lanyards can be run directly to the deck, for they are already elevated by the spreader itself and do not need to be held aloft. Use strong Dacron lines for lanyards. Keep them with your awning so you won't discover one cloudy morning when you go out to raise your awning that you've used them to secure your oars to the grab rails.

Whether you decide to construct your own awning or have an awning maker do it, consider the "checklist" I have mentioned, for it will aid you in the creation of an awning built for your boat and your cruising needs.

Good Stove, Good Cruise

What comprises the best seagoing range　　　　　　　　Lin Pardey

I **may be just** a showoff, but I love to have guests on board for dinner. I bake fresh bread, roast a bird or bake lasagna, and stew a fruit cobbler. No one seems to expect this kind of dinner on a 24′ cutter, so I'm an instant success. But, it was only because my husband Larry had been shipmates with many different types of stoves that he blessed our cruising home with a three-burner stove with oven and grill.

After nine years of cruising, delivering boats and crewing on both sailing and power vessels, I'm convinced that being cook is the hardest job afloat. I've never met a crew that didn't hope for three hot meals a day. Cruising thus becomes a 52-weeks-a-year proposition. If cooking isn't easy and enjoyable, neither is cruising. Good food conveniently prepared is one of the joys of life; and the most important tool the cook has is the stove.

Although a lot of people may disagree with me, I'm sold on butane (propane or bottled gas). Why? It lights instantly. Just turn on the safety valve, light a match and it's burning. No priming; if there's fuel it works. The flame is hot and *extremely* clean. The stove requires very little maintenance other than a monthly check on the valves and connections. Since you can use either butane or propane in the same bottle, supply is no problem.

We have now been in 16 countries and had cooking fuel for an average of three months, including baking our own bread. When we use it for our gas heater as well, it lasts us three weeks during an English winter. Our single tank has a volume gauge on it which is handy. But two smaller tanks can work just as well; when one runs out, switch tanks and refill the empty.

Is an oven essential? One day we were moored in the estuary behind Punta Arenas, Costa Rica. A glorious 58′ Herreshoff-designed ketch flying a French flag anchored near us and we were invited for cocktails. We were dazzled by the polished bronze work and traditional teak finish but when we left we invited her owner to bring her children aboard for tea the next day. I baked fresh cookies for the youngsters. Our very gracious guest said, "I know I am richer than you are, but which one of us is wealthier? You live on a 24′ yacht yet you can serve fresh-baked pastries on china. I serve only things that can be cooked on two burners and we have a 58-footer."

She missed the added enjoyment of cooking with an oven and so do many cruising families I meet. Life without baked potatoes, roast beef or grilled pork chops just wouldn't be the same for us. Besides, a diet of fried foods is just what a sailor doesn't need: too much fat and not enough variety.

The two most common reasons we hear for not using butane are: it's not safe and it weighs too much. To the first I can only say, butane can be dangerous, but so can sailing. Using a stove and sailing both require care, planning, and prudence. A boat stove never should be left unattended. If a pot boils over and puts the flame out, don't re-light the stove until you have checked the bilges for gas.

A butane stove must be well installed *with the tanks on deck*. There must be a convenient shut-off valve near the stove, one that shuts the tank off. Connections through the

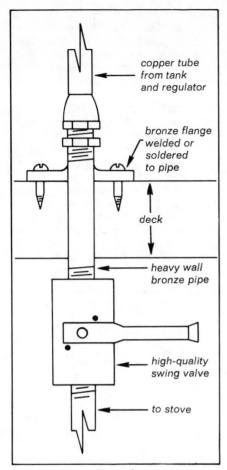

copper tube
from tank
and regulator

bronze flange
welded or
soldered
to pipe

deck

heavy wall
bronze pipe

high-quality
swing valve

to stove

Figure 1

deck should be heavy wall bronze piping. We use a nylon ball swing-type valve. If the handle is at right angles to the piping, the tank is off. It's much quicker and easier to check a swing valve than a gate valve (Fig. 1).

I repeat, the tank must be on deck! So-called vapor-proof cockpit lockers are no go. A very well-built Swedish yacht was running from Trinidad to Cartagena, Columbia. Its butane tank was in a cockpit locker than had two overboard drains near the stern of the boat. After running for four days in heavy wind, the skipper went below to start the engine and charge the batteries. His boat exploded, blowing the skylight through the bottom of his dinghy, and burning and partially blinding him.

The vapor-proof butane locker drains had been covered by his quarter wake. The tank had developed a leak and butane, flowing like water, had overflowed the locker, filled the cockpit, and poured over the companionway filling the bilges. With the tank on deck, leaking butane will run out the scuppers and will flow harmlessly overboard.

We had a small leak in our butane tank. We merely said no one could smoke on deck. We used the stove and oil lamps until we were able to repair the damaged tank which is stored in a bottomless deck box forward of our cabin.

What's wrong with kerosene (paraffin), alcohol, diesel, wood, or electricity? I've used alcohol, kerosene and electricity, but not wood or diesel. I think the disadvantages of wood are obvious for long-distance offshore sailing. I have been told that diesel is great in a northern climate, but roasts you out of the cabin when you head south. I dread electricity because generator failure means no hot food.

Kerosene smells just enough to make a queasy cook seasick. So does alcohol (methylated spirits). Kerosene and alcohol both need priming and priming means waiting before you can cook. So, the man on watch can't just dash down and warm a cup of coffee quickly. With an alcohol stove, the packing glands can dry out and must be adjusted frequently or they will leak. Both alcohol and kerosene must be pressurized and that means remembering to pump the tank before your fire goes out. Otherwise you have to go through the whole re-priming, re-lighting procedure again.

I'm often caught when I'm on a boat with a pressurized stove because the fuel runs out just at the wrong moment. Both fuels must be burning perfectly or they will cause soot. Over a few months your nice white cabin overhead will tell you this by turning grey. Finally, over-priming causes fires. I know you *can* put alcohol fires out with water. But as far as I am concerned any fire is a nuisance unless it's the perfect blue glow of a butane fire underneath a bubbling fish stew.

Can kerosene or alcohol stoves have a good oven? A proper oven needs a fire the whole length of the interior enclosure and a small round burner in the center doesn't radiate properly and can cause a central hot spot. Using priming cups creates more difficulties. With propane, the oven can have a properly shaped burner with a heat-controlling thermometer like ours does. Fiberglass 1½" insulation makes our oven super-efficient and produces evenly browned birds and cakes with no burned bottoms. A grill located under the oven burner gives us space to toast six sandwiches evenly all at once.

If you are worried about the space needed for a stove with an oven, consider not gimbaling it. Except on a boat used for long-distance ocean racing, races where the boat may be on the same tack, bashing to windward for days at a time, gimbaled stoves are a waste of space, an extra expense, and potentially dangerous.

I'm sure no one will argue about the extra space required to gimbal a stove properly. The extra expense involved is the gimbaling brackets, flexible piping and most necessary of all, a proper lock to use on the stove when it is being used in port.

The danger of a gimbaled stove can be divided into two areas. First, since the stove is free to swing, a person accidentally losing balance and falling against it in a seaway can cause a pot to tip over. This happened to a friend of mine during a Transpac race several years ago. She was wearing her oilskin pants, the boat lurched, she bumped the stove and spilled a boiling pot inside her oilskin pants. She had to be flown off by helicopter for treatment of third-degree burns. Cruising

people don't have the support of a Transpac Race Committee and escort vessels, so a burn like this could prove to be fatal.

The second danger of a gimbaled stove is that few come equipped with quick-to-use individual clamps for each burner. So, a pot is set on the stove and is expected to stay in place. A sudden lurch, a change of tack and the free pot slides across the stove, bumps the rails and pours onto the cook or cabin sole. If you must have a gimbaled stove, please have good pot clamps (Fig. 2), a three-inch sea rail and a warning for each new crewman: *Don't grab the stove for support!*

I've a passion for commercial

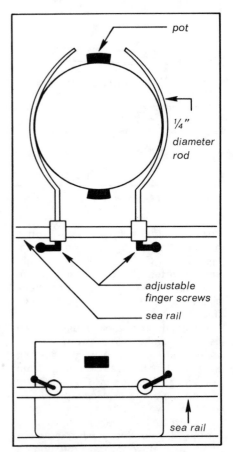

Figure 2: Plan and side view of a good set of pot clamps

boats and I've never been on board one that was outfitted with a gimbaled stove. I had the dubious but very interesting privilege of being cook on a 100-ton Costa Rican shrimp trawler for a month. I fed our crew of six with little difficulty by using oversized deep pots clamped to a three-inch-high sea rail. A shrimp boat may not heel like a sailboat, but it sure can roll.

On our own boat, we have bolted our oversized cooker amidships to the aft side of our forward bulkhead. We've a three-inch-high solid bronze sea rail with great easy-to-use clamps. Twice we've been on our beam ends, once because of an unexpected williwaw and the second time because of a hurricane. Both times our high-profile six-cup coffee percolator stayed put.

What do I do when we're beating to windward? Luckily, *Seraffyn* is a beamy boat and doesn't immediately assume a 30° heel. About 20° is right; any more than that and its time to shorten down. So, slightly deeper pots solve the problem.

Because we live on board that means about 70% to 80% of our cooking is done in port which means only 20% is done at sea. And the odds are that only half of that 20% should be while you are hard on the wind. (The odds have been against us over here in Europe.)

One special advantage of a thwartships-mounted non-gimbaled stove, i.e., the cook is facing either fore or aft when using the stove, is that if the liquid in a pot does chance to overflow or overboil, it spills either to port or starboard and not toward the cook.

People often tease us saying, "Did you build the boat around the stove?" No we didn't, it just happened to fit in the space the designer allowed. But if it hadn't, we would have figured a way to make this a home. Because that's what having a real butane stove with oven and a proper grill means to me: the difference between living on board and just camping out.

It's (Almost) All in Your Mind

Home measures for seasickness prevention Lin Pardey

It **never fails.** Every time we get into a discussion with a new or would-be cruising sailor there comes a moment when a concerned look crosses his or her face and the question is blurted out, "Do you ever get seasick?" I don't think any aspect of sailing causes more worry and certainly nothing is more demoralizing than being seasick. I know; I am one of the sufferers.

There we were, finally on our way after three-and-a-half years of scheming, planning and building. I'd sailed lots of times before, but when we set off from San Diego into a confused cross sea, I was so sick that I finally ended up lying on the cabin sole praying for land. "All my dreams ruined," I said to myself. And even more morbid thoughts rushed through my head for over a day. Larry tried joking with me, holding me, teasing me, but nothing helped. Then to my amazement, the second day out my seasickness began to fade away. By the end of the day, I was more than making up for my lack of interest in food. Even more amazing, after three days, I had forgotten that I ever was seasick.

I still get uncomfortable occasionally and every time it happens I am just as unhappy as the first, but I have learned to minimize the problem. I don't include Larry in this problem because he is one of the outrageously fortunate 10 percent who don't even know what seasickness is. Put him in a boat with bilges full of diesel, odiferous food on the counter, and a vicious sea running and he'll ask where the butter and jam are so he can make a sandwich. But, about 90 percent of all people who go to sea do suffer at one time

or another. So, an active program of prevention is worth considering.

I'm convinced that 30 to 50 percent of the problem is psychological and other long-time sailors have supported me in this belief.

Curiously, I never get seasick when we are working on other boats, only when Larry and I are together alone sailing *Seraffyn*. It must be because I am being paid to cook or crew when we deliver boats. Then I've got important responsibilities and don't want to let the crew down. On board *Seraffyn*, I know Larry will take care of any problems and he handles the boat easily by himself with the aid of our self-steering gear, so I can relax and it doesn't matter. I'm not in any way saying that my seasickness is any less real for being psychological. But by accepting the fact that it is caused by mental processes in our case, we can more actively fight it.

Doctors are forever coming up with new pills to fight the problem. Unfortunately they often forget to put the most important instructions on the package. To work at all, a dramamine or any other anti-motion-sickness pill *must* be taken one hour before the motion starts that causes the problem. Once you are sailing out the marina entrance, it is too late. It takes an hour for some pills to dissolve and spread through your body. If you vomit before then, you lose the medicine.

I personally can't recommend any type of anti-motion pill because I have given up trying to use them. In the excitement of getting under way I usually forget to take one. Or, if I did take one, it always turned out to be lovely, easy sailing and

I had to suffer with the drunk sleepy feeling the pill left. I did try taking a mild tranquilizer (on my doctor's recommendation) an hour before we sailed and it worked even better than any other pill I'd used. I've asked other sailing friends to try this and they report the same.

Whether you want to use anti-motion pills, tranquilizers, or go it without, there definitely are other measures you can take to minimize seasickness.

First: keep your boat very clean. Eliminate any odors you can. It's the odors that do the final trick. A person can be fine until he opens the ice chest and gets a whiff of bleu cheese or sour milk. In fact, we've found that people get seasick less easily on a boat with no engine. There are fewer unusual odors to become accustomed to in a non-auxiliary vessel. If you do have an engine, be careful of over-filling the tanks; check any oil leaks and wipe excess oil off the engine itself to eliminate odors.

Ventilate the boat well and remember that odors you live with day in and day out may not upset you, but they may do the trick for a guest. Don't allow anyone to smoke on board under way if you or one of your guests is prone to seasickness. If you are embarrassed to ask your friends to snub out their cigarettes, put up a sign, "No smoking aft of the headstay."

Second, if you or your guests have a tendency to get queasy, try living on board at anchor for a few days before you head for sea. There always is a slight motion afloat and this seems to help you get acclimatized. People who live on board constantly suffer less when they head to sea.

Third, rest well before you set off. I know now that my first real bout of seasickness was brought on by too many farewell parties and an excitement-induced sleepless night before our departure. At sea, get all the rest you can. Your body will cope with weather changes better and mentally you'll be less annoyed if some queasiness does occur.

Fourth, if you happen to be in charge of cooking, prepare enough meals for two or three days *before* you leave port or, if you are on a long passage, when it is calm. I always make up a pot of stew or spaghetti and sauce or a really thick soup in an eight-quart pot. I mix sandwich fillings and bake fresh bread before each long passage. Then, once we set off, I don't have to put up with the unsettling smells of cooking if it's rough. And if I do get seasick, I don't have to worry for Larry can turn a fire on under the pot of soup or stew and scoop a bowlful for himself. If you have prepared several meals beforehand and you don't get seasick, you end up with a bit of extra free time at sea to sunbath or to read a good book.

Fifth, once you are under way in a rough sea, avoid going into either the forepeak or the engine room. The motion is more pronounced in these parts of the boat. Also, if possible avoid using an enclosed toilet. Head areas are rarely ventilated well enough and the odors multiply when you are in a seaway. Instead use the lee rail or try a bucket with a secure lid if it's really rough. This is very important and even fishermen and seamen on small commercial ships prefer not to use a cramped enclosed head (which probably will be located in a bad spot anyway).

Sixth, keep warm, active and stay out in the fresh air. Because seasickness is partially psychological in many cases, if you put on your foul-weather gear, get out on deck and actually join in the sailing of the boat, you won't have as much time to think about the motion. Very few people who sail dinghies get seasick; they are just too busy.

Seventh, on a very hot still day try to keep cool. It's amazing how many people become upset on glassy calm days when the sails are slatting. Finding some shade, pouring sea-water over yourself or drinking a cool glass of juice will prevent this.

Eighth, if you do become ill, try drinking some sweet fruit juice such as well-chilled apricot or peach nectar. This seems to settle well and provides almost all of the nutrition necessary to keep you from becoming weak or dehydrated.

Ninth, in really bad conditions, if a crew is very seasick try changing the motion of the boat by easing the sheets a bit and reaching, running, or even heaving-to. We know one tough-looking six-footer who becomes as weak as a baby as soon as the sheets are hauled in hard. He lies in his bunk until the sheets are eased. Then he makes up for lost time — and food. He just can't take the motion of being hard on the wind in anything more than 12 knots or so. But, he loves sailing and going places so much that he is willing to put up with the inconvenience.

Finally, if you have a first-time sailor on board and she or he becomes seasick, don't discourage him/her from sailing. One of our best friends spent years learning about boats and building beautiful dinghies which he sold with an aim toward some day having his own yacht. Then he was asked to crew on a 40-foot hot racing machine and, excitedly, he accepted. In 20-knot winds he became helpless. The regular crew of the boat teased him and he never again went sailing. It's rather sad because he would have made a good sailor with his quick mind and strong frame. But in his mind sailing wasn't worth the discomfort and ridicule.

I think that is one of the big secrets: you have to *want* to sail and cruise so much that you'll put up with one or two days of discomfort for the reward of new ports and new people.

Normally, few people stay seasick for more than two or three days except in the most extreme storm conditions. I did hear of one person who reported she was seasick the whole way across the Atlantic. But it turned out she was suffering not from seasickness but from a problem that can be caused by seasickness. I learned about this when I spoke to Dr. Isola, the port doctor in Gibraltar. He told me that in the past two years he has had to assist in the delivery of nine unplanned babies conceived by cruising people who were using the pill.

As Dr. Isola explained it, an oral contraceptive must stay in your stomach for four to eight hours to spread into your bloodstream effectively. He advises that if you want to be sure of not getting pregnant, use other means of contraception if you have been seasick for more than a day. Pregnancy in its second and third month will cause almost the same symptoms as seasickness, and that was what our friend on her transatlantic voyage was suffering from.

No one enjoys being seasick. But for most of us it is an integral part of going to sea. However, the discomfort is quickly forgotten the minute you reach a new port or sail out of a storm into beautiful weather.

Grooming While Cruising

Handy ways to keep clean and fresh Jane Silverman

Happiness is a hot bath! Not a shower, a bath. In a tub. With scads of hot water, and bubbles, and a huge fluffy towel, and clouds of talcum, and cologne, and . . .

I've learned to live with baths or showers in the cockpit, and bathing over the side, and bird-baths in the head or galley, and showers ashore, but a real tub bath is still one of my favorite daydreams. Not that it dominates my life, but it's a nice thought to pull out and luxuriate in every once in a while.

Let's face it, living afloat, whether for a weekend or for a long cruise, simply does involve some degree of "roughing it." In exchange for the freedoms and pleasures of sailing, you do sacrifice some of the conveniences you have in a house. And old man weather can conspire against even the best-planned trip, so that all hands feel lucky if they're able to get warm and dry once in a while, never mind having smooth hands, or smelling good.

But during the seven years we've been living afloat my husband and I have discovered a number of tricks that help us maintain a comfortable level of cleanliness and good grooming without a lot of gadgetry. Maybe all our ideas won't suit you, but perhaps one or another of them will provide a starting point as you think about how to cope with some problem on your boat.

From my own experience, I'd say the first step to good grooming on a boat is simply making up your mind to it — deciding you will not succumb to the temptation to let yourself go all to seed, merely because keeping decent requires adjusting to different routines from those you're used to at home. From there on, it's a matter of learning to make the most of the resources at hand, and this can be fun.

Perhaps the question of bathing is a good place to begin. Whether or not a boat has a shower is not really the key problem. The true limiting factor is the water supply. Trying to take a shower with a teacupful of water can be so tantalizing it's almost worse than none at all. But unless we're talking about really big yachts, not many sailboats are able to carry enough fresh water to provide for satisfying daily showers for everyone aboard, except on very short cruises. At sea, though, or in harbors where the water is clean, your boat is floating in the world's largest bathtub. All you need for a good bath is a bucket, some liquid detergent, and your rubber duck!

Is it possible to use salt water, which is pretty harsh and drying, and *not* end up with hair like an old broom and prune-like skin? Well, that's where some of our tricks come in. Adding fabric softener to sea water makes it less harsh, and makes it smell nice too. You use from a capful or two to a quarter of a cup per bucket. Put it in every bucketful you scoop up, or only in the one you use for rinsing.

Liquid detergent makes fine salt-water soap, but you won't need a laundry detergent formulated for getting ground-in dirt out of jeans. Choose one of those dishwashing liquids that's supposed to be kind to hands — it will be kinder to the rest of you as well.

For washing your hair, any detergent-based shampoo will work fine in salt water. Add the fabric softener, and end up with creme rinse or conditioner just as you would when using fresh water.

If you can't spare *any* fresh water, towel vigorously immediately, before the salt has a chance to dry and cake. We do use a little fresh water. After we've gotten rid of the dirt with sea water, we have a final rinse with a little fresh to get rid of the salt. If we're too far away from the nearest faucet to spare water for an all-over rinse, we concentrate on key areas, like face and bottom. We also use a cupful or two for a final rinse when we shampoo.

Men who aren't comfortable growing a beard and thereby eliminating the shaving problem altogether, probably will want to use fresh water to shave. My husband's shaving routine is the same on a passage as it is at any other time, except that he's a little more frugal with the water. I've found that I can use sea water for shaving my legs and underarms if I use shaving foam rather than soapsuds. Leg skin isn't so sensitive as facial skin, and I don't have to shave every day or two. Salt water is hard on razor blades, though, so you have to carry a few extra. Don't forget to use only stainless blades.

We have found the best substitute for a built-in shower is an insecticide sprayer (Fig. 1). They come in plastic or metal (obviously the plastic will be more satisfactory on a boat) and most hold about two gallons of water. You put in the water, pump for the specified number of strokes, and the water is dispensed in a fine spray when you squeeze the handle on the nozzle. It's amazing how much mileage you can get from those two gallons. We use ours primarily for that final freshwater rinse, but have met a couple who used their sprayer for all baths and hair washing. Though their new boat came with the grating and holding tank for a shower, they were so happy with the sprayer they never bothered to go to the trouble and expense of having the rest of the shower apparatus put in.

We keep our fresh water for bathing in a couple of jerry cans on the deck, or in a cockpit locker. It's easier having it up there handy in the place where we do most of our bathing. Pouring from the jerry can also takes less effort than using the pump in the head or galley. It's easy to see how much water we're using and to ration ourselves if necessary. And when the jerry can is lashed somewhere on deck, the sun makes a dandy water heater.

Saltwater sores, pimples, and fungal infections can produce anything from

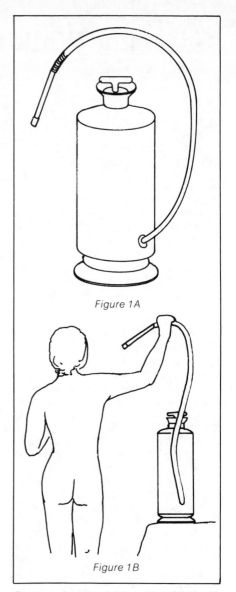

Figure 1A

Figure 1B

Figure 1: An insecticide sprayer filled with fresh water can make a very useful and easy to stow shower arrangement

mild annoyance to near-agony and can be almost impossible to clear up while under way. Worst, they always seem to appear on one's backside. Believe me, you'll never realize how much of your time on a sailboat is spent sitting until you can't do it comfortably. The first line of defense against these problems is prevention. Keep your bottom as clean and dry as possible, washing, or at least rinsing every day with fresh water, drying thoroughly, and perhaps using a touch of powder. Whatever you have to do in economizing on other clothing because of money or space, try to carry enough underwear so that you can change every day.

"Sit test" underclothes and bathing-suit bottoms before you decide which ones to take. There should be no seams to chafe in crucial places and leg elastics should be snug enough to prevent riding up, but loose enough so they don't cut off circulation. I like cotton fabric best, or at least a cotton lining in the crotch. The very stretchy nylon pants with no seams are my second choice.

If you're susceptible to athlete's foot, you already know what you're supposed to do to prevent it—keep your feet clean and dry, be especially careful in drying between your toes, and wear clean socks every day. It's not a bad idea to include anti-fungal cream and powder in your medicine chest. Tinaderm and Tinactin creams are good; Mycolog is very high-powered and should be saved for conditions which won't respond to milder measures.

Most people agree that hot food and rest are important in dirty weather. But really, grooming measures are important too. When a boat is closed up tight around several unwashed bodies, it doesn't take long for the cabin to begin smelling like a laundry bag full of dirty socks. While this may make going on watch a relatively pleasant prospect, it considerably reduces the feeling of the cabin's being a cozy refuge! A squirt of air freshener (unscented!) now and then doesn't hurt, but better yet, try to see to it that all hands pay at least some attention to personal anti-smell measures—deodorant, talcum, an occasional change of socks. You have to grin and bear some things, sure, but the grinning part comes more readily if the bearing part is kept to the lowest possible level.

You may not feel like trying to wash when the boat is leaping around in nasty seas, but the following routine can give you an adequate clean-up job: use cleansing cream for face, neck, ears and hands; brush teeth; comb hair; reach up under your shirt to apply a new layer of deodorant; and dump some talcum down inside the thermals. If you're agile enough to be sailing, you can manage this whole procedure without taking off any more than your outermost top layer. If you *can* strip and change your underwear and socks, and wash before using the deodorant and talcum, so much the better.

I have mentioned cleansing cream. This has become one of the most highly valued items in my good-grooming kit at sea. I first started using it because it seemed like a good way to be stingy with our fresh water, but soon discovered it has other real advantages. It does an unbelievably good job of removing caked-on salt spray and it leaves your skin less dry than does water. It also can be used for hands, neck, ears, even for armpits and legs if they're shaved. It doesn't splash and since it can be used anywhere in the boat you can get cleaned up a bit before leaving your bunk if you want, and don't have to wait to wash your face if the head happens to be occupied.

Cleansing cream also solved a problem I used to have with my hands. Whenever we'd make a passage of more than a few days, I'd get nasty-looking grime embedded in the webs at the base of my fingers and along the edge of my palms. I never did figure out just what caused this but whatever it was, "washing" my hands with cleansing cream or lotion a couple of times a day prevents it.

A word about hair. I've found that mine stays remarkably soft with sea-water shampoos since I've taken up the fabric softener, creme rinse, and final-freshwater-rinse routine. For those times when I can't shampoo just when I'd like to, bits of cotton stuffed between the rows of bristles on my brush help to get out a lot of dirt. Besides cleanliness, another basic aid in avoiding the old-broom look is to get a good haircut. Tell your hairdresser you need a style that can be blown around and still look decent with minimum care. If you wear your hair long, a good cut still helps, and you'll want some bands or scarves for controlling it. Long hair can tie itself into dreadful snarls if it is left free in the wind. And having hair whipped into your face can really hurt.

Clothes also play a part in achieving comfortable good grooming. Even in the tropics you're not likely to want to go topless and bottomless *all* the time. The same basic criteria apply both to sailing clothes and to the ones you'll take to wear ashore. They should be easy to care for and stow, be suitable for the weather conditions you expect, have enough style (or at least color) so they're good for your morale rather than depressing, and of course, be comfortable. If you're sailing in cold weather, remember that several light layers will be warmer than one heavy one. Layering also makes it easier to adjust to changes in temperature. For warm weather, beside your bathing

suits you'll want some lightweight loose-fitting things for covering up when you've had enough sun. And have something warm for cool-to-cold night watches.

Having an outfit that is fit to wear ashore when you reach your destination first depends on how wisely you choose those clothes, then on how carefully you stow them. Dacron knits travel very well. Some Dacron and cotton fabrics are quite wrinkle-resistant, and tightly-woven woolens also are good at retaining their shape. I suggest that you pick out your entire outfit, everything from the skin out, before you ever leave home.

For proper stowing, lay all your clothes out with the largest item on the bottom. Put things that can wrinkle, like underclothes, along any fold line. Then carefully roll them all up together and put the resulting bundle inside a pillow case or plastic bag to keep them dry. Or you can lay your things out on a piece of canvas or a big towel so that when you've rolled them up a protective covering is built right in. Tying a couple of strings around your bundle

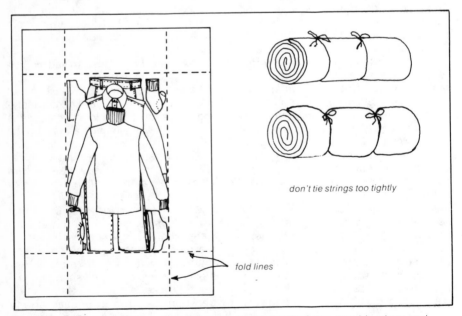

don't tie strings too tightly

fold lines

Figure 2: Arranging clothes so that they don't get crushed can provide clean and unrumpled garments when it is time to go ashore

will keep it neat, but don't tie it too tightly (Fig. 2). Stow in a dry, out-of-the-way spot such as the back of a locker or the bottom of your sea bag. If possible it's good to open your bundle a little before you reach port so you can air out any mustiness that may have developed.

Once you've devised good grooming routines that work for you on your boat, you'll probably forget that, by many people's standards, you are "roughing it." After all, while we sailors daydream about a real bath as we slog along in squally weather, those folks who'd consider a seawater bath too primitive are probably sitting in their hot tubs dreaming about the very bay with the palm-fringed beach we're going to anchor in at the end of our slog. Personally, I'm happy to keep the hot tub in my dream, and have the beautiful bays and interesting harbors my reality!

Methods

The Seamanlike Way

Use the elements instead of battling them   John Mellor

How **often have** you struggled like an idiot on some foredeck in a howling gale, up to your eyebrows in foaming water as you try to change headsails with your boat hammering along to windward, the skipper clocking up miles with the intensity of a stamp collector in a post office?

I spent most of my early deep-water days doing just that, and no matter how hard I tried to convince myself that this was what being a sailor was all about, I failed dismally. Somewhere in my nautically-indoctrinated brain was a little voice that kept saying: Don't be silly. It's wet, cold, uncomfortable, tiring, miserable, and, just for the sake of saving half a mile or so, utterly unnecessary. I grew to agree with that little voice, but it was quite a long time before I realized that there were other ways of doing these things.

It was only after a few months as a delivery skipper, with the sheer boredom and loss of interest in sailing that life can generate, that the last dregs of romance attached to struggling with recalcitrant sails on wet and windy foredecks finally died an irretrievable death. It was only then that I set about finding pleasanter ways of carrying out these jobs.

It occurred to me that changing headsails was always more pleasant and comfortable when sailing down wind; especially when the helmsman sailed a little by the lee so that the foredeck and headsails were sheltered by the mainsail. I know this sounds easy, but in my experience I have come across very few people who do this. By "this" I mean running right off downwind, even when beating, in order to change headsails when conditions are heavy.

You might lose a mile or two, but what's that to a cruising man when weighed against stable, dry and comfortable conditions, all of which go a long way towards combatting the greatest bugbears of any cruising sailor — seasickness, tiredness and cold, bugbears that to a short-handed cruising man, sailing perhaps with only his wife and family, can become literally fatal. At best they can ruin his holiday.

I no longer can remember the last time I got wet changing a jib, and I don't envisage any time in the future when I willingly shall do so. Once you experienced the sheer, unadulterated luxury of working on a stable, dry foredeck, sheltered from the wind, while changing down to a storm jib in a rising gale, you'll know what I mean.

Once I stood on the foredeck of a 50-footer in jeans, T-shirt and slippers and had a smoke and a chat with the foredeck hands as they changed sails in a full and rising Force 7 in the middle of the English Channel. The job took five minutes and no one wore oilskins or seaboots. We were headed into the teeth of the blow at the time, and the trip ultimately took us 43 hours. The beneficial effect on morale of changing jibs in that manner earned me a considerable quantity of free beer when we got to port.

So next time you want to reduce your forward canvas in rising, blustery conditions, get the new sail ready down below, then run the ship off dead before the wind. Don your carpet slippers and change the sail with little more effort than would be required alongside a dock. Try to run her off very slightly by the lee so that the foredeck is completely shel-

Figure 1
A headsail blanketed by
the main is easy to lower

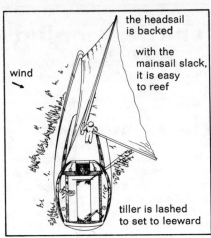

Figure 2
An easy way to reef when
sailing shorthanded

tered behind the main (Fig. 1).

Running off downwind to produce easy, sheltered conditions on the foredeck applies, of course, to any situation where you have to work on deck in rough weather, but it applies particularly when you have to go forward. The one time it doesn't apply, unfortunately, is when you need to reef the main, unless you have an intelligently worked-out slab-reefing system. I have roller-reefed mainsails while running but have never found the situation very satisfactory, even after you put aside the danger of tearing the sail in such a maneuver.

I have found that the best solution here is simply to heave to. Then you can do the job quickly and efficiently in relative comfort and safety. If you're on the wind, just put the boat about without releasing the jib sheet. Then let the mainsheet right off so the sail can find its own position; and lash the tiller to leeward.

This is the basic principle: namely, to allow the backed jib, the tiller, and the slack mainsail to balance each other and hold the boat in equilibrium (Fig. 2). The actual adjustment of tiller and sails will vary with the individual boat. Set her up so that the boat sits quietly with the wind

forward of the beam, and is moving forward through the water as slowly as possible. You will be surprised at how stable a working platform you will have.

While on the subject of heaving to, there are many other times when this maneuver can be useful. Imagine yourself driving the car with family and picnic aboard, down winding roads through a pretty country area. Lunch time comes. What do you do? Of course you stop, find an attractive parking spot with a view, and sit down for a long and leisurely lunch.

What normally happens on a boat? Everyone gathers around in the cockpit, trips over one another and passes around plates and food that are promptly sat upon or trodden on by the helmsman as he desperately tries to peer through the throng to see where he is going. If it's raining, of course, everyone stays below and leaves the helmsman stoically clutching the tiller and a rain-soaked lettuce sandwich while the rest dive into their salads. The net result of all this is that everyone, particularly the helmsman, gets chronic indigestion.

Why not heave to and relax? The boat will look after herself and you can all have a peaceful lunch.

Let's assume you are approaching a strange harbor rather too quickly for your peace of mind and you are having difficulty identifying the necessary marks. Everyone is beginning to panic, rushing back and forth from chart to tiller and back to sailing directions. Rocks may begin to loom up on all sides.

Relax. Heave to while you are still in safe waters and take your time sorting out the approach. Get it all worked out exactly ahead of time with all the marks positively identified. Then sail in, taking your own good time, confidently and in a seamanlike manner.

You can also heave to for a rest, especially when sailing short-handed. If you are alone in the cockpit at night and there are only two of you aboard, you might find yourself nodding off. Heave to for five minutes and go below for a warm-up and a brew-up. You'll be amazed how much better and refreshed you feel. Have a look at the chart while you are there, and see how you are progressing. Ten minutes later you'll return to the tiller a new man. Don't forget to keep a lookout though. Ten minutes is too long to go without checking the horizon.

I remember once being struck by an incredible hailstorm just off Guernsey in the Channel Islands. Hail the size of marbles was hammering on the deck. We had just hove to and put the kettle on. We simply remained below until it passed over. So simple and so effective.

The watchword in all this is *seamanlike*. The seamanlike way of doing things is invariably the easiest and most comfortable. The *seamanlike* thing to do when you are alone in the cockpit and in danger of falling asleep is to heave to for a cup of tea. It is *seamanlike* to heave to off a strange harbor while you get your bearings. It is *seamanlike* to heave to for reefing in bad weather, to run off before the wind when changing jibs, and so on.

Take a new look at things — take it easy at sea. Difficulties come along soon enough without creating unnecessary ones, and it is vital to keep your strength and morale as high as possible all the time you are at sea. Then, if trouble should strike, you would be in good shape to deal with it. Remember, any fool can battle with the elements, but it takes a seaman to use them.

Getting Unstuck

The intelligent response to being stranded   Lindy Lindquist

If you own a 14′ skiff and run aground, you can simply get out and push her into deeper water. However, if you own a boat of, say, 25′ or more, or hope to, then the "push" method of re-floating is no longer going to suffice. Therefore you may be interested in learning little known methods used by experts at this sort of thing — the marine salvage companies.

First aid to a stranded boat, if promptly and properly applied, prevents damage and can often save a total loss. When a stranding is not serious, it will result in getting afloat before outside assistance is either needed or called. Principles behind application of this first aid are the same whether the boat is 25′ or 1200′.

The cardinal rule in *all* strandings, regardless of how slight the danger may seem at the time, is GET THE ANCHORS OUT IMMEDIATELY!

The effect of swells and tides upon any craft aground is always to force her higher, or harder aground. Should the stranding occur on an exposed coast, movement can be very rapid indeed. It is imperative this movement be stopped quickly.

Equally important is that the boat be held end-on to the swell and not allowed to swing broadside, particularly with deep keel sailboats. If you are unfortunate enough to ground in a surf line and the boat is allowed to swing broadside, it will be difficult if not impossible to change her attitude, making the chance of saving her far more remote.

Most strandings occur bow-on, allowing the engine to be used. If the first application of full power fails to back her off, however, there is a 98% chance further engine use alone will never get her off. Moreover, the engine's cooling water intake may suck sand from the bottom and cause overheating. That engine will be needed later, don't burn it up.

Apply only enough power to hold the boat's position, i.e., stern toward deep water, while an anchor is quickly run out. An engine cannot prevent a boat from being driven further ashore.

If two anchors are carried the heaviest, or "bower" should be floated by means of the dinghy as far astern as possible. If there is an on-shore wind, the second anchor should be placed well to windward — but not over four points (45 degrees) off the stern. Assuming the boat is aground bow-on, do not attempt turning her. Take strain on the ground tackle from the stern in order to haul her straight off, stern first.

The initial thought in a stranding is usually to obtain a tow. There are three important reasons why this is not advisable. First, while waiting for a tow the boat is constantly being driven by wind, surf, or tide to higher ground. If she goes high enough, it may be found impossible to haul her off.

Secondly, if a boat willing to tow you arrives, the force she can exert is very small, no matter what amount of horsepower she may have, compared to the power of your own anchors. The reason for this is simple. Pull on a stranded vessel is most effective when she is nearest to being afloat, as when partially lifted by a swell.

Since the towing boat is subjected to the same swell at nearly the same time, her power is nearly all used to overcome swell effects upon herself. Consequently her towing power is at its minimum. When the towing boat recovers full pulling power the stranded boat has lost lift given by the swell and the moment at which she can be moved has passed.

This fact seems virtually unrecognized, even by shipmasters. Furthermore, the towing boat is unable to maintain the steady, efficient strain essential to success. By sudden, uneven jerks, a towing boat is more apt to pull the cleats out of a yacht's deck or part the towline than to be of any real service.

Conversely, pulling power of the stranded vessel's anchors is not affected by surge or swell, but is continuous. It is available with full efficiency when the boat is lifted sufficiently to make movement possible. If strain on the anchors is greater than the sea's pressure, she must move in the direction of her anchors.

The third disadvantage to a tow is that this can lead to a salvage claim — on the strength of the tow line being passed and accepted — even though the real work of refloating was likely done by a yacht's own anchors and the towing boat was of little, if any value other than moral support.

Intelligent use of tide and swell must be made to work for, rather than against you. When a boat strands in an area where significant tidal range exists the skipper must make all possible use of it and not attempt to haul off by main force at an inappropriate time. This latter can result in parting the anchor cables or loss of the anchors. If the tide is rising but the boat cannot immediately be re-floated, efforts in this direction should be stopped until the tide is at a higher stage, while anchors hold her in position.

Meanwhile, whether the tide is rising or falling, it is important the boat rest quietly on the bottom or serious damage may result from pounding. This can best be accomplished by borrowing a tactic used by salvage companies for years: pumping or letting water *into* the boat to hold her down.

The fastest way to do this is disconnect the "head" intake and discharge piping at the thru-hull fittings and open the seacocks. Needless to say, as soon as the yacht stops pounding, close the seacocks.

Then, just before high tide, the heaviest possible strain should be taken on the anchor cables and the engine brought into use; while at the same time the boat is pumped dry and heavy articles jettisoned if necessary. The boat must *not* be lightened under any circumstances until the anchor cables have a heavy strain on them. Otherwise the swell will overpower the relatively ineffective engine and the yacht, her draft reduced, will be driven harder aground.

At high tide draft reduction will be of greatest concern. There are several ways to accomplish this. In sailing yachts it is often advantageous to move the crew as far forward as possible, or swing out the main boom 90° and send a crewman or two out on it to induce heel and thereby reduce draft.

In extreme cases a third anchor can be placed abeam and the cable taken to the mast truck to heave her down. However, this requires continual moving of the third anchor as the yacht is pulled toward deeper water and is of little practical use except with very large sailing craft. If wind is fresh and more or less abeam, setting the main sail and sheeting it flat will also help lay the boat down.

For motor yachts, move crew and heavy articles either well forward or aft — depending upon which end of the boat draws the least. Boats carrying great amounts of fuel and water can reduce the draft, often by quite a bit, by offloading them. However, emptying tanks filled with gasoline is not recommended for it greatly increases the fire hazard.

It is not the purpose of this article to urge that *assistance* of other boats should in all cases be refused. When assistance can be of value it should be used. An assisting boat may help in getting out the heaviest anchor, in standing by to remove crew if this becomes necessary, or helping once the stranded yacht has been re-floated. But the most important use to be made of an assisting vessel is that demonstrated by salvage companies, a trick which shall be explained in a moment.

It is a prevalent but mistaken notion that salvage companies maintain huge tugs for the sole purpose of *towing* stranded ships off the beach. Actually, successful work accomplished by these companies is due to their use of anchors and cables, intelligent use of tides and swell, and very little else. The principles which apply to all craft, regardless of their size, and on which these firms work, are identical with those already outlined.

The tugs are used for various purposes: carrying men and equipment to the stranding, placing anchors (and their subsequent recovery), helping the vessel after she has been re-floated, and occasionally towing her to port — but *never* off the beach. Salvage is accomplished, and here's the trick, in the following manner by which the *greatest effective pulling power is obtained.*

The tug is anchored out as far as possible in deep water and astern of the stranded ship. She then backs down, veering her own cables as she goes, until she can pass or float a towing line to the stranded ship. When this is done the slack is taken out of the tug's anchor cables as well as the towing cable and the procedure previously mentioned is followed, but with the power from the stranded ship's anchors *and* the anchors of the tug giving a tremendous continuous strain.

The tug's engine is rarely used at all, and if so, is run very slowly so propeller wash does not hinder the operation.

At the business of getting unstuck salvage people are expert, and this is one time when big ship prin-ciples can be applied to little ships whether they are grounded on the coast or in a lake. So if you run aground and a well meaning fellow boating enthusiast wants to "rescue" you, consider applying these methods and keep the cleats aboard.

Moreover, after first taking the precaution of obtaining a salvage waiver, the method just described can be put into service by *any* yacht, power or sail, and in the case of the latter, whether she is equipped with an engine or not!

Obviously, since they are so necessary in a stranding, anchors should never be considered sea-going equipment only. Indeed, they may be the only way to free a boat grounded in a lake or river where tides do not exist.

Many lives and boats are lost each year in strandings. Regrettably, the majority of yachtsmen seem inclined to dash for the radiotelephone under such circumstances and shout "Mayday" in the direction of the Coast Guard.

By first taking action, with a little effort and no danger to life and limb, one can get himself back afloat and thereby experience the satisfaction which comes with consummate seamanship. In most cases, however, nothing is done save waiting for the Coast Guard who, by the time they reach the stricken boat, often find her position hopeless.

By then lives of the vessel's crew may also be in danger. Removal of the crew is the Coast Guard's first concern, but by the time this is completed the vessel may be a needless total loss.

The various situations in which a stranded boat may find herself are almost limitless. In general it can be said that if her skipper follows basic principles outlined herein — with variations as may be applicable to his particular circumstances — it is quite likely re-floating can be accomplished or, if help is obtained, it can be successfully rendered the yacht by the Coast Guard or others.

Like the master of an ocean liner,

the skipper of any small boat has an obligation to her safe navigation and to the lives of her crew. If trouble comes he must use all the resourcefulness and seamanship at his command. He must not *rely* on the Coast Guard — or anyone else. He must rely *first and only* upon himself. Only then can he be called a seaman.

Proper Anchoring Methods

Techniques for staying put

John Mellor

Good anchoring technique is perhaps one of the most important requirements of a seaman. In bad weather in a not-too-well-sheltered harbor, it is going to be of paramount importance.

In quiet weather, in a well-sheltered anchorage, you can throw any old thing over the front end of a boat and claim to be anchored. When it is blowing hard down an open reach of water with perhaps a strong tide against the wind, it is a very different situation. The slightest weakness in your anchoring technique will be cruelly uncovered, possibly to the accompaniment of a lot of very expensive noises.

There are various ways of improving your situation when you are anchored in adverse weather. But before I go into them, let us consider the simple, basic business of just anchoring. For unless your boat is properly anchored to

begin with, all the hurricane hawses, sliding weights and everything else will be useless. The vast majority of dragging anchors are caused simply by faulty anchoring.

So, what do I mean by anchoring properly? I mean quite simply, laying out the anchor and rode so that they lie in a nice straight line away from the ship, that the anchor itself is firmly dug into the bottom, and that the rode is long enough so that the pull it exerts on the anchor is always horizontally along the seabed. If this is done properly with a decent size of rode, it will have to blow very hard indeed before any extra measures have to be taken to prevent your dragging.

Dragging in heavy weather, in fact, generally is caused by the boat's lying back so hard on her rode that an excessive amount of it is hauled up off the seabed, thus putting more strain on

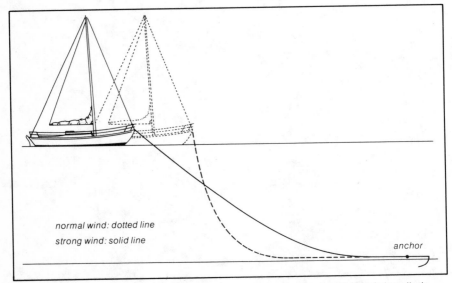

normal wind: dotted line
strong wind: solid line

anchor

Figure 1: Dragging in heavy weather is often caused when large amount of rode is pulled off bottom putting more strain on anchor

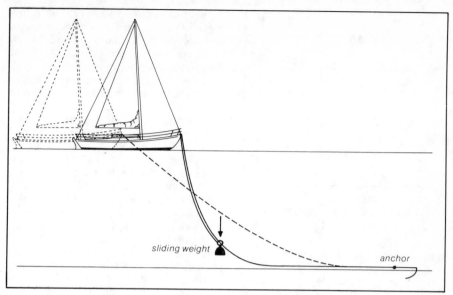

Figure 2: With sliding weight on anchor rode, angle to anchor is reduced

the anchor itself (Fig. 1). The rode then is said to grow on a very long stay. The remedy is simply the opposite of the cause. You must get more weight back onto the seabed between boat and anchor in order to take some of the strain off the latter. With chain, this can be done quite simply just by letting more out. It can also be done (and this is my personal preference) by sliding a weight down in order to reduce the catenary and thus put more chain down on the bottom (Fig. 2).

There are considerable advantages to this technique, particularly if you are using nylon for the anchor rode. Veering miles and miles of nylon to try to prevent dragging is the original "lost cause." The great danger with nylon, unless you have a considerable length of chain leader between the nylon and anchor, is the possibility of lying back so hard that any horizontal pull on the anchor is lost altogether. The anchor will then, very neatly, weigh itself. It can be most embarrassing!

Lowering a weight down the rode will solve this problem very neatly. It will also act as an effective shock absorber, rising and falling to the pitching of the boat and preventing that pitching

from being transmitted directly to the anchor.

In all but the worst conditions, this little device, combined with a careful basic anchoring technique, should solve all your dragging problems. The device can be made quite easily from an old pig of ballast with a hole in it, through which you thread a strap to hang over the cable. Also good, manufactured ones with a well-designed chafe-free slider are available and they are well worth investing in. Using such a device has an advantage over letting out more rode because it does not increase the length of the rode and therefore your swinging circle. In fact, if anything, it will reduce the circle, a most important consideration in a crowded anchorage with a shifting wind or turning tide.

In really dire conditions, an open lee shore, hurricane, etc., something more is needed. The traditional technique is the hurricane hawse shown in Figure 3. Two anchors are laid out separately, one off each bow at a fairly good angle. Thus the strain is shared equally by the two anchors and cables. If you still are dragging, the situation can be alleviated by powering up into the bight of

223

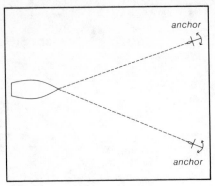

Figure 3: A standard way to anchor when there is a good chance of very high winds

second anchor to the chain a few fathoms back from the main anchor.

Clearly, the theory behind this is sound. The danger lies not in parting the chain (almost unheard of with modern materials), but simply in dragging the anchors along the bottom. With two anchors in line on the same chain, each one must be tremendously effective in reducing the strain on the other. The man in question, whose name escapes me, absolutely swore by it and claimed that he had never dragged once, and would happily lie on a completely open lee shore in a gale!

I have used this method on a few occasions, although not in such hair-raising circumstances, and it certainly seems to be effective. It is also beautifully simple; it creates no problems when the wind shifts, no problems in laying out, no problems in recovery, and it leaves you with twice the amount of chain you can let out should it prove necessary.

You can also shackle on any number of anchors you like, each one digging firmly into the bottom a few fathoms along from the previous one. Its simplicity is such that you could happily use it in borderline situations in a busy anchorage where you would hesitate to go to the steps required in a full hurri-

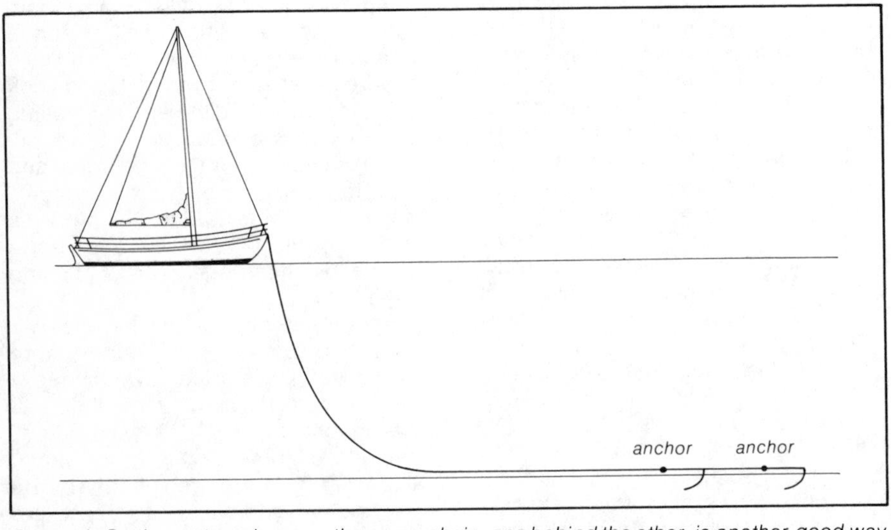

the cables, thus reducing the weight on them.

However, for my money, it is a messy business laying out separate anchors, and, if you wait until the wind is blowing before you do it (which you really have to because of the swinging problem), it is not a very easy business either. I was interested therefore to read about someone who seemed to spend the best part of his time anchoring off open lee coasts around the world, in full gales without ever dragging. What he did was to lay out his anchors in tandem *on the same chain*, shackling the

Figure 4: Putting out anchors on the same chain, one behind the other, is another good way to ride out strong winds

cane moor. You could also slide a weight down the cable to further reduce snatching. It is a very flexible system (Fig. 4).

The second big problem you face when anchored in strong winds is that of yawing or *sailing* back and forth across the rode powered by bare poles. This has a threefold deleterious effect. The constant snubbing, as you come to the end of each yaw, puts extra strain on the rode and mooring gear. It also makes life rather uncomfortable below, and you might collide with a nearby boat that is yawing in the opposite direction.

How do you prevent this? A weight slid down the rode will reduce it somewhat, but there are two other much better ways if the risk is still too bad for peace of mind. One way is to drop your second anchor at the end of a yaw. This is especially useful if there is danger, in the form of a boat moored nearby or shallow water on one side— with the other side clear.

In a case like this you would drop the second anchor at the end of the yaw *away from the danger*, then let out the rode on that second anchor until you return to the central position. The second anchor then prevents you from yawing toward the side of danger (Fig. 5).

If danger is equally close on both sides or if you are concerned with strain on the ground tackle and general discomfort, there is another method you can use. I personally prefer it for I feel it is more effective at generally damping down the violence of the yawing. All you do is drop a second anchor, or any heavy weight for that matter, in case you happen to have the second anchor already on the main rode underfoot. Veer just enough chain or nylon to ensure that the anchor or weight stays on the bottom. Then, whenever the boat yaws off to one side or the other she finds that she has to drag the anchor or weight and the rode with her along the bottom. This reduces the yawing considerably, and at the same time damps down the violence of the snubbing at the end of each yaw.

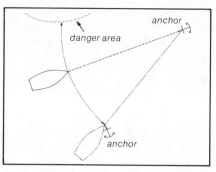

Figure 5: To avoid yawing toward a danger area, wait until boat has swung all the way away from danger, is at end of yaw; then drop anchor

So you can see that this anchoring business, as with so many aspects of sailing, is largely a matter of *common sense*. Thinking ahead about the basic principles involved is a far more profitable occupation than merely slavishly copying something read in a book. More mistakes are made by people who can quote the various seamanship manuals backwards simply because they do not *understand* what they are doing!

Never just glibly throw your anchors around as if they were going out of fashion. Think about what they will be doing and what you want them to do. Try to visualize the anchor and rode on the sea bottom so that you can assess how they will affect you. Don't be one of those people who pompously recite that the correct amount of rode to let out is 1.4 times the square root of the depth at high water in fathoms (or whatever). Unless you are anchoring a fleet of aircraft carriers the difference between that and three times the depth lies only in the difficulty of remembering it.

What *is* important is understanding how the anchor and rode work. If you know this, and take as a basic starting point a minimum rode of three times the depth at *high water* (all too often overlooked when anchoring at low water), then the rest is relatively easy.

Let's go back to the basic operation of anchoring and look at it a bit more closely.

Figure I shows how the anchor and rode should look to an inquisitive diver: a neat, direct pull, horizontally along the seabed on an anchor well dug into the bottom. Just throwing the anchor over the side and piling the chain up on top of it, on the theory that it is just all that weight down there doing the work, is worse than useless. You would be better off using a piece of clothesline and a wooden anchor. At least then you would *know* you were going to drag!

How do you achieve this ideal situation? You do it simply by letting the anchor go on the run. You don't do it when the boat is stopped, and then pay out the rode steadily as you run over or fall back on top of the anchor. If you let it go on the run and make sure, as you are laying it out, that the rode constantly leads away from you toward the anchor and not dropping vertically into the water, you will end up looking like Figure 1.

When the required amount of rode is out, you then must dig the anchor in by giving a good jerk on the rode, until you feel it bite solidly and grip. This can be done either by snubbing the rode up sharp when you have enough out, or you can use the engine to draw back on the rode until you feel the anchor grip hard. If you have a freewheeling windlass with a brake, it is easy. Never try to stop the anchor rode with bare feet or light shoes. Nylon, in particular,

running at high speed will burn you just about as efficiently as an acetylene torch.

If you are anchored efficiently, and you know how to cope if a wind blows up hard from the open end of a creek, the final thing you must think about is chafe. This very easily could be the subject of a complete article, but there is no need for it to be. If you have chain you need only concern yourself with putting a big fat fender under the bow to protect the hull if you ride up over the cable.

If you have nylon rode, things are a little different. It is *vitally* important that you protect the nylon where it passes through fairleads, etc., with some old canvas, plastic hosepipe, or old rope wrapped around it—anything that will chafe in preference to the nylon. Keep an eye on it and replace it before it chafes through and the fairlead goes to work on the nylon.

Finally, make sure the rode is secured to a very strong point on board. The weak little mooring cleats on some modern boats will be totally useless in a strong blow. Secure the rode to a strong samson post, windlass, or hefty cleat properly bolted through the deck with a good solid backing plate. If you are still in doubt, secure the line to the base of the mast. Perhaps, more than anything else, good anchoring methods are always the sign of the good seaman.

Working Aloft

How to go up and down safe and sound

Mike Macdonald

For many centuries the basic skill of seamanship was the ability to work aloft safely and efficiently. Rigs and tasks above the deck have changed greatly since the days of square riggers and gaff-headed schooners, but it is still necessary to work up the mast at sea. Whether you are racing or cruising; daysailing or making a long passage; eventually you or a member of your crew will have to go aloft.

It may be routine maintenance on a sunny afternoon or it might be an emergency in the middle of a rough night. Whatever the circumstances, placing yourself 30 to 100 feet over the deck can be the most hazardous job on a boat. Forethought and planning can greatly reduce the danger, increase comfort and efficiency, and shorten the time spent in the chair.

Who should go?

There are few sailors who really like going up the mast, for obvious reasons. When the work has to be done, the best man for the job is the lightest experienced hand. Know your own capabilities before you volunteer. If you get nosebleeds on a stepladder, are prone to motion sickness or feel uncomfortable up the mast at the dock, working aloft at sea probably isn't for you. Don't let some romantic image of old Errol Flynn movies overpower your good judgment. It's better to acknowledge limitations on deck than to endanger yourself and your shipmates by getting in trouble up the spar.

Even if you feel comfortable as a squirrel in an oak tree, mast work should never be taken lightly. Smooth teamwork between a qualified and responsible man in the bosun's chair and the crew on deck is a mark of good seamanship.

The chair

Always use a bosun's chair. It's easy climbing to the first set of spreaders, but it will be a long tiring shimmy to the mast head. The only thing preventing a fall is the strength of your grip. Bad odds any way you look at it. No skipper should ever permit an over-eager crew to monkey up to retrieve a lost halyard except on small boats in light air. Even then, the risks are great.

The standard plank bosun's chair is marginally safe in the slip, but useless at sea. There are a number of good "diaper" type chairs on the market which offer more security. The cardinal rule of mast work is: stay in the chair. A slippery plank invites an accident.

The best diaper chairs feature a wraparound design with a stiff seat sewn in. There should be a sturdy backstrap and some provision to keep the wearer from slipping out the front. If a crotch strap is not built into your chair, make one with a length of gasket or Dacron which can be tied to the back of the chair. The only acceptable design is one which will contain an unconscious man.

It is the responsibility of the person in the chair to insure that he won't come out and the chair won't release from the halyard. Inspect the halyard, especially the knot or splice on the shackle. Don't trust the holding power of a snap shackle alone. A screw-pin shackle through the thimble is the safest method of attachment. If you have to switch halyards while aloft, use the snap shackle, but tape the pin closed and back that up with a gasket tied between chair and thimble. You can't be too cautious with your own body.

A short piece of line with a carabineer (the snap fitting on a safety harness) on the bitter end is a valuable extra fitting on the chair. Use it to hook onto shrouds or belayed halyards to secure yourself. Make sure the fitting can be opened and closed with one hand (Fig. 1).

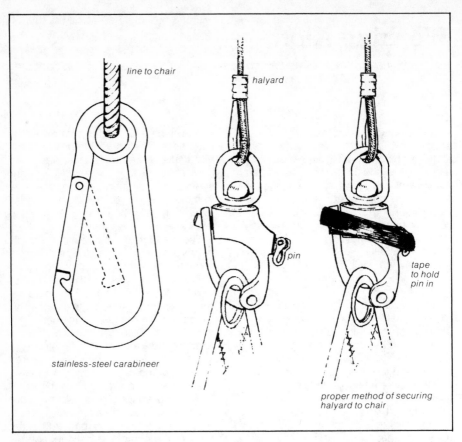

line to chair

halyard

pin

tape
to hold
pin in

stainless-steel carabineer

proper method of securing
halyard to chair

Figure 1: When you are working aloft, always have short piece of line and carabineer to hook onto a shroud or secured halyard to prevent swinging

Staying in the chair is only half the safety problem. Anything dropped from the masthead is a potential lethal missile. A canvas bucket should be tied to the chair for all tools and spare parts. Screwdrivers, hammers, wrenches and other heavy objects should be secured with lanyards.

Going aloft

Before going up the mast, the skipper or watch captain and the mastman should confer on the job to be done. Whether it is maintenance or repair, work out a plan to minimize the shouting. Whistles or prearranged hand signals may be necessary with a tall mast or lots of wind. Make sure you have all the proper tools and parts. It's easier to take it with you than to have it hoisted later. Every minute up the stick slows

the boat and tires the man, so plan ahead.

The most powerful winch available should be used to hoist the person. If mast-mounted halyard winches are not big enough or are awkward to crank, lead the tail to a cockpit winch. Use the grinders if you have them. Make certain the fairlead blocks are stout enough for the job. Some crewmen would rather hand-over-hand you up the mast. In calm weather this works with a light person, but a winch is safer, if slower.

I would rather trust a hungry shark than a reel halyard winch. It will get you up all right, but when was the brake last serviced? On some boats with a three-quarter rig, for example, the main halyard is the only way to get to the masthead. Make sure a strong man, preferably a close friend or relative, lowers you with a handle. Never use a reel halyard winch if a regular action winch is at hand.

One man on deck should watch the mastman at all times. On the way up and down he relays instructions to the crankers. Getting over and around shrouds, spreaders and lifts will take teamwork if the sea is lumpy.

The weather side of the mast is usually the best route up. Shrouds can be used for support and the angle of heel makes it easier to "walk" up the mast. Once past the lowers, a belayed halyard might help as a handhold. Use your feet to fend off the mast. Signal the observer when you want to slow or stop. Leave yourself enough slack to perform the necessary task.

If possible, both the observer and trailer should be men who have worked up on a mast. They will better realize the problems the man in the air has to face and how they can aid him from the deck. Even in a racing situation the observer should keep his eyes on the man aloft while the rest of the crew works the boat. It goes without saying that the tailer should double-check when he cleats the halyard. Overwrapping the winch plus two half-hitches on the cleat might seem excessive, but you'd want the same if you were at the top of the mast.

Working aloft

Simple jobs, such as inspecting, switching, or clearing halyards can be completed in a few minutes. Several consecutive spinnaker changes without a gybe in the interim will foul the halyards on themselves and the headstay. After you reach the masthead and are secured, call for the fouled halyard to be topped. Hold it away from your body with your foot; it will accelerate from the weight of the tail and the shackle might hit you. After clearing the working halyard and the headstay, clip it to the chair and have the tailer lower you. Make sure you bring it and yourself down on the proper side of the headstay, topping lift, staysail halyard and spinnaker pole.

On a long downwind leg, it may be necessary to change spinnaker halyards while the kite is flying. In a race like the Transpac, this is done at least once a day to check for chafe. If there is a free jib halyard, use it to go aloft. But if the staysail is on the jib halyard, you'll have to go aloft on the new spinnaker halyard. In this case, after reaching the top, tie yourself to the masthead with a gasket or the short line and carabineer. Remove the new halyard from the chair, hook it to the head of the spinnaker, tape the shackle and call for tension on the new halyard. When the old halyard slackens, remove and inspect it for wear. Check the shackle, knot or splice and especially the spot where it was riding in the block. If anything looks suspect, tie the halyard into the chair *above the worn spot*.

If you have to re-lead a broken internal halyard, use a leader line and weight. This is better than your trying to drop the tail of the halyard down the mast. Heavy monofilament fishing line or smooth Dacron of at least 100-

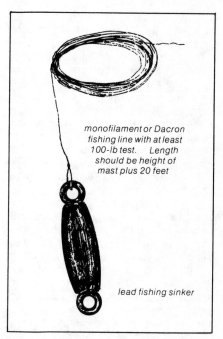

monofilament or Dacron fishing line with at least 100-lb test.   Length should be height of mast plus 20 feet

lead fishing sinker

Figure 2: Fishing line and weight are good emergency gear for releading broken internal halyard

pound test tied to an oblong fishing sinker makes an effective leader. Remember, the weight has to be small enough to fit through the mast-head sheaves. The men on deck should remove the bottom sheave box and use a bent wire coat hanger to fish the leader out of the mast (Fig. 2).

Wind guides, antennae and lights may occasionally need repairs at sea. Unless the piece of equipment is vital, don't try to do the impossible. Standing up in the chair to reach an aerial is bad enough at the dock. In a seaway, it could be the last repair you ever make.

Heavy-weather mast work

The best way to work up the spar during adverse weather is to wait until things calm down. If it's imperative to fix something when the stick is dancing, every possible aid should be given to make the volunteer's task easier.

A preserver or vest will help to protect your ribs if you slam into the mast. Slip another one over your legs to guard your thighs and groin. Sea boots will grip the mast better than shoes and will ease some of the pain when you hook your legs under the shrouds at the mast head. Wear full-fingered gloves on the trip up and down, removing them to work.

Planning and communication are doubly important when conditions are nasty. Discuss the anticipated problems and make a plan. As the person starts up the mast, the boat should be taken to that course which provides the easiest motion, usually a beam or broad reach. Don't heave-to, for boat speed and heel will reduce the snap-roll of the mast. The best helmsman aboard should have the wheel (Fig. 3).

If you are the lucky fellow in the chair, don't try to hang onto the upper shroud and walk up the spar. If you lose your grip on that skinny piece of rod or wire, you will crash into the mast and could injure knees, ribs or elbows. Once past the lowers, it seems best to wrap one leg around the mast and drag the other on the mainsail while hugging the mast with both arms. Work your way past the spreaders with care. Don't be timid about yelling *Stop* if you feel yourself breaking loose. Fear can be a

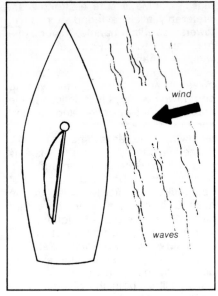

Figure 3: Proper course to steer when sending someone aloft; roll is easier to deal with than pitch

powerful amplifier of the human voice. As the boat rolls to leeward you have more control, so the crankers can raise you faster. Slow down as the boat snaps to weather.

When you are topped, wedge, wriggle and strap yourself into the most secure position you can attain. Get the job done quickly since you will be expending tremendous amounts of energy just hanging on. Don't exhaust yourself, because you still have to get down.

After re-leading an internal jib halyard broken during a storm in the 1969 La Paz Race, I lost my grip just below the top spreader on the way down. The next roll of the boat sent me flying around the headstay, crashing into the main sail on the leeward side. On the following lurch I flew back around to hit the cap shroud before banging into the mast and hanging on. This registered Force 9 on the fear scale and was an incident I don't care to repeat. A line tied to the bottom of the chair and carefully tended might have prevented this breakaway.

Night work

Before you go aloft at night, inspect the situation from the deck with the most powerful light available. Plan which halyards you will clear and which you will bring down. Any repairs should probably be left until morning. Take a small flashlight to hold in your teeth or tape a regular light to your forearm so both hands will be free. If you're helping to sort fouled halyards on deck, don't shine the big light on the person aloft. The head of the mast is no place to go night blind.

Getting up and down the stick with the job completed takes skill, team-work, strength and sometimes a lot of guts. Anticipating the expected problems and planning how to deal with them before you leave the deck will shorten time aloft and make mast work a safe, and almost ordinary sailing chore.

Provisioning for the Voyage

How to fill your boat to the brim   Lin Pardey

Buying **sufficient stores** for your voyage takes planning. But they can make the difference between pleasurable living on board and just getting there. I refrain from saying pleasant eating because "stores" include much more than food. Toilet paper, writing paper, flashlight batteries, bicarbonate of soda. All are stores and on most voyages I've been on they've been the responsibility of the cook or whoever is assigned the job of buying food.

It's obvious that running low on stores on a long ocean voyage can ruin your fun. But on a coastal cruise, at home or abroad, having proper stores on board really adds pleasure to the trip. Instead of having to spend your cruising time finding a shop to buy dinner fixings, you can spend your time touring and enjoying yourself.

Six months before we actually bought stores for our first long voyage, I kept a list of everything we bought for our house that wasn't main-course food. I kept track of the amount of salt, Worcestershire sauce, flour, soap, scouring pads and towels we used. I was surprised to find items on my list such as toothbrushes, Scotch tape, toothpicks, black mending thread, erasers and flashlight bulbs. And the survey showed a surprising amount of peanut butter consumed over the six-month period.

At the same time we started a custom we call *can night*. At least one night a week we ate a meal

It's well worth taking the time to look at prices and contents of different packages in different stores. I've found that supermarkets often have lower prices than cash and carry firms, especially on their own brands. But store brands also should be tried beforehand, for they can vary quite a bit.

Look at the ingredients and weights on different packages. A canned whole chicken is no bargain. You are paying for bone, water and skin. Three small tins of chicken meat cost about the same; they contain solid meat, and take half the space and preparation. Condensed soup gives you twice the soup for only 10% extra cost. Some freeze-dried products provide excellent results but they do take extra time, fuel and water to prepare. Try all of them beforehand.

Try the canned goods sold in stores' refrigerated section. Most keep extremely well when stowed low in the boat. Canned Brie and Camembert cheeses keep for two or three months if stowed just below 70°. If the lockers below your waterline will keep at water temperature, you can be assured of having canned, refrigerated goods last well, except of course in very tropical waters.

Economy sizes have no place on a boat. A small container of dish soap is easier to handle and easier to store; if it breaks open it makes a smaller mess. Leftovers are difficult to keep on board. A can just large enough for one meal means you can clean up the galley without trying to find a way to preserve half a cup of corn. This is especially important in the tropics where food that isn't refrigerated rarely lasts two days.

Check the different types of packaging. Cans are heavy and take more space than flexible foil packages. I buy a brand of coffee that comes in well-sealed bags, and I get sugar, flour and rice in five-lb bags and then seal them in two plastic bags, one inside the other. This way if one bag goes bad or breaks, I haven't lost my whole supply.

Once you have done your price and product research, how do you do your actual shopping? I never make a detailed list. Instead I go to the shops I've found to have the best value and buy main-course meats for the expected length of our voyage plus 50%. In other words, our boat holds stores for 60 days of offshore cruising, so I buy about 90 cans of meat products. I stock up on corned beef more than, for example, on ham because we like corned beef better. I buy at least 24 cans of stewing beef because it can be used so many different ways.

I purchase fruit, rice, powdered potatoes, flour, noodles and non-food stores for the same period. I take all this back to the boat and store it. This way I can see how much space I have left over. Then I go back to the shops and buy our luxury items to fill the empty space. Tins of nuts, canned pate, Brie cheese, candy, what we call fun foods, are what add variety to our menu as we cruise.

My final purchase is 12 complete very easy to prepare meals that I store in the most accessible place possible, meals such as hot dogs and baked beans that simply can be opened and heated in one pan. These are for those times when it's too rough for anything else. When I'm too seasick to cook, Larry knows exactly where to look for something to ward off his starvation. Then I feel a bit better about being seasick because I've done my bit when I shopped for stores.

Fresh vegetables and fruit are the last thing I buy, and I wait until the last possible day to actually pick them out. I prefer to shop at an open market for this way I can have a choice of the farmers' best and see each vegetable I'm buying.

New potatoes last virtually forever, so we buy 30 lbs for the two of us whenever our stocks get low. Onions the same. Tomatoes, purchased green, ripen slowly and can be good three or four weeks later. Lemons wrapped in foil and stored in a sealed container are good for two months. Other fresh produce is a gamble, but nice to have so I always buy some. I rarely waste it, but there have been times when we had apple fritters, apple-sauce and apple fruit salad all in one day to use up apples before they turned rotten.

Eggs are the life saver for us on long voyages. They'll keep fresh for four months if they are carefully purchased. Farm eggs, laid within four days of purchasing and never refrigerated, are what you want. I don't do anything to them once I've bought them other than store them away safely in their cartons and then turn each carton upside down every three days. Turning the eggs keeps the whole inside of the shell damp and solid. The eggs stay sealed and don't rot. We usually carry 12 to 15 dozen and in the past six years have tossed out only about six eggs. Remember to keep your plastic or paper egg cartons; most countries don't supply them free.

When the boat is full to the brim and I can't think of anything I've forgotten, I do one last thing. I take a stroll through one or two different markets and drugstores looking at each item they sell. This often perks my memory or else reassures me that we haven't forgotten anything.

Once you go foreign, shopping becomes a bit more of a challenge. Now language differences add another dimension to your problem. Arm yourself with a translating dictionary and a good cookbook that describes vegetables and foods from all parts of the world and ways to use them. Both books will be invaluable.

We've learned one very important thing about buying stores in foreign countries: canned and packaged foods are extremely expensive in less-developed countries, and in Scandinavia. In Costa Rica we could buy three lbs of beefsteak or one small can of peaches for the same price. Colombia, South America, had almost no canned foods at all. Prices in Sweden, Germany and Denmark were fantastically high, triple those of England. So, stock up at home to be sure.

When you are near a free port, check prices. As a yacht going foreign, you are eligible for the same treatment as a commercial ship. We filled up at duty-free stores in Panama and in Poland, and we ended up with top quality goods at wholesale prices.

Finally, a bit of advice that is often repeated by Larry: Over-buy. Fill the boat to the brim. Keep it full and refill it every chance you get. The food and stores never will be wasted. Prices won't come down. With extra food on board, you are free to change your plans, extend your stay, and avoid civilization for just that extra bit of time that will make your cruise a joy.

7

Improvements

Make Your Boat Safer

Preparing for an extended cruise   Edward Brewer

If this is your year to make that extended cruise, then it is time you started thinking about the boat that is going to take you there and bring you back. The sea is an unforgiving adversary and an ill prepared vessel can be an invitation to disaster.

One point to keep in mind about today's boats is that the vast majority are built to suit the average sailor and not necessarily the globe girdler. Many do not have the basic necessities of a deep sea yacht in order that they may be reasonably and competitively priced. This is not a criticism of mass production boats, for without them the joys of cruising would be limited to a very few.

Strengthening a fiberglass hull for ocean passages is not difficult as long as the interior of the hull is accessible. Where access is restricted either by joinerwork or a hull liner, it will be necessary to do some tearing out before rebuilding can commence. In any case such work is best performed with the advice of a competent yacht designer or marine surveyor, and in a yard that is experienced in fiberglass work and repairs.

Let's go over the points that an owner can inspect and, to a large extent, rectify himself to better prepare his boat for sea. Seaworthiness is the ability to keep water out of the boat and keep the crew aboard. Windows, hatches, handrails and liferails are vital components in this effort.

No production boat is fitted with window covers (shutters) or deadlights (hinged metal covers that can snap down to close off a broken portlight) yet most boats today have large and vulnerable expanses of glass in their saloon windows. These could let enormous quantities of water aboard if they were broken in heavy weather. Some of these windows are not mechanically fastened in place but just held by a rubber gasket that clips over the glass and cabin edge; they could pop out of place if a large sea fell on them. Shutters, therefore, are essential for any true seagoing yacht.

Shutters can be held in place over large windows with machine screws driven into matching plates bolted to the cabin side (figure 1). However, a slight clearance between the window and shutter to give a bit under a heavy blow without breaking the glass. On portlights, the shutters or deadlights can be fitted inside or outside by machine screws fastening into holes drilled and tapped into the metal portlight frames. Material for shutters can be either $3/8$ to $1/2''$ plywood or $1/8''$ aluminum plate. Small slits can be cut into the center to let light through. Alternately, 5/16 to $3/8''$ plexiglass can be used, but is difficult to store without scratching it.

Hatches that cannot be fastened solidly in place are another vulnerable spot. While cruising in a small auxiliary a few years ago I had the distinct displeasure of seeing the foredeck hatch drift off rapidly astern during a blow; a sound lesson in the value of having strong tie-downs. Simple eye hooks can shake loose!

While on the subject of hatches it is not amiss to point out that many modern yachts have clear plexiglass hatch and skylight tops, wonderful for light below but slippery underfoot when wet. These should have the foot gripping self-adhesive sand strip applied and the same strips

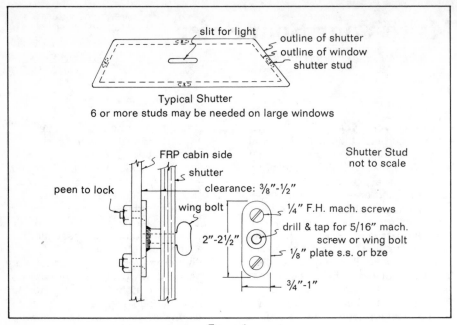

slit for light

outline of shutter
outline of window
shutter stud

Typical Shutter
6 or more studs may be needed on large windows

FRP cabin side

shutter

Shutter Stud
not to scale

peen to lock

clearance: 3/8"-1/2"

wing bolt

1/4" F.H. mach. screws

drill & tap for 5/16" mach.
screw or wing bolt

2"-2½"

1/8" plate s.s. or bze

3/4"-1"

Figure 1

should be laid down wherever there are large areas of smooth fiberglass — hatch slide covers, deck centerlines, even cockpit seats. Better to have a worn out trouser seat than a broken leg at sea!

When it comes to keeping the crew aboard, some craft fail to have adequate lifelines. They may be too low, insufficiently strong, poorly fastened or all three. It's a sure invitation to disaster. Better no life lines at all than bad ones, for they always give a psychological feeling of security that may prompt a sailor to take chances he would not otherwise consider; such as going forward in heavy weather without a safety belt.

A lifeline height of 24" is too low for safety on a short handed cruising yacht, 26" is barely adequate, 28" is better and 30" is good. Check yours. Most lifeline stanchions and pulpits are made of thin wall stainless steel or chromed brass tubing of 3/4 to 1" diameter. The 1" size is just strong enough but the 3/4" size is not up to the job of holding a falling human body.

The best material for stanchions and pulpits is 3/4" IPS stainless steel or bronze pipe. Its outside diameter is just over 1" and most stanchion bases can be readily reamed out to accept it. Pipe also has a relatively heavy wall thickness that provides the necessary safety factor over the thinner walled tubing.

Stanchions and pulpits always must be through bolted for strength. Fortunately this is more common on fiberglass than on older wood boats, for it is all too easy to use a screw instead of a bolt on a wood boat. Few fiberglass craft have any member that will take a screw fastening at their deck edge so bolts are used. Still it is worthwhile to double check that your stanchion bases are, indeed, through bolted and that the nuts are snugged up tight.

Another failing of some craft is the way their handrails are fastened. These also should be through bolted, not just fastened with screws from below, and they should have heavy washers on the inside of the deck or cabin roof. If your handrails feel loose or wobbly, check the fastenings and either add more or replace screws with through bolts.

Take a look at your rigging. Replace any chafed lines and lock and tape your turnbuckles. If you are strictly a cruising man you may not be rigged out with spinnaker gear, scoffing at it as a racer's nightmare (which it can be). Still the spinnaker halyard can serve many useful purposes in a pinch. It can get a man aloft, be a spare headsail halyard, even an emergency headstay.

Most stock boats have stock masthead fittings that will accept a spinnaker halyard block. If your boat doesn't have spinnaker gear rigged, now is the time to get that very useful halyard up there. If you don't want the halyard aloft, at least rig a messenger line in the block so the halyard can be sent up when needed.

Another common rig failure occurs in the fastenings holding the spinnaker track, gooseneck and sail track. I have seen spinnaker track slowly peeling off the mast under the prolonged stress of extended periods of heavy weather. Many small craft have this hardware held in place with aluminum pop rivets.

But if the mast wall is sufficiently thick (.150" or more) a hole drilled and tapped for a machine screw is stronger. Of course, a bolt is the strongest of all, if access can be had to hold the nut while it is being tightened. However, even pop rivets can do the job if there are enough of them, and extra fastenings at points of strain are a wise precaution.

Other points include the sail track where a storm trysail would be set, the lower part of the gooseneck track where the gooseneck normally sits, the spinnaker track, spinnaker pad eyes or any other fitting subject to a twisting strain that tends to stretch and deform the metal.

Below decks, let's consider the engine first. It is one of the most neglected items on the average auxiliary sailboat, but a reliable engine has saved many a craft from being pounded to pieces on the beach. More engines have quit though through dirt or water in the fuel than for all other reasons put together. Unfortunately the small fuel filters that come attached to most engines as standard equipment simply are not up to the job, except as a secondary filter.

The main filtering should be taken care of by a combination fuel filter and water separator installed between the tank(s) and the engine filter. On a number of boats we have fitted two of these filters in parallel, arranging the valves so either filter can feed the engine while the other one is being drained of water or having its element replaced. Of course, extra filter elements must be included in your spare parts kit. Good filter-separators are available at any well stocked dealer or boat yard and easily installed at a reasonable cost. They are wonderful insurance against engine failure.

The best filter in the world is useless, though, if there is so much water in the tank that the fuel outlet tube is immersed in water. It can happen. A simple trip to Bermuda turned into a royal foul-up when water entered the fuel tanks through the tank vents in heavy weather.

The result was that, two days out, we had no engine, dead batteries and consequently, no radio or navigation equipment. A completely overcast sky put the kibosh on any sights and as Bermuda is a very tiny spot in the ocean to find by dead reckoning alone we were a few days overdue on our arrival.

Tank fills and vents are weak spots that must be attended to. The usual flush deck fills, often placed outboard along the rail, are an invitation to water to creep into the fuel. Heavy waterproof pump grease on the screw threads is a must but a raised fill is an even better answer; one with a gasketed screw type cap.

Vents are another problem since they must be open to the air for the engine to draw fuel. Obviously they should be as high up as possible and preferably close to the centerline. On one new design the vent is led up inside the mizzen mast to a loop 10′ above the deck! Another design has a vent loop up inside the winch handle boxes. Take a look at your fuel tank vent and if it seems prone to water intake move it up and inboard.

A good spot on many boats is in the small corner alongside the companionway hatch trim. The vent can run almost up to the cabin roof height there and loop back down to the cockpit seat.

Neoprene or rubber tubing can be used to quickly extend the vent outlet to a safer location. A vent cover is used by many yachtsmen but it should not be airtight, for vacuum could collapse the fuel tank if the engine ran without the cover removed.

The fuel tank can give trouble in another way. It can break loose in a heavy sea. Most tanks are well secured but inspect yours to ensure the straps and blocking are adequate to take the weight of possibly hundreds of pounds of fuel charging about in rough weather. Straps should be insulated from the tank with neoprene strips to prevent chafe and possible leaks. Give these a once over.

Another source of water in the engine is through the exhaust pipe. In heavy weather, following seas can force their way into the exhaust and flood the engine manifold and cylinders in some installations.

A high loop in the exhaust should prevent this but a large gate valve that can close off the exhaust at the through hull is absolute insurance against trouble from this source. The valve should be installed so that it is easily accessible, usually through the lazarette hatch, and the crew must get into the habit of opening and closing it whenever the engine is run.

Speaking of the exhaust, ensure that the sections of pipe that are not water cooled or water jacketed are heavily lagged with asbestos. Hot exhaust pipe is a danger source

on any boat and on two separate occasions I have seen it start a fire. One fire was in a large coil of manila line which burned a big, costly hole in a dacron genoa. Check your pipe thoroughly and asbestos wrap all hot pipe including the hot joints between sections of water jacketed piping.

This is a good place to reiterate that *all* through hull fittings should have a seacock or gate valve on them to prevent flooding in case a hose ruptures. This includes deck and cockpit scuppers as well as the other water inlets and outlets.

Some through hulls are threaded so that a seacock can be screwed onto them, but this mounting is not sufficiently strong, particularly on a relatively thin fiberglass hull. The seacock must be fitted onto a doubler or otherwise reinforced section of the hull and solidly through bolted even if it is screwed onto a husky through hull fitting.

It may not be feasible, financially or practically, to mount seacocks in a completed boat and the only alternative is to have a tapered softwood plug permanently tied beside each through hull so that it is instantly available to seal the hole in case of trouble.

The other main bugaboo in modern craft is the electrical system, largely due to the dependence modern sailors place on electricity for lights, navigation gear, engine starting and even refrigeration. The battery(s) are the main source of power and must be cared for. This requires that they be solidly clamped into place so they cannot break loose in heavy weather.

A deep battery box just is not good enough when the boat rolls onto its beam ends: a positive hold down is a necessity. A ventilated plastic or wood cover also must be fitted to prevent accidental short circuits from tools or equipment falling across the terminals. A dead short in a fully charged 12 volt battery can be a very exciting affair while it lasts! Rubber terminal covers are available, though I prefer a solid cover across the complete battery. Terminal covers though, are the next best thing.

If two batteries are carried, there should be some arrangement made so that either can be used for engine starting in a pinch. A crossover switch is preferable but a pair of jumper cables will do in an emergency. If only one battery is fitted then you would be wise to carry a spare, also firmly fastened in place and protected, of course.

Dry charged batteries are available but I would not care to think of that bottle of acid bouncing around in my boat. Nor would I like to fill the battery in a heavy sea. Any spare battery should be wet and fully charged so it will be ready instantly when needed.

Most wiring today is hidden behind fiberglass headliners or joinery-work so it is impossible to inspect and difficult to repair. Howard Chapelle wrote that "exposed piping in a boat is a seamanlike feature." The same could be said about wiring.

Check all the wiring that is accessible. See that it is firmly fastened in place by closely spaced clips and, where possible, put identification tags on it. A marine electrician can be of assistance here and can, at the same time, check the various circuits against minor current leaks that could cause a dead battery over a long period.

Even with all these precautions it is still wise to carry a huge store of spare parts on any protracted voyage. And even then, things will go wrong. That is when seamanship and ingenuity come into play. But it is much better to see beforehand what might fail, and to take preventive measures before it does. Take a look around your boat.

Proper Ventilation

Ways to keep fresh air moving

Dick Cumiskey

Mildew looks terrible in a boat and it may cause a lot of effort to get rid of it. But that effort is not half so bad as being cooped up in the confines of an unventilated cabin during a rain shower. With a carefully designed ventilation system, any boat can be comfortable below decks no matter what the weather is like. And that system can virtually eliminate mildew and dampness as well as moisture in the engine's electrical system and the musty smell that occurs in a closed-up boat.

In a wooden boat a steady supply of fresh air reduces the chance of wood rotting. With modern materials such as fiberglass, ferrocement, and metal, rot is not a problem but odors, mildew, and dampness are at least as much a threat as they are in wood construction.

The basic concept of a ventilation system is to keep changing the air below decks. To accomplish this, air needs a way to get out of a boat as well as into a boat. Moreover, the air in all parts of the boat needs to undergo constant change.

A boat is divided into two or more compartments such as the main saloon, the forward cabin, the head, and possibly an aft cabin. Each of these must have adequate ventilation for the comfort of those living aboard. In addition, the lockers, drawers, bilge, and engine compartment must have air circulated through them.

To perform its function properly, a ventilation system should operate under three conditions. First is to provide for air circulation when the boat is unattended. Second is to provide for comfort in generally mild weather for the people aboard while the boat is at the mooring or in a slip. The third and most difficult requirement is to provide adequate air to make the quarters as comfortable as possible during adverse weather conditions especially at sea. The costs will naturally be higher for more sophisticated ventilating systems and certainly not every boat needs a system to meet the third requirement. Each boat, however, does need at least some form of ventilation.

There are generally enough hatches and opening ports in most boats to provide a satisfactory system if they can all be left open. However, for security reasons few owners can leave their boats open and inevitably rain will require hatches and ports to be closed.

The more important function of air movement is the exhaust. Merely forcing air into the boat is not an efficient way to change the stale, moist or warm air already there.

There are two ways to get air out of the boat. One way is to mechanically draw it out with a motorized blower or fan of some sort. In general this is not an acceptable method. The electrical drain and the objectionable noise limit the use of these motors to problem areas.

The more practical method is to utilize the natural flow of air over the exterior of the boat to help draw air from the interior. To do this effectively one must realize that in a boat moored with her bow into the wind the flow of air below will be forward, not aft as might be supposed.

The dorade vent is the most common way to remove air from below decks. A dorade vent allows the passage of air but prevents water from entering the compartment by using a system of baffles (Fig. 1). At

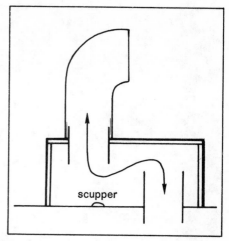

scupper

Figure 1
Dorade vent

least one of these vents should be mounted on the highest portions of each compartment. Moreover, each vent should be as large in diameter as possible; a vent 4″ in diameter admits 4 times the volume of air as a vent 2″ in diameter. These vents serve primarily to draw air from cabins and they should be aimed away from the prevailing breeze, not towards it. It is the suction created by the breeze traveling around the cowl that draws the warm, moist air from the upper reaches of the cabin. Blowing air down these vents only serves to agitate the trapped air inside.

The drawing of the air from within the compartment creates a negative pressure which will tend to return to a balance as new air moves in to replace the old.

To replace the air drawn out, the cooler exterior air flows in through a series of openings and ducts and travels to the bottom of the lower compartments. Air intakes require no special orientation to wind direction but should be protected from rain and spray.

A good spot for a permanent intake or two is in the cockpit well or on the afterdeck to take advantage of the forward flow of air. Use the

same type of corrugated hose used for Coast Guard-approved engine vents, available at most marine hardware stores. A flanged ring is available at the same store and will secure the hose at the opening. This opening can be made with either a holesaw or a sabresaw. The hose leads from the intake to the lowest points of each area needing ventilation.

Closed places such as lockers should have openings cut into them to permit passage of the fresh air. Where these cut-outs are visible they may be decorated with grills, louvers, screens, or simply attractively shaped holes.

There are more sophisticated air intake systems, one of which is the *Myth of Malham*-type vents as used on many of Gary Mull's latest designs. They are relatively expensive to build into an existing boat but they remain usable under virtually all conditions (Fig. 2).

When people are aboard the boat, security no longer becomes the dictating factor and more options are available to move air with, and indeed, become necessary since people require a greater air flow than does the boat itself.

The most common methods of in-

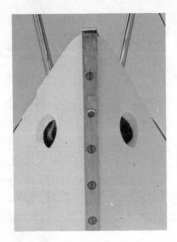
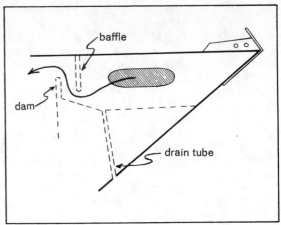

Figure 2
Myth of Malham vents

creasing air flow are to leave the companionway open and to raise the deck hatches. Again, the most effective way to remove air from the cabin is not to raise a forward hatch into the wind, but to raise it against the breeze and obtain a suction effect to remove the air, making use of the tendency of fresh air to flow toward the bow.

The companionway will serve effectively to let new air into the boat and cowls or other sources of intake air at the ends of the boat, ducted below, will supplement the source from the companionway to give a generous flow throughout the boat. Opening ports in the cabin will also help.

These systems can become useless, however, when the rain forces hatches to be shut. Unless you have a companionway dodger or hatch dodger, it will be necessary to close off all of these hatches. Dorade vents alone may not suffice and conditions may become intolerable below decks. Most canvas shops can make hoods to fit over opened hatches, effectively keeping the rain out, but still letting air move. These range from some very simple flap covers with limited usefulness to highly sophisticated venturi hoods

that can be used under many adverse conditions.

To be effective both venturi covers and dorades must be as high off the deck as possible. Air flow close over the deck is restricted. The higher you can get the opening off the deck, the more effective it will be. Many modern ventilators are of the low profile type since they look more racy. You will have to make the decision which is more important, a clean, unobstructed deckline or increased ventilation capacity.

Ventilation may seem to be of secondary importance on the racing boat with its emphasis on low windage and uncluttered decks. Thus the desire for a clean deckline has led to some ingenious ventilation systems on the racing boats. In contrast, the cruising sailor often seems to accept the loss of valuable deck space to vents as a simple solution to his requirements for air movement below decks.

Within the last few years manufacturers have been striving to find innovative ventilation methods for both types of sailors. For instance, the latest custom boats have some ingenious ventilators built into the cabin faces and low deck hatches that are actually flattened out dorade vents. These systems are not so effective as vents opening well above the deck but they do work in a variety of conditions, keep water out, and leave the deck unobstructed — the basic goals of any ventilation system.

The need to increase ventilation in a boat is a common problem. The concerned skipper should look carefully over his boat and consider what type of ventilation can make his boat more pleasant to live aboard and less effort to maintain.

Toward a Quieter Boat

A program for noise control   Lewis Bell

The **scene may** be familiar. A fine mist is falling as a 32-foot auxiliary sailboat powers to windward against a light breeze and a sloppy sea. Periodically, spray from the bow joins the mist as it falls on the deck and cockpit.

In the cockpit the crew sits huddled and wet. No one is below. The reason? The noise created by the engine below decks is intolerable, more objectionable than the discomfort of sitting topside.

Many boat owners object to the noise levels associated with their auxiliary engine or a power generator, but few owners realize the number or complexity of the noise problems that exist aboard a modern yacht. The requirements for maximum auxiliary power and continuous electrical usage have pushed designers and builders to specify and install larger engines and generators. As space is at a premium and cost a factor, less attention is paid to reducing the increased noise levels and many otherwise well fitted boats are annoying if not uninhabitable below when machinery is in operation.

Despite the widespread problem no formal text or design manual exists for dealing with noise control on small boats. A glance at the engine room construction or bulkhead treatment of many recently built boats reveals a basic lack of understanding of the problem by many designers and builders. In most cases, the problem of noise control is only considered in the final stages of design or construction and often consists of attaching ceiling tile or patches of polyurethane foam to the hatch covers, bulkheads, and any available bare spots of the engine compartment. This kind of treatment is superficial and provides about as much noise reduction as a screen door. In addition, many of the materials used present a serious safety hazard in that

they form a porous sponge for soaking up flammable fluids or they can be a source of noxious or poisonous fumes in the presence of heat or fire. On a positive note, with the application of a few basic design and construction principles and continuous attention to detail through construction, most of the unwanted sound can be reduced to a level of little or no annoyance.

Moreover, it should be emphasized that there is no mystique needed nor "gimmicks" available to solve the noise problem. As in any other precise nautical or engineering discipline, "you get nothing for nothing."

Let us take a look at a systematic approach and some fundamental guidelines to the control of noise particularly below decks.

Source of noise. By far, the major source on modern yachts is the internal combustion engine used for propulsion or to drive electrical generators. And, by far, the diesel engine is the worst offender. In the case of the diesel, the noise emanates from the intake, the exhaust, and from the block itself. Or, in short, from everywhere. For gasoline engines, block-radiated and intake noise are minimal, leaving only the exhaust noise that needs to be treated. The quality of engine noise is dominantly discrete (i.e., pure tones at the piston-firing frequency and higher harmonics) and in a range of peak annoyance (200 to 4000 Hz) to most people's ears. Other noise sources associated with mechanical equipment include gear boxes, hydraulic pumps, superchargers, etc., but these are generally of a lower sound level, although of a similar pure tone character.

Fortunately, these sources are almost always located in the engine compartment or in close proximity. Treating them need not be formidable.

On sailboats, the clanging of the

source, then the only other avenue is to isolate the source.

Consider, first, source reduction for the engine compartment equipment. It is usually possible to install a filter-silencer on the air intake of diesel engines. These combinations are sold both by filter and silencer manufacturers and provide significant engine room noise reduction. Basically, they consist of a filter coupled to a tuned, reactive expansion chamber silencer. Installation is simple and usually only requires a pipe coupling and a support bracket. With respect to the block-radiated noise from diesel engines, total enclosure is the only approach that is effective. Enclosures, however, present additional problems with accessibility, visibility, air flow, temperature control and maintenance that halyards against the mast, both at sea and at anchor, can also be a source of noise and very annoying both to crew and neighbors. I have also heard a few complaints that impacting seas can excite some "ringing," especially on aluminum hulls, but, to be sure, halyards and sea noise are secondary and easy

to solve compared to the noise created by propulsion and generating equipment. Therefore, most attention must be focused on the latter sources.

Noise paths. There are two paths that noise must follow to reach the ears of the crew or those aboard nearby boats. First, airborne noise insidiously travels through small holes or penetrations in the engine room bulkhead, engine exhaust ducts, the bilges, or any other air-coupled route. Secondly, structure-borne noise is noise carried through the hull, superstructure, bulkheads, or any mechanically-coupled route and re-radiated into the saloon, galley, head and staterooms as well as up to the deck and cockpit. In addition, complex combinations of both airborne and structure-borne paths exist and are common carriers of the unwanted sound. With dozens of maze-like routes available, it is obvious that only through strict attention to detail during boat design and construction can the noise be contained.

Noise control measures. It is a basic premise of noise control that if you can't reduce the noise at its

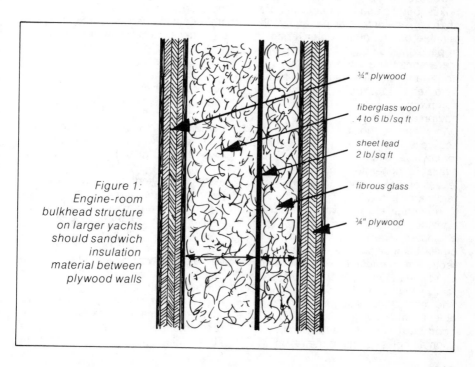

Figure 1:
Engine-room
bulkhead structure
on larger yachts
should sandwich
insulation
material between
plywood walls

¾" plywood

fiberglass wool
4 to 6 lb/sq ft

sheet lead
2 lb/sq ft

fibrous glass

¾" plywood

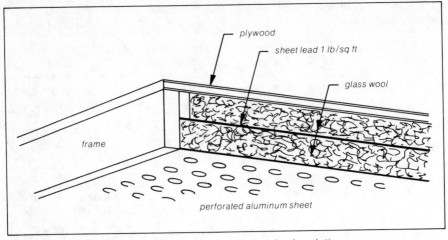

Figure 2: Engine-room ceiling insulation may involve insulating underside of cockpit on smaller craft

are difficult to solve. Most leading manufacturers of generating equipment do sell a total enclosure as an option. Generally, these enclosures are of a molded fiberglass construction and work well. Partial enclosures provide little or no noise reduction and are better left at the dock.

Source noise reduction at gear boxes, pumps and other ancillary mechanical equipment is generally obtainable only through major redesign or part replacement. In short, rarely is there something simple that can be done, and usually amateurish antics here result in serious damage or a compromise in the reliability of the equipment.

In summary, noise reduction at the source is, at best, meager and difficult to achieve except for commercially available generator enclosures; this leaves engine room isolation the most fertile area to pursue.

The engine compartment can be considered as a large noise source enclosure. Therefore, the basic principles of enclosure design apply directly. In particular, two necessary conditions must be met to assure effective engine room noise isolation: (1) The enclosure walls must be sufficiently massive (or dense) to be a good barrier; (2) the acoustical leaks such as holes, ducts, penetrations, or

areas where walls are lightweight must be treated. The importance of strict attention to those two conditions cannot be overemphasized. All others are secondary.

For engine compartment bulkheads, masonry blocks or bricks would be the first choice of materials to reduce noise. However, for obvious reasons, the following construction guidelines are recommended for boat bulkheads on larger craft with larger mechanical systems.

The surface density of the bulkheads must be a *minimum* of eight to 10 pounds per square foot. The construction should be composite in nature as illustrated in Figure 1 for optimum barrier performance. The external materials are plywood, the likely choice in a wood or fiberglass boat. However, for an aluminum or steel hull design, metal materials of equal surface density (weight/square foot) may be used.

For the absorbing material, the readily available and inexpensive 2'x4'x1" fibrous glass ceiling acoustic tile panels do very well. These panels can be obtained wrapped in a transparent plastic film at no extra cost, and the plastic simplifies handling and minimizes the possibility of soaking or wicking flammable fluids. Note that the recommended absorbing material is fibrous glass. Tiles or panels made of

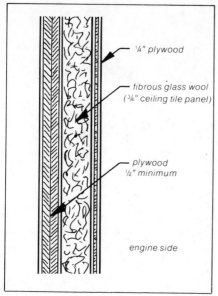

Figure 3: Smaller boats with less space can use this minimum insulation and structure

provide the noise insulation of the glass fibers.

This engine-room treatment can be extended directly to an engine compartment on smaller boats. However, with smaller engines the wall composite construction can generally be reduced somewhat in weight and thickness as shown in Figure 3. Here, again, the absorbing material can be fibrous glass ceiling tiles wrapped in plastic film. The top of the engine compartment should be similar in construction to the overhead treatment as shown in Figure 2. For small gasoline engines, the lead septum and one layer of fiber absorbing material can be deleted.

All openings for ventilation should be no larger than necessary and should be "trapped" with a labyrinth (Fig. 4). For these small traps, polyurethane foam (acoustical quality) can be used. It is much easier to form, cut and shape than fibrous glass.

With respect to acoustical leaks, all penetrations through conduits, ducts, pipes, etc., must be sealed. Sheet lead one pound per square foot is quite malleable and makes an excellent,

paper pulp, polyurethane, and other foam-like materials sold as ceiling paneling or thermal insulation are not suitable for use in a boat nor do they

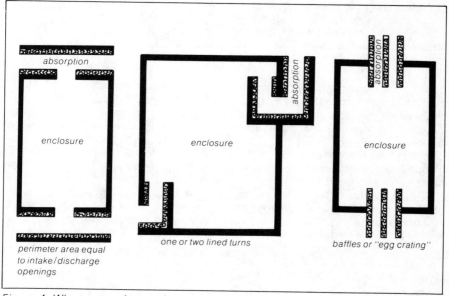

Figure 4: When an engine enclosure requires openings for air flow and ventilation, sound traps are easy to construct using sound-absorbing materials in a system of baffles

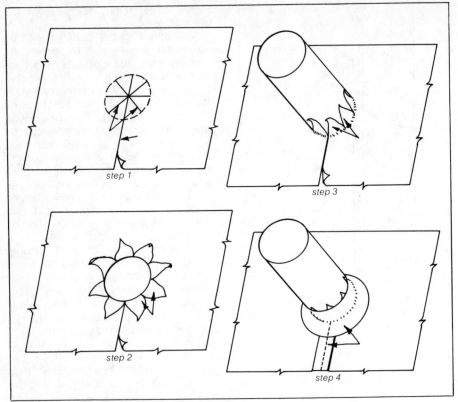

Figure 5: One method of sealing penetrations through insulated structure using sheet lead. Slit piece of lead from bottom and cut segments slightly larger than diameter of pipe. Work lead over pipe and press segments tightly against it. Then tape segments and slit securely

easily worked material for such applications as penetration seals (Fig. 5).

Moreover, all doors must have an overlap with a good rubber seal, and be capable of being dogged tight. A good, positive seal not only adds to the integrity of the enclosure, but eliminates the possibility of door rattles.

Frequently, the bilges provide an airborne path for the noise to reach accommodation areas. Therefore, the bulkhead noise-reduction treatment must extend to the bilges. However, the fibrous glass should not extend to where it can get soaked and possibly present a wicking problem.

Other measures are strongly recommended but are usually easier to handle. For instance, engines and all

rotating equipment should be installed on high-quality, vibration isolation mounts. Great care, along with some engineering analysis, is required to avoid potential problems with shaft misalignment and subsequent chronic bearing failures. Therefore, it is strongly suggested that isolators and installation methods recommended by the engine or generator manufacturers always be followed very closely. Elastomeric-type neoprene mounts are generally the choice with a durometer in the range of 50 to 60.

Both diesel and gas engine exhausts should incorporate a high-quality, heavy-duty reactive muffler. Here, again, engine or muffler manufacturers generally provide specific recommendations and, in some cases, guarantee results. The basic guidelines on muffler selection are rather straightforward:

1. The muffler material must be heavy-duty cast iron or ¼-inch (minimum) Monel.

2. The diameter of the expansion chamber should be at least five times the diameter of the inlet.

3. For water-cooled exhausts, the exit port must be at the lowest point on the muffler or water accumulation will detune the muffler and seriously reduce the acoustical performance.

It is generally good design practice to have the mufflers as close to the engine as possible and preferably in the engine room. In this way, most of the noise will be eliminated before entering the exhaust ducts which may pass through or by accommodations.

Frequently, the exhaust ducts downstream of the muffler are lightweight and flexible for ease in routing. Since their ducts still contain substantial amounts of acoustical energy and may pass within inches of a bunk, some additional treatment may be required. I recommend the exhaust ducts be heavy-wall (¼-inch minimum) rubber pipe. For lightweight, flexible duct materials already installed, the sound transmission loss through the duct walls can be increased by wrapping the duct with a commercially available dense vinyl (one pound/square foot) composite (Fig. 6).

Incidental, non-mechanical noise is usually simple to reduce, in some cases merely by a crewmember's taking some care. For example, in dealing with halyard noise at anchor, nothing works better or cheaper than tying them off to a shroud. At sea, either tightening, easing, or realigning the halyard will often stop or reduce a self-exciting resonance condition.

With respect to the "ring" of a metal hull, little acoustical treatment of a practical nature is available to the builder, designer or owner. I feel that

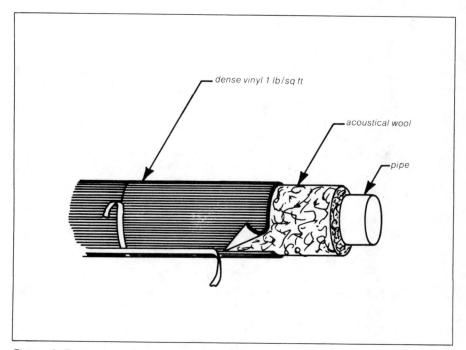

dense vinyl 1 lb/sq ft

acoustical wool

pipe

Figure 6: To insulate pipe wrap pipe first with acoustical wool and then sheath wool with dense vinyl

this problem really exists primarily on stripped-out ocean racers where the interior is acoustically hard (i.e., it contains little or no absorbing materials). Here, the clang of a dropped winch handle does reverberate longer than on a cruising-type boat whose cabin contains headliners, hull ceiling, cushions, etc.

To reduce the structure-borne noise from lines being eased off a winch or led through a block mounted on a metal deck, fittings can be fitted with wooden or plastic pads and back-up blocks. Deck blocks and track-mounted blocks should be spring-loaded at their base to keep them from falling over.

To be sure, the metal hulls do not contain the internal viscous damping of a fiberglass, composite, or wooden hull. However, by the time the hulls are painted and submerged in water, the addition of some superficial damping treatment is expensive, heavy, and for the most part, worthless. Can you imagine the "ring" of a bell half submerged in water?

In summary, the first-order noise problems are the engines and associated mechanical equipment. It is here that attention must be focused to assure a comfortable acoustical environment. It should be emphasized, however, that a boat is a small, compact space and to render the noise of diesel generators or auxiliary engine inaudible on deck or in adjacent accommodations is far too ambitious a design goal. However, by following basic guidelines with care, resultant sound levels can be sufficiently low that in no way will there be any annoying interference with the pleasant sound of laughter, the sea, or the tinkle of an ice cube hitting the side of a glass.

Pumps Can Save Your Boat

Proper equipment for emergencies   Robert Del Morris

An often quoted equivalent of Murphy's Law states that malfunctions occur at the worst possible time. A howling gale, heavy seas coupled with spray, noise and unaccustomed severe motion, constitute a fairly good description of the phrase, "worst possible time." It does not take a psychiatrist to describe the trauma of a skipper when, in the midst of this scenario, someone discovers three feet of water over the cabin sole. Something has failed and the available crew — often the wife and children of the skipper — are set to the pumps. The boat, however, becomes increasingly unstable and the crew, growing even more apprehensive, become confused and less efficient. Eventually the decision is made to abandon and the boat is lost.

The above situation has happened more than once and will probably happen again. The immediate questions raised are: What caused the leak? And did that leak have to result in the loss of a good boat? One subject worth considering in answering the second question particularly is the available bilge-pumping system and under what conditions that system would be adequate to handle emergencies.

The owner of a sailing craft equipped with a bilge pump will, in general, feel a sense of ensured safety knowing that for emergency purposes he has a built-in device for removing in-hull water. Many boats, in fact, are equipped with multiple pumps, either electrical, manual or a combination. This leads to a doubly ensured feeling of safety which, for the most part, is justified since it is not likely that all pumps would fail simultaneously; and the alternate pumps significantly increase the pumping system capacity when needed.

However, most commonly found bilge-pumping systems are of value in the removal of casual water only. In-hull water is defined as *casual* if the capacity of the available bilge-pumping system is equal to or greater than the sustained water in-flow rate. Casual water is usually the result of condensation, spills, seepage through fittings and the like, and the pumping system can easily remove, in minutes, water that may have taken days to accumulate. Casual water might also include more serious water intake such as that resulting from pooping or broaching. In this case the amount of water taken aboard, while large, is essentially fixed in quantity and will be handled by the pumping system in due time, although obviously the quicker the better.

The capacity of most bilge pumps is given either in the manufacturer's data sheet or is labelled on the pump itself. This is the value the pump was designed for, and implies no pick-up losses, back pressure, improper installation, or aging — all factors that can reduce capacity of that pump when installed in a boat. It is not difficult to measure the output capacity of any already installed pump in terms of gallons per minute (GPM) flow rate. A suggested procedure is as follows:

1. When the boat is level, put sufficient water into the bilge to cover the pump intake.

2. Operate the pump until essentially it can remove no further water.

3. Fill the bilge with (say) five gallons as measured from a one-gallon bucket and; finally,

4. Note the time (T), in seconds, it takes to pump that five gallons of water out of the hull and restore the bilge water level to that which it had in step 2.

The flow rate in GPM is 60 times the amount of water of step 3, divided by the time noted in step 4.

This measurement can be done for

253

all on-board bilge pumps—one at a time—and the GPM of each added together for the total capacity. For example, if three pumps on a given boat measure 8.5 GPM, 17.2 GPM and 13.4 GPM, the total pumping system capacity would be 39.1 GPM. A sustained input flow rate of this value or less would then be defined as casual water. Obviously, a wave breaking over the stern could dump 100 gallons of water into the boat in five seconds (calculated input flow rate of 1200 GPM). However, after the initial dump, the actual flow rate is zero and a quick calculation, using the above example of a system, shows that in about 10 minutes all the water would be pumped out; this is an effective out-flow rate equal to the in-flow rate as measured over 10 minutes of time.

Now examine the case where the sustained in-flow rate will exceed the system capacity, and the term casual can no longer be applied. In this case, the term emergency water is used. In-hull water is defined as *emergency* if the capacity of the available bilge-pumping system is less than the sustained water in-flow rate.

When attempting rationally to derive charts or calculations applicable to water in-flow, one is tempted to consider such drastic cases as groundings, collisions or major structural flaws. In these cases the damage may vary between a hole of minimal diameter (i.e., virtually no damage at all) to a hole of very large diameter (i.e., the entire hull has been opened). While these cases are certainly of interest, they thwart any attempt at precise analysis. There are, however, cases of equal interest that may be handled with numbers, the essence of this approach being to treat the holes in the hull that *are*, rather than the holes in the hull that *might be*, although the conclusions can be applied to comparable in-flow from ruptures of the hull skin.

Borrowing from fluid-flow theory, it is possible to derive a simple equation for water in-flow applicable to small boats. Figure 1 is a family of curves from such an equation showing the initial in-flow rate F (GPM) for a hole of

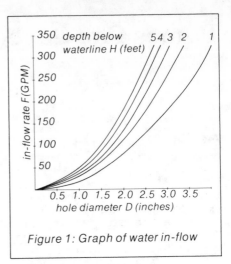

Figure 1: Graph of water in-flow

diameter D (inches), located H (feet) below the waterline.

The scaling shown in Figure 1 is specifically aimed at something that all boats have in common, namely, through-hull fittings. Examination of these curves will show that for a large number of boats, a leak caused by the failure of even a single through-hull fitting (or connecting hose) is classifiable as emergency water. This merits concern because these fittings can fail and, apart from collisions and grounding, the failure of a through-hull fitting is the most common cause of sinkings. For example, a pounding sea and the resultant hull flexure and vibration are just the kinds of additional stress that a fitting with undetected electrolytic corrosion neeeds in order to break completely.

Take as an example a two-inch through-hull fitting for a cockpit drain that lies about 1.5 feet below the water line. In the worst case, if the boat is heeled about 25-30 degrees towards the side the fitting is on, the below-water-line depth becomes 3.5 feet. For this case H equals 3.5 feet, D equals two inches and the resultant value of F (from Figure 1) is over 135 GPM. This is three times the pumping system capacity of a pumping system capable of handling 39.1 GPM and is clearly emergency water. The problem is made worse by the fact that in all likelihood, the fitting failed some time before it was noticed and the pumping system is already behind. Note that no matter how efficiently the pumps are manned, they cannot keep up with the in-flow, and unless the leak can be found (and plugged) immediately, the outcome is already determined.

The use of Figure 1 and the knowledge of the depth and size of through-hull fittings on any given boat will permit a quick comparison between pumping system capacity and in-flow rate obtainable with each fitting considered at its deepest possible position below the waterline. The comparison thus obtained is a pessimistic one since it assumes tne in-flow rate is constant (it will decrease as the in-hull water rises above the hole) and that the failed fitting is always at its lowest position. However, the comparison will serve as a measure of the pumping system's adequacy.

Based upon such data, several choices are possible:

a) The present pumping system is adequate to comply with the casual water definition for an existing below-waterline hole. No action required.

b) The present pumping system is not adequate in the sense of a) above but the conscious decision is to leave the system as is.

c) As per b) above but additional pumping capacity will be added.

Of the decision choices listed above, only the third requires positive action. This then leads to another set of choices involving the type of pump (or pumps) to be added. In general, there are five categories to be considered:

a) Manual operated pump
b) Electrically operated pump
c) Engine-cooling water pump
d) Engine-driven auxiliary pump
e) Self-contained engine-driven pump (pump and engine in one unit)

The list is not exhaustive but most types of pumping systems can be placed under one of the above headings (e.g., a bucket goes under a).

Figure 2 is a relative comparison of some key features of each of the five types listed. Again, the features are not exhaustive but have been selected for their practicality. In conjunction with the data of Figure 2, the following points are offered for consideration, keeping in mind that their purpose is to

	MANUAL PUMP	ELECTRICAL PUMP	ENGINE-COOLING WATER PUMP	ENGINE-DRIVEN AUXILIARY PUMP	SELF-CONTAINED AUXILIARY PUMP
NOMINAL CAPACITY (GPM)	10-25	10-25	5-20	100-500	150-1000
SIZE	0.1-0.3 CU. FT.	0.2-0.5 CU. FT.	0.1 CU. FT.	1 CU. FT.	2-6 CU. FT.
COST (DOLLARS)	100 OR LESS	100 OR LESS	NONE	150-350	450-1500
RELATIVE EASE OF INSTALLATION	EASY TO MODERATE	EASY TO MODERATE	EASY	MODERATE TO DIFFICULT	EASY TO MODERATE
RELATIVE SUSCEPTIBILITY TO CLOGGING	VARIES	MODERATE TO HIGH	MODERATE TO HIGH	SMALL	SMALL

Figure 2: Typical pump characteristics

convert emergency water into casual water, and in some cases they augment, not replace existing on-board pumps.

1. Manually operated pumps are attractive on nearly all counts. However, manual power is, of course, required at the end of the pump handle. For an ocean racing yacht with a full and seaworthy crew, this may not be a handicap. For a short-handed crew, however, with little or no chance of relief, such may not be the case. The energy required to raise and discharge a given flow rate of water equal to the pump's design limits is fixed. In order for the pump to be effective in emergency use, the energy input to it must be sustained for as long as necessary. While it is true that a frightened person with a bucket is a great bilge pump, it is also true that the ability to sustain a high energy expenditure is limited. This feature cannot be taken lightly.

2. Electrically operated pumps should be self-priming and submersible. Automatic turn-on is desirable but should always be backed up with a manual switch. They are more subject to clogging than modern manual pumps of equal capacity and, as with any pump type, they should have a readily accessible intake or equivalent. If the boat's batteries are reasonably charged, they will operate at, or close to, their rated (or measured) output for hours, which makes them, in this sense, more desirable than manual pumps.

Bear in mind, however, that in the power cycle from engine-to-altenator-to - battery - to - electric - motor - to - pump impeller, the cycle has gone from mechanical energy (engine) back to mechanical energy (pump impeller). The conversions to electrical/chemical energy are for convenience and are not without some loss in efficiency. This is another feature which must not be taken lightly.

3. Engine-cooling water pumps have been used for some time. A valve selects as the cooling water supply either sea water or in-hull water. Engine-cooling pumps are convenient and will run efficiently. However, they are subject to clogging which may cause pump damage (which can obviously make further engine use difficult and clearing them is time consuming). Second, they are not high capacity pumps; they are cooling pumps and the fluid they pump must remain in contact with the hot surfaces of the engine block long enough for adequate heat transfer to take place. Engines of 10 to 50 horsepower have pump flow rate values of five to 20 GPM.

4. Engine-driven auxiliary pumps are high to very high capacity pumps (i.e., 100 to 500 GPM). Generally, they are belt driven from the main engine and may be engaged manually or with a magnetic clutch. It takes from three to five horsepower to drive a 200 GPM pump, a value well within the capability of in-board auxiliary engines. They should be self-priming (many are not) and will digest most of the floating materials that would clog other pump types. Their cost and problems of installation are a drawback, but they excel for high volume water discharge.

A sometimes-mentioned concern about auxiliary engine pumps is that if the failed fitting happens to be the engine-cooling intake, the engine could not be run very long before overheating. However, a moment's reflection would suggest that a soaring temperature gauge on an otherwise normally running engine is in itself a good clue as to where the problem is.

5. Self-contained engine-driven pumps have the same advantages as those of 4 above. Their cost is higher and installation may or may not be an even more significant problem. It would seem that an auxiliary pump which is hopefully never used is expensive insurance. An auxiliary engine plus a pump which is similarly never used may be excessively expensive unless another use for either the pump or engine is found or where installation difficulties prohibit the use of the belt-driven pump.

From the foregoing discussion, one tends to lean heavily towards the engine-driven auxiliary pump choices (i.e., choices 4 and 5) as being the most purposeful since they efficiently employ the best power source available, they are not easily clogged, and they provide, in one unit, the out-flow rate needed to render as casual water, the in-flow rate of any hull fitting that should fail. The final choice depends on the individual boat.

Most of these pumps have a specified output GPM for a given discharge head (i.e., the distance the water must be lifted before it is discharged from the outlet). For bilge-pump purposes the discharge head is small (but should not be zero). This means that a pump specified at 100 GPM with 30-foot head may deliver 170 GPM or more at a 10-foot head. Thus, a lower cost and smaller size unit may be sufficient for the particular application and full advantage should be taken of that sort of trade-off.

Pumps such as these are sensitive to being operated "dry" (i.e., no water available at the intake). The usual problem that occurs is damage to the pump seal, causing it to leak and reducing the pump flow rate. To guard against running dry, the pump selected should be self-priming. A minor handicap of the inability to run the pump dry is the reluctance to test the pump occasionally. A suggested alternative to this is to engage the pump clutch and turn the engine over with the starter only (do not run the engine) to check that the pump is not frozen, the belt is not slipping under no load, and that the clutch will engage. Follow this operation with a check of the pump's priming water level and refill with fresh water if necessary. A good pump will hold its prime for months or even years. Assuming that the pump chosen is of proven design and that the installation details have been properly attended to, these simple periodic checks should reasonably guarantee performance should the need arise.

A final thought: The opening paragraph of this paper used the word trauma in describing a disastrous situation. The mental strain imposed on any skipper during those times can, in itself, be disastrous. A potential for alleviating some of the mental strain, it would seem, would be to substitute some degree of familiar actions into a situation full of unfamiliar happenings. For instance, the procedure of starting an engine (familiar) and of flipping a switch and hearing an engine load down (familiar) as a high capacity pump engages is a direct and positive action. The skipper knows that his system will discharge more water than any fitting in his boat, by its failure, could put in, and, further, may very well keep him afloat in case of grounding or collision. There has to be some feeling of comfort from the knowledge that strong measures have been taken to buy the time with which to combat an emergency, rather than to see a difficult situation turn hopeless.

Inflatable Raft Care and Repair

Preventive maintenance for long life   Dag Pike

From its hesitant beginnings after the war, the inflatable has developed into an accepted part of the boating scene. From a temperamental, unreliable craft, it has developed into a craft which invites neglect simply because it seems to keep going forever with remarkably little attention.

It therefore comes as a disappointment to find one day that one compartment is not holding air or the floor is letting in water, which may happen just when you want to use your inflatable tender to get ashore from an anchorage. Don't blame the boat. The signs of deterioration have probably been there for some time if you only knew what to look for.

Leaks in air tubes come from three sources. There is the obvious puncture when the fabric of the boat has come against a sharp object. This type of puncture is much more likely to occur when the boat is inflated and the material is under tension. Being careful prevents this.

Another type of leak is that caused through wear. The fabric from which these boats are made is nylon coated on each side with Neoprene or Hypalon synthetic rubber. The rubber provides the air seal; the nylon fabric, the strength. Abrasion when the boat is dragged across a beach or where the wooden or metal parts of the boat rub against the fabric can wear the rubber coating thin. This increases the chance of a small leak and this is the type of leak that may suddenly let you down.

Finally there is leakage from porosity which happens with age when the fabric crystalizes and shrinks because of chemical change.

A little care in how you handle the boat can reduce all this wear. Most of the vulnerable parts are protected by doubled pieces so that wear is not so critical. The bearing areas for the wooden floors in particular are protected in this way. The enemy is sand lodging between the wood and the fabric. This acts as a marvelous abrasive when the boat moves in a seaway. Fortunately, most of the wear is on the wood.

Regular washing with fresh water can help to keep down the amount of sand which collects in the boat. To do this properly, stand the boat vertically on the transom or even suspend it upside down so that it will drain completely. Washing with fresh water also gets rid of the accumulated salt, a good idea if the boat is being left unused for some time.

Sharp edges and abrasion from the floors is predictable. Where damage can be done in unlikely areas is when the inflatable is stowed on board its mother craft or when it is being transported by car or trailer. The fabric's chafing against fixtures on the yacht or trailer, or the lashing ropes, soon can wear through on even the best boat. It is all too easy to roll up the inflatable and stuff it into a locker when you are getting under way. Just stop to think what the constant movement of the boat will do to the fabric. Stowing the inflatable in a bag or box can help a lot since the container takes the wear and tear. But also have a check around the locker for projections and sharp edges.

Many people keep their inflatable inflated and lashed on deck. If you do this, watch the lashings *very carefully* and check what the boat is sitting on so that there is no chance of its chafing.

Most of the general wear and tear on an inflatable boat can be taken care of during its annual overhaul. You can do this yourself or better yet you can take the boat to an authorized center that specializes in servicing inflatables.

The boats are tested for leaks and any worn areas are fitted with doubled

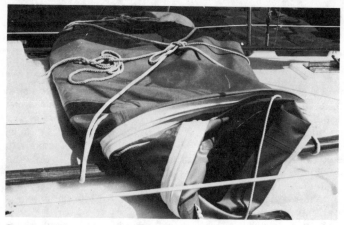

*Ropes securing an inflatable on deck
can chafe the fabric if there
is any movement*

pieces. The woodwork is checked and finally the boat is cleaned so that it comes back looking like new.

The owner who wants to do things himself can easily carry out the examination. Look carefully for areas where the white fabric is showing through the rubber covering. This means a close examination of all parts of the boat. By close, I mean *very close*, not just a quick glance. Overhaul centers test boats for leaks with a very sensitive pressure device. They must be able to maintain their pressure within close limits for a period of time. You can check your own boat by inflating it hard and leaving it for 48 hours. To do this get a pressure gauge to test compartments from a dealer who sells inflatables.

If the raft still seems hard after this time then you don't have many problems, but the air temperature must be the same at each check. The pressure varies considerably with temperature.

If one compartment deflates slightly then you have to start searching for a leak. Small pin-prick leaks can be found by mixing up a solution of soapy water and brushing this over the surface of the tube. Any leaks will show up by bubbling of the soap. Once found, mark the leaking area so that you can find it when the boat is deflated.

Repairing minor leaks in inflatables is within the capabilities of the average owner. But there are no short cuts, and it requires great care if the final result is to be satisfactory. A car inner tube has the tire on the outside to support the patch. On the inflatable boat, the patch is on its own. Apart from the pressure trying to force the patch off, there is also the water trying to peel it off, and possibly gasoline from the outboard attacking the adhesive.

In tackling any leak, whether it's a large hole from damage, or a pin-prick leak, first wash the area thoroughly with Tolulene. Any hole over about two inches long can be repaired by first cementing on an inside patch that overlaps one inch all around the cut. Let the inside patch cure for 12-24 hours, then apply an outside patch in the same fashion. All patching should be done using the same material the boat is built from. Tolulene is generally available and any inflatable repair facility will stock it. Make sure that the repair area is thoroughly ventilated and that there are no naked fumes around.

To apply, lay the patch onto (or inside) the buoyancy tube and mark its edge. Apply a coat of adhesive to both the tube and the patch. When this is dry, after about 15 minutes, apply a second coat to both areas. When these are tacky, the patch should be carefully applied. Test tackiness by using your knuckle. If you hit it with your knuckle and it sticks, you know it is ready.

A small roller is good for applying pressure to the patch and also helps to remove any air bubbles. Once firmly in place, the patch should be left for a minimum of 12 hours before use, and preferably 24 hours. Any surplus adhesive around the edge of the patch can be removed with Tolulene immediately after the patch has been applied. This gives a tidy appearance.

Most inflatable-boat manufacturers supply a repair kit with their boats. It includes a tube of one-part adhesive, usable straight from the tube. This adhesive will do the job, but the professionals always use a two-part adhesive which is much stronger. The one-part adhesive is more suited to emergency repairs to keep the boat going during the summer. Always make sure you use an adhesive recommended by the manufacturer. You must also plan your overhaul work so that it can all be done at once.

For really effective repairs the work should be done in a warm dry area.

Air leaks may also come from the inflation valves which benefit from a regular check. Dirt and grit are the big enemies of valves, although these are usually cleared when the valve is used to inflate the boat. A spray from one of the silicone grease aerosols can keep the valve working freely, particularly when there are metal parts in the valve. Do not use grease at any time.

Water leaks in the bottom of the boat can be just as frustrating as air leaks. You can find them by putting water (not too much) in the boat while it is supported on chocks. These leaks are repaired in the same way as leaks in the air tube except that in this case you can get to both sides. It is good practice to patch both sides to make a stronger job.

One of the difficulties with inflatables is maintaining their appearance over the years. Boats coated solely in Neoprene rubber lose their showroom finish fairly quickly. Neoprene is softer and less abrasion-resistant than the Hypalon finish. Hypalon, with its smooth shiny finish, is being used more as appearance becomes more important.

Hypalon rubber is more difficult to repair than Neoprene. It may require several coats of adhesive to get a good bond and surface preparation is very important. Repair of these boats is usually a job for the specialist, but you can still make emergency repairs.

The appearance of an inflatable can be restored by painting. There are sev-

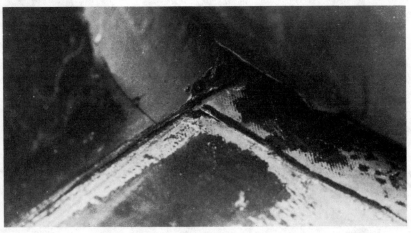

The corner between the transom and the buoyancy tube is a favorite area for chafe to start

eral special paints for this purpose on the market, many Hypalon based. The instructions must be followed closely for good results. These paints depend on getting a proper bond between the paint film and the skin of the boat, the main difficulty being cleaning the fabric surface thoroughly. This is particularly difficult on older boats where the paint is usually required. One snag with painting a boat is that all of the paint has to be removed before a patch can be applied. In general, painting is not recommended and a good cleaning with a Tolulene solvent will do much to restore the appearance.

The way you treat an inflatable, whether it is a small yacht tender or a high-speed runabout, largely determines the life expectancy it will have. New transoms and fabric floors can be fitted if these get damaged. In fact even the most serious damage can usually be fixed if necessary.

What eventually finishes off an inflatable is deterioration of the rubber-impregnated fabric. The rubber slowly oxidizes and changes its chemical composition. It then becomes difficult

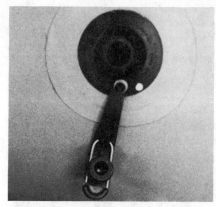

Check inflation valves. With this type of valve, the metal prongs must not be left in the valve after deflation otherwise damage will result

to get patches to stick and some strength is lost. It may take 10 or 15 years for this point to be reached by which time you should have had more than your money's worth out of the boat. My inflatable is still going strong after 15 years.

Galley Accessories

Considerations for a compact kitchen

Lin Pardey

Now that cruising is more and more becoming a husband and wife affair, builders and designers are giving galleys a bit more consideration. No longer is it normal to see a cruiser with only a two-burner primus stove and a dishpan for a sink. Some of the well-planned popular cruising boats we see advertised have the galley out of the way of the companionway complete with a proper stove and oven and generous counters for preparing foods. This is as it should be if you are planning to live on board for more than a week each year. Everything must be done to make the cook's job easier because that virtually guarantees good meals for the crew.

Each time Larry and I board another yacht or ship of any kind I survey the galley immediately. Over the past nine years I've seen some details that work and some that don't. We've adapted the most interesting ideas to our cruising galley when and where we could. Most of the small and seemingly inconspicuous conveniences have become so important to us that I couldn't imagine being without them.

Because 60% of galley time is spent doing dishes, first have a look at your drainboard and sink. Is the sink large enough to put your biggest frying pan into for a good scrubbing? Does the drainboard have sides high enough to keep dishes from falling as they drain? Does water from washed dishes run back into the sink or does it pour onto the floorboards?

I've seen some lovely stainless-steel molded units with the ultimate in luxuries, a double sink. My second choice after stainless steel is a laminated maple drainboard with a stainless-steel sink. This really looks beautiful and I only have to scrub mine once a week with chlorine bleach to keep it looking fresh and clean. My last choice would be Formica or molded fiberglass. On every new boat we see the Formica looks great. But one year later the top is full of scratches from each knife cut. The corners are delaminating from the constant damp a drainboard suffers and rot often sets in on the plywood that is used under the Formica.

Whatever material you use for a drainboard, a separate chopping board is a treat. Not only will it protect your drainboard surface, it can be carried out on deck on those balmy days when it's nicer to peel carrots directly overboard. Bare laminated maple is best for this and, like a butchers block, it should be sanded or planed smooth once a year. My cutting board is small and has little rubber feet on it so it stays put on the drainboard unless we get knocked down. A bigger board should have a convenient peg for hanging.

I dislike galley freshwater pumps. Have you ever been heeled in a stiff breeze with a bit of a sea running and tried to fill a large soup pot with water? If the pot is already hot you add a third dimension. One hand for the cook, one hand for the pot, one hand for the pump; it just doesn't add up. Electric pumps are impractical except on a boat with a large generator and a willing engineer. A foot pump is only a bit better.

One easy solution is a gravity-feed system. A 10-gallon day tank stored in a deck locker above the galley gives you water just by turning a swing valve. The plumbing can be extremely simple and straightforward. Each time the day tank is empty you just transfer water into a five-gallon jug from your main tank and put it in the day tank. If you are near a dock you can fill the day tank directly and save your main tank water for emergencies. At sea, this gives you a way of keeping exact track of your water usage. If you have to transfer water three times in one week you know you are using too much, and you know it immediately, before you near the danger point.

The day tank gravity-feed system has other benefits. Because your water is in two different tanks, it can't all become contaminated. We've been in places where we've had to take on water with rather poor flavor. So, we just filled our day tank and kept the main tank full of sweeter water.

By putting a T in the water line you can use the same plumbing for a shower; or, the ultimate in boating luxuries, a hot water heater. There is no complicated plumbing and no broken pumps. Gravity isn't terribly sophisticated, it just works.

Paper towels. We use at least a roll a week, so Larry has installed a paper-towel rack on the underside of the deck, above the sink and a good distance from the stove. Because paper-towel sizes are different in almost every country, a standard holder doesn't work. The simplest solution is two pieces of wood fastened to the deck 12½" apart with holes drilled for a ½" wood rod to slip through (Fig. 1).

Plastic dishes aren't appealing to us; they always remind us of camping out. Instead we use ironstone or stonewear china and have been pleased with its durability. China must have snug holders to prevent it from rattling, and it should be convenient to the galley sink.

Less durable, but an addition to enjoyable dining afloat are wine glasses. We buy inexpensive ones by the dozen. When we were at the Erickson museum in Mariehamn, Aland, touring the *Pommern* we saw at last a way of storing wine glasses that should reduce our breakage rate. Once again, the rack can be secured to the underside of the deck near the galley, using space that might otherwise be wasted (Fig. 2). Each glass in the rack can be removed individually and if one of the set breaks it doesn't matter. Properly built, the rack should hold any size or design of glass provided the glass has a stem.

A spice rack with holes for each of my 12 favorite spices had been on our work list for five and a half years. It wasn't until I was ill on a passage from Germany to England that Larry had to find the cracked pepper for himself with a fresh breeze blowing. My spice rack is now being designed and built.

Equally important is a place to

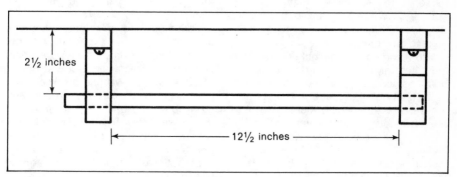

Figure 1
Simple Installation for a Paper-Towel Holder

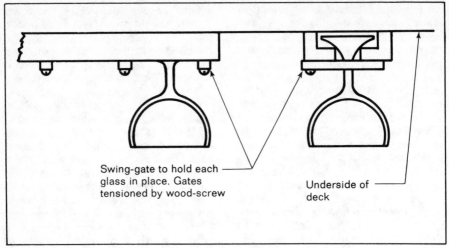

Swing-gate to hold each glass in place. Gates tensioned by wood-screw

Underside of deck

Figure 2
Wine-glass rack for as many glasses as you wish to have. Inside of rack must be lined with heavy felt to prevent glasses from making a racket

store a carving knife and its steel sharpener. Ideally, this should be right in reach of the cook when she stands by the sink. A loose knife can be potentially very dangerous. A knife stored in a drawer can be gripped accidentally and result in serious injuries. A holder that you stick the whole blade of the knife into, like a holster, is not only a convenience for the cook, but safety for the crew.

Large deep pots are a must for an ocean-going boat. I've one nine inches deep that is great for stews. But, storing it is a problem. I've had to settle for storing it in the oven, but all the other pots and pans have very convenient places on shelves next to the stove.

A top-loading storage locker is by far the safest and most economical on a boat. As long as the cook does not have to lift half the boat apart to get at the cans, a top-loading locker also is the easiest to live with. Cans don't fall as you tack or go over a wave. The locker can be opened safely on either tack and you can see at a glance what you have. On a fiberglass hull, large lockers should have dividers to keep

cans from setting up their own symphony by rolling about. The frames on a wooden hull serve this purpose well.

One cruising boat we delivered advertised 25 storage lockers. It had them, but they had neither bottoms nor backs, and everything we put in them ended up in the bilge. Another boat had fine molded lockers but no drains in them. Water collected in each locker and we had to mop them out with a sponge.

Drawers are nice but they are a great waste of space. The framing is heavy and with changes in humidity, they shrink and swell so that one day they will open; the next day they won't.

There is one problem I haven't been able to solve except on a large Costa Rican shrimp trawler we once worked on: fresh vegetable storage. On the trawler, we had a three-foot-wide wicker basket sitting on another basket right in the corner of the galley. With fresh air circulating around each vegetable, we never had to toss anything out because of rot. That was a four-week voyage in the tropics.

I have to settle for airing my vegetables every three days and throwing out the rotten ones. Ideally, a bin on deck built of slats with ¼" air space between each one and a solid top to provide shade would be my choice. A good second choice would be a section of a well-ventilated chain locker where I could hang baskets of fruit and vegetables.

One thing most galleys lack is a good permanent garbage bin. On a luxurious 43′ racer-cruiser, a hole had been cut through the locker front and a frame fitted to hold a standard-size plastic bag. The full bag can be removed through the main door of the locker. On another boat with the companionway right next to the galley, one of the steps lifted to expose a removable garbage box.

There are always new ways to improve your own galley. Try to visit as many boats as you can and look them over carefully. You will be surprised how many different solutions there may be to a single problem. You may even find that your own ideas are the best!

Galley Storage from the Inside

Making the most of locker space

Joan Wendling

Although most sailors know well the importance of a safe, efficient and seaworthy galley, there is an area of the galley that seems to be totally neglected: the inside of storage lockers. You can find some articles on how to make galleys in general efficient and safe, what to cook in them, and a dozen different layouts for the perfect sea-going galley. But I've never seen drawings from the *inside* out. And if you take the time to peek inside one of those large cabinets labeled "Utensils"—under the sink or off to the side—what you usually find is—nothing! They're often very large, usually odd-shaped with the hull of the boat forming one side of the locker, and filled with nothing.

Picture the incredible amount of utensils you can fit in this cavern: pots and pans, baking dishes, roasting pans, pressure cooker, bowls—all the things you need and lots you don't. And they're all stacked neatly inside one another and then jammed together so they don't jostle about. Fantastic! But *invariably* the one particular item you need is under six others, and its removal signals the rhythmic destruction of whatever order had prevailed, in perfect time with the roll and bounce of your boat. It is a completely inefficient, noisy, and unseaworthy locker. And a few shelves make it little better. Everything bumps and slides noisily along the shelf as the boat rolls, and usually ends up out of reach against the hull at the back of the cabinet.

But these empty, cavernous lockers are the perfect beginning for designing a galley locker that suits *your* own particular utensils and style of cooking, a locker where every item has a place of its own that is handy and quiet, and the removal of one thing affects no others. It's easy if you use the shape of the locker to advantage, make a careful selection of minimum galley equipment, and keep your handles up!

Just exactly what constitutes minimum galley equipment depends on how much room you have; on whether you cruise weekends or weeks; on whether you live aboard; and on the type of cooking you like to do. What's essential for one cook may be excess to another. I suggest starting with the barest complement of cooking equipment. You can always add an item or two, but you'll never take something off once it's aboard.

When we moved aboard six years ago, I sold or gave away all my kitchen utensils and appliances except the following:

- 1 10″ frying pan—fairly deep
- 1 10″ omelet pan
- 1 2-qt. saucepan w/lid
- 1 1-qt. saucepan w/lid
- 1 4-qt. pressure cooker
- 1 Dutch oven
- 2 pie tins
- 2 square cake tins (that fit side by side in oven)
- 1 muffin tin
- 2 loaf pans (both fit in oven at same time)

Since then I have added only the following:

- 1 11″ square griddle
- 1 small roasting pan w/lid
- 1 cookie sheet that just fits the oven

There is virtually nothing I could prepare in our apartment that I can't prepare on board with the above utensils. In fact, the second week we were aboard, I fixed Cornish hens with a flaming brandy, sour cream sauce and permanently put to rest any fears my husband may have had that we would end up on a canned stew diet.

Figure 1 shows the galley locker I inherited on our new boat, a 35-foot sloop. After living with the locker a few

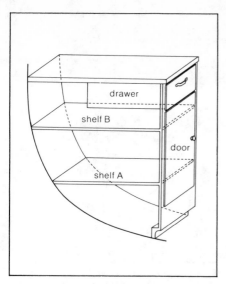

Figure 1: The galley locker I inherited

months I decided that (1) The top shelf was useless as there were only 4½ inches from the bottom of the drawer to the shelf, barely enough space to put your hand in, let alone to store objects in. Also the space behind the drawer was inaccessible and tended to trap objects out of reach. (2) The lower shelf, though easily accessible, was too low to allow good utilization of the space below it. My decision was to tear out both shelves and begin again.

And so I began, as I suggest you do, sitting on a comfortable cushion in front of the empty locker, with pencil, paper, tape measure, and a cool drink handy, and surrounded by all my cooking utensils. After several hours of holding pots and pans in various positions, measuring, visualizing the most accessible positions for the most-used items, I came up with the final arrangement as shown in Figure 2.

The lower section of the cabinet is what makes it unique and so handy. Across the front of the cabinet I have five slots ranging from 1½ inches to four inches in width, with each slot extending 11 inches deep into the cabinet (which will hold my widest utensil, a 11-inch griddle; if I'd had a 12-inch skillet, I'd have made all the slots 12 inches deep). As partially illustrated in

Figure 3, these slots hold my griddle and 10-inch omelet pan in one slot, then my 10-inch-deep skillet, my baking tins (except loaf pans), my two saucepans in one slot, and finally lids. This is the handiest section of the cabinet; you should put in there the things you use most often. You can reach any item easily; just grab the handle (Fig. 3). The hull shape dictated that my larger items be on the left (forward side) and the smaller-diameter items to the right (aft end). You will want the utensils with the longest handles (skillets) to be on one side or the other; if they are in the middle, they may interfere somewhat with access to the back of the cabinet.

The next shelf to be designed was Shelf A, directly above and behind the Handles Up section. I had decided to put my Dutch oven (diameter of 9½ inches) on Shelf A. This shelf is merely quarter-inch plywood with a hole cut out the same diameter as the Dutch oven. I made the whole shelf 13 inches wide (the width of the cabinet) and 12 inches deep and placed it high enough to accommodate the 12-inch depth. Figure 4 shows how the Dutch oven fits securely in the shelf. To retrieve this item I just reach in, grab an ear of the

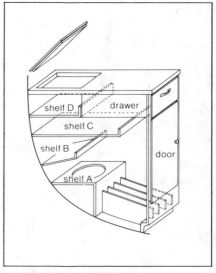

Figure 2: The final arrangement

pot, lift up and out. If any handles are in the way from the front section, they are easily tilted forward out of the way.

Shelf B was next. I had decided to put my pressure cooker there for several reasons: (1) it is an item I don't use often; and (2) though that shelf is far back in the cabinet, the pressure cooker has a long handle which makes it easy to put in and out (Fig. 4). By giving the shelf a rakish angle, just a small lip on the front edge is enough to keep the pressure cooker secure in any seaway. (I could also have made this shelf like Shelf A with a hole the diameter of the pressure cooker.) I placed Shelf B as low as possible without its interfering with the Dutch oven below.

Now in just the lower half of a previously useless locker, I had homes for nearly all my cooking utensils.

As I still had quite a lot of room, I put in Shelf C taking care: (1) to place it as low as possible without its interfering at all with the pressure cooker below; and (2) to move the edge of the shelf back a good six to eight inches from the front of the cabinet to keep good access to the storage below. I put a higher lip on this shelf to keep from losing things on the wrong tack. I will utilize this shelf by putting the roasting pan (seldom used) at the back, then my loaf pans, and flat,

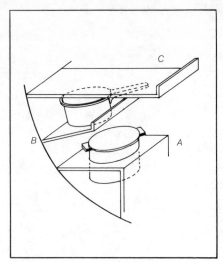

Figure 4: The Dutch oven fits securely in the shelf. The pressure cooker has a long handle which makes it easy to put in and out

quiet things, such as paper plates and cartons of plastic wrap and aluminum foil, to the front.

That still left me with a tantalizing, inaccessible space behind the drawer. Is there anything I can do with it—cut a door in the side of the cabinet into the aft end of the settee, or the forward end of the quarter berth? Better yet, I put in Shelf D and cut an access hole in the counter top. Finally, we have a good place to put our thermoses—safe yet handy (Fig. 2).

It's a good idea to line at least the lower section of the cabinet (before you have everything built in) with a thin layer of foam. Closed-cell foam is best because it won't hold moisture. With a fiberglass or steel hull you'll prevent "sweating" and have a drier locker. It will also prevent pots and pans from scratching and enamel pans from chipping; and best of all you'll have a really quiet storage locker.

Figure 5 shows how I used the same design approach on an entirely different locker (our last boat) to accommodate the same utensils. And it will work for you on your boat.

Building a galley locker like this one is a great project for the beginning carpenter. It can be a sort of test case to

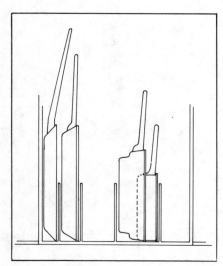

Figure 3: You can reach any item easily. Just grab the handle

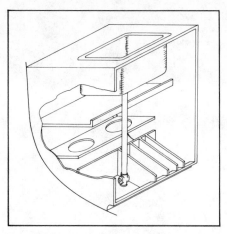

Figure 5: The same design approach on an entirely different locker

see if you enjoy that kind of work, or perhaps a desperation move when the galley locker is a low-priority item for the regular ship's carpenter. You can do the whole thing with—perhaps skilled craftsmen should put their hands over their ears so they can't hear what comes next—a saw (preferably saber), glue, hammer and nails. Honest. Well, you'll need tape measure and pencil, too. Oh, and don't forget the plywood and 1″ X 1½″ wood strips (approximately) for shelf supports. Find someone to show you how to use any equipment you're unsure of, then have at it.

When you're finished and you have personalized cubbyholes for all your cooking utensils, you have a safe, handy, quiet, and efficient galley locker. Then paint it all with several coats of white paint and put everything in place. No one will even *notice* if something is a little crooked or a few nails don't go in perfectly straight. They'll just say, "It's fantastic! Why you've got all your handles up!"

Contributors

D. A. Bamford is an electronics engineer, presently working as an industrial consultant. In the late Fifties his teen-age son introduced him to sailing; he began in a 14' dinghy and gradually moved up to his present 34' ketch, *Foudroyant* of Toronto. Being a manufacturer of fiberglass boats for four years, he maintains a close interest in boatbuilding methods and quality of construction. He has been a member of the American Boat and Yacht Council and is currently the chairman of the Cruising Standards Committee of the Canadian Yachting Association. His principal interest is cruising, and his years of sailing have taken him to all the Great Lakes (except Superior), English waters, both coasts of North America, the Gulf of Mexico, the Caribbean, as well as Australian and Chinese waters. One day he hopes to visit some of these places again on one long cruise. He is now under a contract with a Canadian publisher for a book introducing beginners to cruising.

Lewis H. Bell is Vice President of Harold R. Mull, Bell and Associates, a leading consulting and engineering firm dealing with applied acoustics, noise control, and research. Over the last fifteen years, Mr. Bell has been active in research and development in all phases of aerospace, industrial, and architectural acoustics. He has presented numerous technical papers on sources and control of noise in the marine industry and has acted as a consulting engineer to many leading naval architects and builders. He is an avid sailor and sails his Ranger 26, *Decibell,* on Long Island Sound; and each year he goes on one or two ocean races as navigator.

Edward S. Brewer of Brooklin, Maine, a yacht designer for twenty years, has been in private practice since 1967. His designs include the Whitby 42, Morgan 38, Aloha 28 and 34, Cabot 36, Quickstep 24, Olympic 47 and 42, Cape North 43, plus many custom yachts ranging up to the 62' ketch *Traveller III.* He has cruised and raced in the Great Lakes, Aegean, Atlantic and Pacific, including the Transpac races in 1969 and 1973. He has also written two books: *Understanding Boat Design* and *Cruising Designs.*

Jerry B. Cartwright was raised on a ranch in Texas and first saw the ocean at age 17 when he shipped out on a Danish freighter. In 1956 he took his first offshore passage on a small boat along the coast of Mexico and Central America. Since then he has cruised in many parts of the world, including the Pacific, the Far East, the Indian Ocean, the Mediterranean, the East Coast of Africa, the Baltic Sea, and the Caribbean, and has crossed the Atlantic four times. He participated in the 1969 Single-handed Trans-Pacific Race and the 1972 OSTAR, and organized SOLOS — Society of Lone Offshore Sailors — which ran the inaugural Bermuda One-Two race in the summer of 1977. Mr. Cartwright has been designing boats since 1968 and set up an office in Newport, Rhode Island, in 1972.

Dick Cumiskey's first taste of sailing was around 1948 when he was invited to cruise on a neighbor's Alden-designed schooner in Long Island Sound. This exposure was enough to hook him, and he worked his way up from a Dyer Dhow to his present Ranger 22, *Bandwagon*, out of Newport Beach. His work has always been in the boating industry: he began as a boat boy during the summers, then went into marina work in the '50s, freelanced in boat maintenance, and worked in a number of boatyards on Long Island Sound. In 1968 Mr. Cumiskey moved to California and began work in production control for Jensen Marine. Recently he became Product Director, responsible for design and product specifications for Cal Boats and Ranger Yachts.

Bob Del Morris spent his early childhood sailing in Long Island Sound waters with family and friends. By the time of high school graduation, he had crossed the Atlantic three times as a crew-member aboard various sailing craft. Following college and the pursuit of a career in engineering, Bob began boating again, this time cruising the waters off Southern California. At present, sailing aboard his 37′ sloop, *Ruff Life*, he enjoys cruising the California and Mexican coasts and has sailed his boat to Hawaii and back. He lives in Marina Del Rey, and heads a team designing automated communications systems for the U.S. Navy.

Paul Dodson sailed the New England coast extensively as a child on boats from 23′ to 36′. After college he entered the Navy, where he developed a strong navigational background through nine years of sea duty in small ships and patrol boats. He served as navigator aboard a destroyer and an ocean minesweeper, on which he conducted a hydrographic survey of the Aegean Sea and the Libyan Coast. At Annapolis Mr. Dodson taught Advanced Navigation, served as an ocean racing safety officer, and was in charge of the plebe summer sailing program. He is now the owner-manager of the Newport International Sailboat Show, and has continued his billet as navigator in ocean racing. Mr. Dodson assisted in the editing of a seamanship text published by the U.S. Naval Institute and was technical editor for a text on practical navigation.

Michel Emmanuel was born and raised in the sponge-fishing village of Tarpon Springs on the west coast of Florida and today is a practicing lawyer in Tampa. He has cruised the Gulf coast from the Yucatan to the Dry Tortugas, Cuba and the Bahamas. He owns a Tartan 34, *Reef Runner*, and enjoys filling in as navigator on ocean racers. Mr. Emmanuel was a young Navy ensign in the Philippines at the beginning of World War II. His ship, the *USS Langley*, was sunk in February, 1942, during the Battle of the Java Sea. Two days later he was aboard the *USS Pecos* when she was sunk by Japanese dive bombers. One of a handful of survivors of this double tragedy, he has been interested in survival techniques to this day.

Don Grayson first became interested in sailing in the Orient while he was an electronics technician in the Navy. Upon discharge, his first cruise with his new bride was in a homemade 12′ sloop, complete with cabin, stove, and bunks. He is a charter member of the Interstate Swing Keel Association (ISKA), a group dedicated to trailerable cruising sailboats. He has led or participated in cruises to North Channel, Lakes Michigan and Erie as well as the Gulf Coast of Florida and the Bahamas from his home port of Indianapolis. Don is an electronics engineer for the Navy with experience in both theoretical analysis and hardware design of a number of aircraft and shipboard radars. His current boat, an O'Day 25 called *Boat #7*, is conspicuous for her 8′ galley counter top and her non-reliance on electronics. His latest goal is a cruise from the Great Lakes down the Intercoastal Waterway to the Bahamas.

Glenn Housley is a sailmaker with a loft in Annapolis, Maryland, specializing in the design and building of cruising sails especially for use in offshore and passage cruising.

Joel H. Jacobs is president of Nautech Maritime Corporation of Chicago. He has been sailing on and off for 33 years and has owned a variety of sailboats and auxiliaries. He graduated from the U.S. Naval Honor School and then attended Tulane University, where he was one of the founders of the sailing club. His sailing and racing experience has included Barnegat Bay, Lake Michigan, Lake Pontchartrain, the Gulf of Mexico, the Pacific and Atlantic Oceans, and the Caribbean. Since 1965 most of his sailing has been on Lake Michigan and throughout the West Indies, where he keeps his 41′ ketch, *Nereus*. Captain Jacobs holds current licenses issued by the U.S. Coast Guard and the Republic of Panama to command auxiliary-sailing, sailing, steam and mechanically propelled passenger-carrying vessels. His original Merchant Mariner's document dates back to 1948. He is the author of *Selecting a Marine Sextant* and has been a guest lecturer on navigation at the U.S. Naval Academy and U.S. Merchant Marine Academy.

James B. Kane first became interested in sailing at the age of 18 while serving as an apprentice seaman on a three-masted schooner and later as a cadet on a three-masted bark. After graduating from King's Point in 1943, he began going to sea on cargo ships. Today, he holds an unlimited Master's License with first-class pilot endorsements for many of the East Coast ports of the U.S. and is now the captain of one of the largest sandsuckers owned by the Army Corps of Engineers for dredging harbors and inlets. Because of his life at sea he never had enough time for a boat of his own, but has chartered boats in many ports throughout the world, adapting navigational practices used on large ships as well as those methods used by ancient mariners, such as the Polynesians.

William V. Kielhorn's first sea-going experience was as a cabin boy aboard a destroyer during the "rum war" of the 1920s, and he later served as a seaman aboard various ships engaged in the Bering Sea Patrol during the 1930s. Immediately after Pearl Harbor he was commissioned in the Coast Guard and served as a ship's officer on a dozen or more craft ranging in size from 100′ schooners to 300′ cutters and destroyers and up to a 20,000-ton transport.

Mr. Kielhorn has a master's degree in oceanography and during his career he has been affiliated with the International Ice Patrol, the Woods Hole Oceanographic Institute, the U.S.N. Hydrographic Office, the Office of Naval Research, and was Manager of Lockheed's Oceanics Division. He has also held teaching positions at the U.S. Coast Guard Academy and at U.C.L.A. Presently Mr. Kielhorn is the chief scientist of Aero-Marine Surveys, Inc., of Groton, Connecticut, which specializes in airborne oceanography.

Christopher Knight began messing about in boats at age two and taking photographs at age 13. During college he and his brother paddled kayaks from Alaska to Seattle, and in 1964 he canoed down the Danube River, visiting seven countries and taking photographs for a 47-page article in *National Geographic Magazine*. This long adventure began a career in photography which resulted in more stories for *National Geographic* on Alaska, Japan, and Rumania. He received a master of architecture degree from Harvard in 1969. Looking for a way to combine the fun of photography with the leisurely design elements of architecture, he decided to go into documentary film production and formed the New Film Company, Inc., of Boston. In 1971 he married Kathryn Lasky, creating a writer-photographer team. Their 30' ketch *Leucothea* became the vehicle for a series of sailing voyages, including two crossings of the Atlantic and cruising in Scandinavia, inland Europe via the canals, the Mediterranean, and the Caribbean.

Murray Lesser took up sailing after more than 40 years of leading an essentially sedentary life, because his wife Jean insisted that he either learn how to sail or else stop talking about retiring to a sailboat. Fifteen years later, he hasn't yet retired. Now the Lessers spend their vacations cruising the New England coast between Long Island Sound and Mt. Desert Island, in their third (and ultimate) *Apsara*, a four-berth, six-ton Pilot 35 yawl.

John Letcher, now in his 30s took up cruising when he purchased *Island Girl*, a 20' hard-chine cutter of unknown lineage, in San Pedro, California, at age 19. After graduating from Cal Tech, he sailed her alone to Hawaii, thence to Alaska, and returned to California, in three successive summers. At 24, he completed his doctorate at Cal Tech in aeronautical engineering and applied math, and began construction of *Aleutka*, a 25' cutter of his design. Since launching her in 1967, Mr. Letcher and his wife have spent nearly half their time afloat in *Aleutka*, cruising to Hawaii and Alaska, and on both the east and west coasts of Mexico, the U.S., and Canada. Since 1973, they have operated a technically based yacht design office, Letcher Offshore Design, located in Southwest Harbor, Maine. John is a member of S.N.A.M.E. and a registered Professional Engineer. His many journal and symposium publications have established him as an authority on mathematical analysis of sailing vessels. His articles and two books, *Self-Steering for Sailing Craft* and *Self-Contained Celestial Navigation*, have carried his findings on the technical side of cruising to a wide popular readership.

Lindy Lindquist has owned various types of boats and has been involved in many phases of the marine industry: chandlery, ship delivery, maintenance, and international yacht brokerage. He also has been a professional captain whose largest command under sail was an 86′ schooner; he was master for three years. Among a hitch in the Navy, professional sailing, and his own numerous voyages, there are not many countries bordering upon the sea that he has not visited. He has also travelled extensively on the European river and canal system. He started writing professionally in 1966; his articles have appeared in many nautical publications, and he uses his own photography for illustrations.

Mike Macdonald lives in Manhattan Beach, California, and first started sailing as a teenager in 1961 when his parents bought a Finn for him and his brother to keep them off the streets. Since 1967, Mr. Macdonald has concentrated on ocean racing, going along as crewman, watch captain, and sometimes cook. The Channel Islands are his local cruising grounds, but after races he has explored the Bahamas, the French Riviera, the Hawaiian Islands, the Sea of Cortez, Vancouver, the San Juans, and the west coast of Mexico. He has recently completed a screenplay about swordfishing in California and has written for most of the major yachting publications. He accounts for all his time spent with boats by having worked as a yard laborer, deckhand, sailing instructor, charter skipper, yacht corporation marketing director, and marine photographer.

Bob Martin has cruised and raced extensively in the Pacific northwest for 15 years. He has sailed offshore in the Transpac and helped crew the Spencer 51 *Odusa* to her record-setting passage in the 1972 Victoria-Maui Race. He was also a crew member aboard the Swan 65 *Sayula II*, which won the first Whitbread Round-the-World Race in 1973–1974.

Fred Martini and *Russ Nilson* form a research team with complimentary talents. They both have an interest in marine science; Nilson looks at things from an engineer's point of view and Martini takes the biologist's viewpoint. They started Marine Environmental Research, Incorporated, and are now engaged in a four-year research cruise working in collaboration with biologists in over 30 countries. They began working in the South Pacific aboard *Serenity*, a 37′ ketch, and their operation has now expanded to include a land base in Pago Pago and *Varua*, the famous brigantine of William A. Robinson. *Varua* is currently being outfitted in Pago Pago as a floating lab for her new career as a research vessel.

John Mellor has been sailing since the age of 13 and served in the Royal Navy as a junior officer for five years. During these years he received professional training in navigation and did quite a bit of cruising. After getting out of the Navy in 1968 he spent three years as a professional delivery skipper and another year as a yacht captain in the Mediterranean. He has also been captain of some of the Island Cruising Club's (Devon) large sailing vessels. As a captain he sailed over 1000 miles a month and called at three or four ports a week in the English Channel, Bay of Biscay, Ireland, and West Scotland; his favorite cruising grounds are the Western Isles of Scotland. His first book, *Sailing Can Be Simple*, was published in 1977. This book is for beginners and a follow-up book, *Cruising Safe and Simple,* will be out in the spring of 1978. Mr. Mellor is currently working on a book on navigation when not rebuilding an 80' trawler. This boat was built in 1920, and as far as he knows there is only one other left from 2000-odd that were working at the turn of the century. He hopes to be at sea in about three years for a prolonged world cruise.

George Nichols' memory of sailing goes back 50 years, but he began before that, thanks to his father. He has sailed on all types of boats and has owned four cruising boats; his most recent is the Carter-designed two-tonner *Airmail.* He has raced and cruised extensively on his own boat as well as on others. His travels have taken him from Haiti to Labrador, to Scandinavia, the British Isles, the Shetland and Faroe Islands, and the Pacific area from San Francisco to the Galapagos Islands. Most recently Dr. Nichols has temporarily "retired" from his teaching position at Harvard Medical School to work in ocean ecology and marine mammal biology. In 1976 he and others of the Ocean Research and Education Society bought a 144' three-masted wooden barkentine, *Regina Maris,* as a research vehicle. So far Dr. Nichols has served as *Regina's* master from Piraeus, Greece, to Boston (including the Tall Ships Races and OpSail in 1976) and on two voyages to Labrador and one to Bequia in the Grenadines and back to Boston.

Lin and *Larry Pardey* have been cruising aboard their 24' engineless cutter, *Seraffyn* for nine years. *Seraffyn* is a Lyle Hess design which they built themselves. Their sailing has taken them from California to Panama, through the Caribbean to Europe, into the Baltic and then the Mediterranean. During the past year they have sailed down the Red Sea and across the Indian Ocean to Malaysia and Indonesia. The Pardeys earn their way as they go by delivering yachts, doing carpentry and rigging work, and writing articles. They have written two books: *Cruising in* Seraffyn and *Seraffyn's European Adventures.* So far they have visited 28 countries and are now looking toward their final destination of Vancouver and California, where their families are.

Dag Pike built his first boat, a canvas-covered kayak, as a child in wartime Britain. He went to sea as a deck apprentice at age 16 and spent five years in the British Merchant Marine. This was followed by a ten-year spell as deck officer with the British Lighthouse Authority. He then spent another ten years as an inspector of lifeboats with the Royal National Lifeboat Institution; part of this time was used in developing and testing new designs of lifeboats, particularly inflatables. He is a freelance writer and undertakes boat deliveries to maintain experience. His published books include *Powerboats in Rough Seas, Motor Sailers,* and *Electronic Navigation for Small Craft;* his pending books are *History of Motor Boats* and *Fishing Boats and Their Equipment.* He is qualified as a Master Mariner and is a member of the Royal Institute of Navigation and an Associate of the Royal Institute of Naval Architects.

Peter W. Rogers, in his 30s, is a marine artist living in Cambridge, Massachusetts. He has sailed all his life, principally in New England, the Great Lakes, and Nova Scotia. He acquired extensive navigational experience in Greenland, the Western Arctic, and the

Antarctic while in the Coast Guard and was awarded two letters of commendation for polar diving. His current boat is a 20' Corinthian moored in Boston, a short walk from his studio. He describes her as "a boat while I'm waiting for time and money for *the* boat." Painted in oils, his work primarily depicts working vessels — old tramp steamers, fishing boats, and tugs. A special project is to do a book with full-color oil illustrations someday to accompany great passages in nautical literature. His paintings have been exhibited in the U.S. and in England.

Michael Saunders was born in South Africa and brought up in Mozambique, where most of his free time was spent in a variety of little boats, from trading dhows to stitched-bark canoes. Later, while living in Rhodesia, Mr. Saunders and his wife built a 20' trimaran and sailed in the Mozambique Channel and on the Lakes of Rhodesia. In 1972, as a result of the political scene and other circumstances he gave up his job, sold all his family's possessions, and bought an old 33' ketch. The boat was called *Walkabout,* and with his wife and four children he set sail round the Cape of Good Hope to St. Helena, South America, the West Indies, and Azores, and finally England. The voyage took two years and is related in Mr. Saunders' book, *The Walkabouts.* On reaching England, the Saunders continued to live afloat, first on *Walkabout* and later on a converted trawler. They are now building a 45' ferro-cement cutter, specially designed for a long voyage. Mr. Saunders writes for a living and makes yacht deliveries, which has provided thousands of miles' experience in many craft. He also runs a firm that offers design and consulting service.

Jane Silverman and her husband met while working for the Department of Health in St. Thomas, Virgin Islands. Since their marriage they have lived aboard *Daemon,* a 37', S&S designed, fiberglass sloop. In 1972 they spent a year cruising the Caribbean, down to the Grenadines and back. The following year they set out for Europe with a planned stop in the Azores. When they arrived in Faial in the Azores, they found it so beautiful that they bought a cottage and stayed for a year. Since then they have cruised the south coast of England, the Mediterranean, the Canaries, back to the West Indies, and have spent most of their summers in Faial. The Silvermans are now in Fort Lauderdale living on shore for the first time in their married life. *Daemon* has been sold, but they are actively looking for a new boat.

Jeff Spranger is an editor at SAIL magazine.

Chet Swenson, President of Chet Swenson Marine Engineers, Inc., of St. Petersburg, Florida, is a member of the Society of Naval Architects and Marine Engineers. Originally from New England, Mr. Swenson has sailed the length of America's Atlantic and Gulf coasts, and has cruised the Bahamian and Caribbean waters and the coastal areas of the Mediterranean and western Pacific. Although his firm is primarily engaged in the design of shipboard energy systems for small commercial vessels and large yachts, Mr. Swenson's reputation in the design of rigging and sail systems has kept the firm active in the design of sail and spar plans for a select transoceanic clientele. His considerable offshore experience has provided his engineering firm with insight into the special needs of the single-handed or short-handed sailor.

Joan Wendling and her husband began sailing together about ten years ago and in 1969 they moved aboard a Chinook 35, *Arima*. Their experience on boats includes two years of cruising along the west coasts of California and Mexico and the Sea of Cortez; sailing with friends in the Puget Sound area; commercial fishing in the Florida Keys for a year; a powerboat passage from California to Bermuda; a six-month cruise of the Caribbean on *Arima II*, their 35' fiberglass sloop; and a transatlantic delivery of a 32' Endeavor from Lisbon, Portugal, to Tampa, Florida. Mrs. Wendling holds a Coast Guard six-passenger license so she and her husband can run the sailing school for Underwood Marine in Miami where she has taught beginning through advanced sailing and a bareboat charter qualification program. She has also organized celestial navigation classes and developed a workbook of problems for HO 249 students which she hopes to publish.

Tisha Whitney has been sailing most of her life, and for the past six years she and her husband have lived aboard their 32' cutter *Tenbrooks*. They are both teachers and have spent their summer months cruising the coast of southern California and its off-lying islands. In December 1976 they left their jobs and set off from Newport Beach. After several months of cruising along the coasts of Mexico and Central America, they passed through the Panama Canal and slowly made their way to Melbourne, Florida, where they are now earning future cruising funds.

Bebe Wunderlich sailed around the world from 1963 to 1967 aboard a 42' ketch, an Atkin double-ender. There were four in crew, travelling westward and using both canals. Presently, she is an anesthesiologist in Boston. Her sailing activities range from local sailing on a Cal 28 to charters in Seattle and other ''exotic'' spots. She plans to return to the South Pacific someday.